ODDBALL WISCONSIN

A Guide to 400 Really
STRANGE PLACES

2nd Edition

T0206658

JEROME POHLEN

CHICAGO
REVIEW
PRESS

Copyright © 2001, 2013 by Jerome Pohlen
Second edition
Published by Chicago Review Press, Incorporated
814 North Franklin Street
Chicago, Illinois 60610

ISBN 978-1-61374-666-0

The author has made every effort to secure permissions for all the material in this book. If any acknowledgment has inadvertently been omitted, please contact the author.

Cover and interior design: Jonathan Hahn
Map design: Chris Erichsen
Cover photograph: North Country Taxidermy, Hazelhurst
All interior images from the author's collection unless otherwise noted.

Library of Congress Cataloging-in-Publication Data
Pohlen, Jerome.
  Oddball Wisconsin : a guide to 400 really strange places / Jerome Pohlen. — Second edition.
    pages cm
  Includes bibliographical references and index.
  ISBN 978-1-61374-666-0 (trade paper)
  1. Wisconsin—Guidebooks. 2. Wisconsin—History, Local—Miscellanea. 3. Curiosities and wonders—Wisconsin—Guidebooks. I. Title.

  F579.3.P64 2013
  977.5—dc23

                    2013002262

Printed in the United States of America
5 4 3 2 1

ODDBALL WISCONSIN

TO MY PARENTS,
JOSEPH AND BARBARA POHLEN,
FOR ALL THE FAMILY TRIPS IN
THE BIG, ORANGE DODGE

Contents

INTRODUCTION

*L*et's be honest: Wisconsin is a state of oddballs. Where else do citizens proudly wear foam cheese wedges on their heads? Where have voters elected both the infamous senator Joseph McCarthy and the nation's longest-running Socialist big-city mayor? And which state's official song was once owned by Michael Jackson? The answer to all these questions is the same: Wisconsin.

And what do these odd folk do with their time? They build elaborate concrete shrines in their front yards or erect enormous fiberglass statues of fish, corkscrews, chickens, and cows, cows, cows. They open museums to honor mustard, angels, honey, paper coffee cups, accordions, and cheese. And they organize festivals to celebrate pot roasts, UFOs, rutabagas, watermelon seed spitting, and cow-chip tossing. These weird folk are willing to break free of Midwestern conformity. They are people I admire.

When the first edition of this book came out in 2001, I thought to myself, Wisconsin couldn't be any weirder. And boy was I wrong. A few months after it was published, I got a kind letter from Mark "Mad Man" Madson, asking if I would include his Chevy pickup—the one he had suspended 50 feet in the air between two trees—in the next edition. I most definitely would! So, too, Chainsaw Gordy's Garden of Saws, Big Al Capone's of Pipe, Smokey Bear's head, and Top Secret, the world's only upside-down White House. And on and on and on.

As before, where other travel guides might bore you with scenic driving tours, homey bed-and-breakfasts, and where to find the fall colors, this new edition of *Oddball Wisconsin* offers you road trip information you're not likely to find anywhere else. Where was Liberace born? How do you catch a Hodag? Who invented the hamburger, and what has his hometown done to honor this visionary man? And which rodent is a better weather forecaster, Jimmy the Groundhog or Punxsutawney Phil?

So forget antiquing in Door County, fly-fishing in the North Woods, and bicycling along the Mississippi. You've eaten far too many waffle cones in Lake Geneva. It's time to live a little, and laugh a lot, on your vacation.

While I've tried to give clear directions from major streets and landmarks, you could still make a wrong turn. Bigfoot might be out there, so it's not a time to panic. Remember these Oddball travel tips:

1. **Stop and ask!** For a lot of communities, their Oddball attraction might be their only claim to fame. Locals are often thrilled that you'd drive out of your way to marvel at their underappreciated shrine. But be careful who you ask. Old cranks at the town cafe are good for information; teenage clerks at the Gas-n-Go are not.
2. **Call ahead.** Few Oddball sites keep regular hours, but most owners or operators will gladly wait around if they know you're coming. Wisconsin is a seasonal travel state, and sites can be closed for the winter at a moment's notice or if the fish are biting. Always call.
3. **Don't give up.** Think of the person who's sitting in a tiny museum dedicated to an obscure topic, and know that they're waiting just for you. Actually, they're waiting for anyone . . . so you'll do.
4. **Don't trespass!** Don't become a Terrible Tourist. Just because somebody built a sculpture garden in their front yard doesn't mean they're looking for visitors.

Do you have an Oddball site of your own? Have I missed anything? Do you know of an oddball site that should be included in an updated version? Please write and let me know: Jerome Pohlen, c/o Chicago Review Press, 814 North Franklin Street, Chicago, IL 60610.

ODDBALL WISCONSIN

NOrtHErN WiSCONSiN

When you think of northern Wisconsin, think big—Paul Bunyan big. Everywhere you turn, there are enormous monuments to everyday objects and wildlife. A giant corkscrew. A colossal penny. A two-story loon. A massive badger. A titanic chicken. A Chrysler-size whitetail deer. Huge black bears, manmade and stuffed. And the world's largest fiberglass animal: a gargantuan muskie at the National Freshwater Fishing Hall of Fame in Hayward.

To properly display these mammoth structures, they've been placed at great distances from one another, and are not the kind of things you can visit on a Sunday drive in the country. You need a full tank of gas, a good map, and an alarm clock to hit the road early—it's going to be a full weekend.

And you won't just see fiberglass monstrosities. There are things up in those woods, things you'll never see anywhere else: UFO parades, crowds of concrete people, card-playing raccoons, hippie colonies, a Bong Memorial, an enormous ball of twine, and the exact geographic center of the northern half of the western-freakin' hemisphere . . . so what are you waiting for?!

Amery
The Haunted Lutheran Church

If you're driving along Route 46 south of Amery and you hear the toll of a church bell, STOP! But only if it is coming from a Lutheran church atop a hill.

Old Norwegian ghosts from East Immanuel's adjoining cemetery have refused to go to their final resting place, choosing instead to congregate in the chapel after hours. Oftentimes they ring the bell to call their other-worldly neighbors to their spirit services.

Many parishioners have heard the noisy throng over the years, but the voices would fade as they approached the building. Others have heard murmurs in the basement, and one church trustee had a light fixture reassemble itself when he turned his back for a moment. As of yet, they dead have not harmed anyone . . . though there is no guarantee that they won't.

East Immanuel Lutheran Church, 207 120th St., Amery, WI 54001

Phone: (715) 268-2143

Hours: Always visible

Cost: Free

Website: www.eastimmanuel-lutheran.org

Directions: Five miles south of town on Rte. 46, turn west on 30th Ave. for one mile, turn south
on 120th St.

Augusta
Big Beaver

The sign on the statue's base says it all: WHEN YOU'RE IN AUGUSTA YOU'RE IN BEAVER TERRITORY. It's not that beavers are particularly territorial, but high school students certainly are—and in Augusta, their mascot is the beaver.

And what a beaver it is! Eight feet tall, it holds a gnawed-off length of birch in its paws. It looks friendly enough, until you realize that it probably chewed that tree down with just a few bites.

Augusta High School, E 19320
  Bartig Rd., Augusta, WI 54722

Phone: (715) 286-3352

Hours: Always visible

Cost: Free

Website: www.augusta.k12.wi.us

Directions: West of town, just
  north of Rte. 12.

The jokes write themselves.

Bayfield
Maggie's

Flamingos aren't traditionally found in these northern climes, but they do exist . . . mostly at Maggie's, a shock-pink eatery that's hard to miss among its duller neighbors. Maggie's has collected hundreds of the long-legged birds and other tropical gewgaws to decorate its walls, tables, windows, and doors. What better way to brighten up a bitter Wisconsin winter?

Maggie's has burgers, salads, and pizza, though they also serve something called a Flamingo Sandwich. Have no fear—the "flamingo" refers to the hot sauce, not the meat. It's chicken. Or at least it *tastes* like chicken.

257 Manypenny Ave., Bayfield, WI 54814

Phone: (715) 779-3117

Hours: Daily 11 AM–10 PM

Cost: Meals, $6–12

Website: www.maggies-bayfield.com

Directions: One block south of Rittenhouse Ave. (Rte. 13) at Fourth St.

Birnamwood
Big Chicken

Talk about sleeping with the enemy! This traitorous clucker shamelessly lures hungry travelers along Route 45 to a killing field two blocks west of the highway, where its feathered kin are roasted, fried, and carved up into breaded strips. Sure, the food at Chet & Emil's is tasty, and yes, they do offer nonpoultry meals. But the notion that this large fiberglass chicken would participate in this carnage—it's nothing short of cannibalism!

In the chicken's defense, it is obviously wired to the top of its sign and probably couldn't escape if it wanted to, and if it didn't act as the restaurant's spokes-hen, whose head do you think would be next on the chopping block? This bird could feed the whole town!

Chet & Emil's Broasted Chicken, 388 Main St., PO Box 207, Birnamwood, WI 54414

Phone: (715) 449-2226 or (715) 449-2297

Hours: Always visible; restaurant, Monday–Saturday 8 AM–bar close, Sunday 9:30 AM–bar close

Cost: Free; meals, $4–17

Website: http://chetandemils.webs.com/

Directions: Sign at the intersection of Rte. 45 and Elm St.; Chet & Emil's is two blocks west on Main.

BIG CLUCKERS

The chicken at Chet & Emil's comes from a larger fiberglass flock scattered across the Cheese State. Check out these other colossal cluckers:

Gas Station Chicken

City Limits BP Gas Station, N3900 Hwy. 180, Marinette, (715) 735-0720

This large white rooster once advertised Ellis's Big Chicken Restaurant, but now it pumps gas.

Angry Chef Chicken

Moe's Diner, 12701 Tenth St., Osseo, (715) 597-3912

The large fiberglass chicken in the parking lot of Moe's Diner doesn't seem happy in its chef's hat and apron. Can you blame it? The bird's relatives are on the menu!

Eddie, the Beer-Swigging Giant Chicken

Ed & Sharon's Chicken, N1294 State Hwy. 64/107, Merrill, (715) 536-3429, www.edandsharons.com

Ed and Sharon don't just served fried chicken—they also serve hamburgers and booze, which is why their big bird holds a burger and a mug of beer in its outstretched wing/hands.

Remains of the World's Largest Badger

He's not what he used to be, but he's still ferocious. The World's Largest Badger once loomed over a mound-shaped gas station north of Birnamwood. The station's pumps were located inside a large, hollow log with an equally impressive squirrel crawling on top. Customers could park their cars inside the log while they filled up; then they could snap a picture and say, "Honey, I shrunk the minivan!"

But the gas station closed several years ago. The new owners pulled the badger off the roof and buried him chest deep, closer to the road, emerging from behind a fence to startle drivers on Route 45. The log was converted to a storage shed, though the squirrel is still up there. The badger mound was leveled, and in its place an architecturally uninspired "exotic dance club" was erected.

Badger Country Lounge, N11004 Rte. 45, Birnamwood, WI 54414

No phone

Hours: Always visible

Cost: Free

Directions: Just north of the County Rd. ZZ intersection, north of town.

Wisconsin's Godzilla.

Bonduel
Doc's Harley-Davidson

If there's any place in Wisconsin more revered by motorcyclists, outside of the Harley-Davidson plant and museum (page 267), it's Doc's, the closest thing to a biker theme park you'll ever find. In addition to the dealership and retail shop (both of which are enormous) and its driving school, they've got the Timeline Saloon and BBQ Restaurant, the Classic Car &

Cycle Museum, and a miniature zoo. You can pet some of the animals, but you should pass on the alligators.

Now step outside. What's that, a pirate ship in the rear parking lot? Yep, and beyond that a lighthouse B&B on its own lake, a 15-foot-long chopper, and a police car chasing the General Lee over the roof of the building.

W2709 State Hwy. 29, Bonduel, WI 54107

Phone: (715) 758-9080

Hours: Monday and Thursday 9 AM–5 PM, Tuesday and Wednesday 9 AM–6 PM, Friday 9 AM–8 PM, Saturday 9 AM–4 PM, Sunday 10 AM–3 PM

Cost: Free

Website: www.docshd.com

Directions: South of town on Rte. 29/55, west of County Rd. F.

Eagle River
Albino Deer

One of the distinct evolutionary challenges faced by an albino deer is trying to stay hidden in a forest of greens and browns. But during the winter, when predators are at their hungriest, it might work to the deer's advantage in the snow. You'd also think it would be easier for drivers to spot its shock-white coat crossing a highway, and avoid running it down.

Apparently, not in this case. A not-so-fast, two-year-old albino buck was hit by a car on Highway 45 near Eagle River in the spring of 1982. This roadkill was then stuffed in a fleet-footed pose (certainly more fleet-footed than when he was on that highway) and placed in the local library for all to enjoy, staring at patrons with his glassy pink eyes.

Olson Memorial Library, 203 N. Main St., PO Box 69, Eagle River, WI 54521

Phone: (715) 479-8070

Hours: Monday 9 AM–7 PM, Tuesday–Thursday 9 AM–6 PM, Friday 9 AM–5 PM, Saturday 9 AM–3 PM

Cost: Free

Website: http://olson.wislib.org/

Directions: Two blocks north of Wall St. (Rte. 70), two blocks east of Railroad St. (Rte. 17).

Ice Palace

This is the type of oddball attraction that can be standing one day and gone the next, literally. Depending on the weather and the snowpack, the Eagle

River Fire Department builds an ice palace after Christmas using ice blocks cut from local lakes. When finished, the structure is illuminated from the inside for a sparkling nighttime display. If the temperature cooperates, they try to finish it by New Year's Day.

But then there's the problem of global warming. Not only will the world's coastal regions be flooded as our atmosphere heats up, but the ice palace might go the way of the dodo bird. And even if the thing is erected, there's no guarantee it will stay up for long; once the melting palace appears unstable, the walls are knocked in so that nobody gets injured.

Eagle River Chamber of Commerce, PO Box 1917, Eagle River, WI 54521

Phone: (800) 359-6315

Hours: Depends on the weather; call ahead

Cost: Free

Website: www.eagleriver.org/icecastle.asp

Directions: Call ahead for this year's location.

Eau Claire
Joel's Donut Chef

When you see the large fiberglass mascot outside Joel's, you might think this is a Dunkin' Donuts. A mustachioed baker in a chef's hat holds an enormous chocolate donut in his outstretched hands. But no, it's a car repair shop. Maybe that's a tire he's holding, a radial covered in vanilla icing, perhaps? Never has a whitewall looked so yummy.

Joel's Water Street Auto, 702 Water St., Eau Claire, WI 54703

Phone: (715) 833-2120

Hours: Always visible

Cost: Free

Website: www.facebook.com/pages/Joels-Water-St-Auto/256740489374

Directions: Five blocks east of Rte. 12 on Water St.

Paul Bunyan Statue

Many states, from Maine to California, claim Paul Bunyan as their native son. Given his size and roaming area, and his role in digging the Grand Canyon, pushing up the Rocky Mountains, and filling the Great Lakes, many could make a strong case. The guy got around. Some say when he died he was buried beneath Rib Mountain near Wausau, but the people who tell this tale are usually from the Badger State.

Whatever. Putting aside the Great Bunyan State Debate, it bears noting the largest tribute to Paul within Wisconsin is in Eau Claire. It was erected in 1982 outside the interpretive center that bears his name. Babe the Blue Ox is by his side. (Though Paul was damaged by hoodlums in 2002, he has since been repaired, and now his fiberglass legs are filled with concrete.)

The Paul Bunyan Logging Camp Museum has plenty to offer those with lumberjack fetishes. You get a feel for the industry in the Bunkhouse, Cook Shanty, and Blacksmith Shop displays. And for more on Paul, stop by the Tall Tales Room where you'll skate in a flapjack skillet and find a replica of Paul's full-size boot. It dwarfs the statues outside, and you know what they say about big boots: Big boots? Big feet!

Paul Bunyan Logging Camp Museum, Carson Park, 1110 Carson Park Dr., PO Box 221, Eau
Claire, WI 54702

Phone: (715) 835-6200

Hours: May–September, daily 10 AM–4:30 PM

Cost: Adults $5, kids (5–17) $2

Website: www.paulbunyancamp.org

Directions: Take Menomonie St. one block east from Claremont Ave. (Rte. 12), turn north into
Carson Park and follow the signs.

He's a lumberjack and he's OK.

BUNYANS AND BABES

Not only have Paul and Babe gotten around, they seem to have multiplied. In addition to the Bunyans found in Eau Claire, Minocqua, and the Wisconsin Dells (page 31), other versions of the bluesome twosome can be found statewide.

Babe Gets a Workout

Vilas County Historical Museum, 217 N. Main St., Sayner, (715) 542-3388, www.northern-wisconsin.com/museum

You can find a small version of the big, happy couple in front of Sayner's local history museum. Babe is yoked to a sled full of logs, while Paul stands by, whip in hand. (OK, so maybe things aren't as happy as they used to be.)

Babe All Alone

Maple Heights Campground, 16091 E. Chain Lake Rd., Lakewood, (715) 276-6441, www.facebook.com/pages/MAPLE-HEIGHTS -CAMPGROUND/56872703110

A giant Paul (a Muffler Man, see page 40) and Babe once stood in front of Lakewood's Paul Bunyan Corner Pub, but when the bar burned to the ground, Paul was sold off and Babe was moved to a local campground. You can see Babe here today . . . all alone.

Bunyan Murals

Memorial Union, University of Wisconsin–Madison, 800 Langdon St., Madison, (608) 265-3000, www.union.wisc.edu

Tucked away in the University of Wisconsin–Madison's Memorial Union are 20 Works Progress Administration (WPA)–era murals depicting the life and exploits of Paul Bunyan and his blue best friend. They were painted by James Watrous, starting in 1933.

Ship Shape

Arrrgh, mateys! If ye be adrift looking fer a port to properly wash yer skiff, sail on in to Ship Shape to get yer land craft shipshape. Aye, and Ship Shape 'tis the shape o' a ship to boot! Pull into th' stern and turn over yer keys to the first mate; then squawk with the parrots in the captain's quarters. By the time yer ship reaches the bow, these buccaneers will have swabbed th' decks, 'n fenders, too. If ye be pleased, maybe ye could gift these poor gobs a doubloon or two.

1241 W. Clairemont Ave., Eau Claire, WI 54701

Phone: (715) 836-9274

Hours: Always visible; car wash, Monday–Saturday 8 AM–6 PM, Sunday 9 AM–4 PM

Cost: Free; washes, $5–21

Website: www.shipshapeec.com

Directions: On the southwest side of Rte. 12 (Clairemont Ave.), just south of the river.

Thar she blows!

Elk Mound
The Castle

The unofficial motto of the US Postal Service—"Neither snow nor rain nor heat nor gloom of night stays these couriers from the swift completion of their appointed rounds"—doesn't say anything about *death*. And, to be fair, can you blame your postal carrier for failing to deliver your junk mail if he or she has suffered a fatal heart attack in the process?

Well, the folks who built this castle didn't think so. This three-story structure was erected by the Works Progress Administration in 1937 to honor all those Dunn County rural letter carriers who perished while on their routes. How many? Nobody quite knows.

Today the castle-like shell is mostly used as an observation tower to survey the surrounding countryside. There are local rumors, likely started by drunk or stoned visitors, that the castle is built atop the grave of a dragon.

Mound Hill Park, 435 N. Holly Ave., Elk Mound, WI 54739

Phone: (715) 879-5011

Hours: May–October, daily 8 AM–10 PM

Cost: Free

Website: www.elk-mound.org/content/parks

Directions: One half mile north of town.

Elmwood
UFO Capital of the World

Stop through Elmwood at any time of year other than the last full weekend in July, and you'll think the aliens have already come and gone . . . and took everyone with them! Not much seems to be happening in this sleepy little burg. But that hasn't always been the case.

The first UFO sighting near Elmwood occurred on March 2, 1975. A star-shaped light chased a local woman and eventually landed on her car's hood when she stopped to get a better look. A year later, in April 1976, another fireball—this one the size of a football field—shot out a blue light beam that blasted all the sparkplugs in a police cruiser driven by officer George Wheeler. Little green men seem to have trained their laser sights on Elmwood.

And Elmwood welcomes the extraterrestrial attention. A few years ago Tomas Weber of the UFO Site Center Corporation in Chippewa Falls proposed that a two-square-mile UFO landing pad be built near town. The price? Twenty-five million dollars. The project has yet to get off the ground, or on the ground. Nobody talks much about it anymore, perhaps due to some type of black-ops "shadow government" cover-up.

In the meantime, the town throws an annual UFO Days celebration to let the Martians know they're still invited. UFO Days has earthly events like beer tents, bands, and a fun run, which might be a not-so-fun run if a flying saucer shows up! They also crown a UFO Queen and have a parade featuring kids dressed up as aliens.

If you come during the off-season, you can find a collection of UFOs, all human-made, in the parking lot of Sailer's Meat Market, a grocery store at the west end of town.

Elmwood Village Office, 320 W. Winter Ave., Elmwood, WI 54740
Phone: (715) 639-3792
Hours: Last full weekend in July
Cost: Free
Directions: All over town; watch the skies.

Sailer's Meat Market, 600 W. Winter Ave., Elmwood, WI 54740
Phone: (715) 639-2191
Hours: Always visible
Cost: Free
Website: www.sailersmeats.com
Directions: On Rte. 72, at Scott St.

A CLOSE ENCOUNTER IN EAGLE RIVER

Elmwood may have had multiple UFO sightings, but none of them compare to a widely reported encounter in Eagle River on April 18, 1961. Local chicken farmer Joe Simonton discovered a chrome-plated saucer near his farmhouse west of town on Perch Lake Road. While inspecting the craft, three aliens emerged. They were five feet tall, wore black turtlenecks, and "resembled Italians." One held a two-handled jug and motioned to Joe that he would like it filled. Upon returning, Joe noticed the aliens were cooking pancakes on a barbecue grill. In exchange for the water, Joe received four steaming-hot flapjacks. He ate one, claiming it tasted like cardboard. The remaining three were later analyzed by the US Food Laboratory and found to contain common baking materials . . . *but absolutely no salt.* Were these health-conscious Martians, sent to warn us of our impending cardiac doom, or puny Italians out for a low-sodium picnic in their hovercraft? We may never know.

Fifield
Big Jumping Deer

You've got to watch where you're going in these parts, particularly at dusk. Suddenly, out of nowhere, you can come across a deer in the middle of the road. No matter the size, deer and cars do not mix. Better pull off and settle your nerves. What's that up ahead, a supper club? And is that a . . . aiiiii!!! . . . an enormous deer jumping into traffic?!

Don't worry—it doesn't move. This 15-foot fiberglass whitetail is only an attention getter for this restaurant. Did it work?

Northwoods Supper Club, N 14066 Flambeau Ave., Fifield, WI 54524

Phone: (715) 762-4447

Hours: Always visible; restaurant, Tuesday–Friday 11 AM–2 PM and 4–8 PM, Saturday 4–9 PM

Cost: Free

Directions: At the intersection of Rtes. 13 and 70.

RATS WITH ANTLERS

North Woods types aren't nearly as sentimental about deer as city folk. Truth is, these critters are everywhere—"rats with antlers," some say. And not just the real kind; you can find plenty of fiberglass deer in these parts, too, and most look identical to the jumping stag in Fifield. There's one outside the **Northwoods Inn** in St. Germain (9038 Hwy. 70 W., (715) 542-2541, www.st-germain.com/whitetailinn/). Another can be found at the **Golden Fawn Lodge** in Hayward (8774 N. Fawn Tr., (715) 462-3185, http://goldenfawnlodge.com). A third hangs way atop the tall sign outside the **Refuge Restaurant & Northwoods Bar** in Antigo (510 Hwy. 64 E., (715) 623-2249, www.antigorestaurant.com). And finally, another deer can be found in the parking lot of the **Black River Crossing Oasis** in Black River Falls (600 Oasis Rd., (715) 284-9471, www.bwarrowhead lodge.com), though it is dwarfed by an even larger traffic-cone-orange moose.

Glidden

World's Largest Stuffed Black Bear and World's Largest White Pine Log

On November 23, 1963, the day after president John F. Kennedy was assassinated in Dallas, a huge black bear was shot in the head in its winter den by Otto Hedbany, five miles north of Glidden. The 12-year-old bear weighed 665 pounds when dressed out, and measured 7 feet 10 inches from tail to snout—a world's record! Glidden then proclaimed itself the "Black Bear Capital of the World," which might seem odd given the way the town treated its biggest attraction.

Not that the bear went to waste. No, it was stuffed and mounted, and locals would haul it out to "march" in local parades. After a few decades of this, the bear got a new home at a local restaurant before a permanent home was built on the town's main drag. You can see it there today, as dead as it ever was . . . or at least since 1963.

But wait! Before you leave town you'll want to go two blocks east to see the World's Largest White Pine Log. Experts estimate that it contains about 1,950 board feet of lumber, but nobody in Glidden is so callous as to carve it up. The log was dragged to Mill Street on December 21, 1984, and given its own protective shed and another honor: the "Biggest and Last Sleigh-Hauled Log."

Black Bear, Grant St. and Broadway, Glidden, WI 54527

White Pine Log, Grant St. and Mill St., Glidden, WI 54527

No phone

Hours: Always visible

Cost: Free

Website: http://gliddenwi.org/attractions-events.html

Directions: Both north of Broadway (Rte. 13)—for the bear, just north; for the log, two blocks north.

WORLD'S SECOND-LARGEST STUFFED BLACK BEAR

You could argue that it's no great honor to be the largest black bear ever shot and stuffed, but imagine how the *second* largest stuffed black bear must feel. Gunned down in 2009, this critter weighed in at 660 pounds, just five pounds lighter than the Glidden bear, earning it a dubious silver medal. It was mounted in a ferocious, upright pose by the owner of the Tri-Mart BP Gas Station (11069 US Hwy. 8, Tripoli, (715) 564-2440), where you can see it in a glass-encased minidiorama today.

Grantsburg

Big Gust

Life was not good for troublemakers in turn-of-the-century Grantsburg. Other towns had police officers, but only Grantsburg had Anders Gustaf Anderson, a 7-foot-6-inch, 360-pound town marshal. Born in 1872, he was the law in these parts for the last quarter century of his life. When he died in 1926, he was also president of the fire department.

Though few today remember Big Gust firsthand, the town still celebrates Big Gust Days each June. In 1980, local carver Alf Olson fashioned a life-size replica of Anderson in his police uniform, which you can find in a glass case outside the town's community center. The local historical society has Gust's old uniform, his size 18 shoes, and the colossal crutch he used after an injury.

Community Center Building, 416 S. Pine St., Grantsburg, WI 54840

Phone: (715) 463-2405

Hours: Always visible

Cost: Free

Website: www.grantsburgwi.com/history.html

Directions: Four blocks north of Rte. 70, at Wisconsin Ave.

Grantsburg Area Historical Society, 133 W. Wisconsin Ave., Grantsburg, WI 54840

Phone: (715) 463-5660

Hours: June–August, Sunday 1–4 PM, or by appointment

Cost: Free

Website: www.grantsburgareahistoricalsociety.com

Directions: Just west of Pine St. (County Rd. F).

WISCONSIN'S TALLEST COUPLE

Anders Gustaf Anderson might have been Wisconsin's tallest town marshal, but Frederick and Jane Shadick of Belmont hold the record for the state's tallest couple. Frederick topped out at seven feet four inches, while Jane was an even seven. They toured for a while with P. T. Barnum's circus—Frederick was dubbed the Scotch Giant—and then with other sideshows throughout the country. Both died in 1854 and were buried in oversize plots in a Rewey cemetery.

Hayward
Moccasin Bar & Wildlife Museum

The Moccasin Bar is one of those rare private institutions that are bold enough to explore uncharted artistic territory: the world of anthropomorphic taxidermy!

Four dioramas depict local wildlife in human settings as never seen before. Two bear cubs play a game of poker. One cub slips a carrot to a bunny in an apron for an ace of hearts to complete a royal flush. The other bear, eyes glazed in a drunken stupor, is served beer by an otter. In another scene, a beaver referee declares one boxing raccoon the victor while another lies outside the ring in a bloody pool. Its skunk manager cries over its limp body. A third diorama depicts dozens of chain-smoking, beer-guzzling Tyrolean chipmunks on a fishing trip. And the final diorama is of a Northwoods Kangaroo Court, yet there are no kangaroos in Wisconsin. Instead, Judge Wolf comes down hard on a handcuffed badger who has been hunting out of season. Who caught the poaching badger? Sheriff Bobcat, that's who!

The dioramas almost detract from the fifth wonder of the Moccasin Bar: the world-record muskie mounted over the pool table. It's a 60.25-inch, 67.5 pounder that was caught by Cal Johnson in 1949. Just imagine this fish swimming around your legs the next time you take a dip in a local lake.

Moccasin Bar, 15820 W. First St., Hayward, WI 54843

Phone: (715) 634-4211

Hours: Daily 9 AM–2 AM

Cost: Free

Directions: Downtown at the intersection of Rtes. 27 and 63.

The Moccasin Bar has a sister establishment with a Wildlife Museum attached, but unlike the Moccasin, this place puts the animals in traditional settings. They've got even larger muskies, but these ones died of natural causes and are not as impressive as Cal Johnson's. The World's Largest Dead Muskie was found floating in the nearby Chippewa Flowage. The Wildlife Museum does have a few oddities, including a stuffed, now-extinct passenger pigeon, as well as albino specimens of a peacock, skunk, mink, pheasant, squirrel, and raccoon.

Wildlife Museum & Bar, 15708 Rte. B, Hayward, WI 54843

Phone: (715) 634-3386

Hours: Daily 9 AM–10 PM

Cost: Bar, free; museum, adults $3, kids $2

Directions: Three blocks east of Rtes. 27 on County Rd. B.

Keep a close eye on the bunny. Photo by author, courtesy of the Moccasin Bar

ANOTHER FISH TALE?

Is the muskie in the Moccasin Bar *really* the state's largest? Not if you ask the folks at **Dun Rovin Lodge Restaurant** (9404 N. Dun Rovin Rd., (715) 462-3834, http://dunrovinlodge.com) in Hayward. Caught by Bob Malo on June 6, 1954, it reportedly weighed a whopping 70 pounds 4 ounces.

There are other big 'uns around here, too. If you want to see the world's largest (stuffed and mounted) speared sturgeon, a 7-foot-1-inch, 195-pound monster, visit the **George W. Brown Ojibwe Museum** (603 Peace Pipe Rd., (715) 588-3333, www. lacduflambeauchamber.com/culture.htm) in Lac du Flambeau.

National Freshwater Fishing Hall of Fame

Bob Kutz had a vision in 1960 of an angler's shrine in the heart of the upper Midwest, and to humankind's benefit he decided to build it. The most impressive part of this tribute to freshwater fishing is the 143-foot-long, 500-ton muskie that rises above a pool filled with live fish and snapping turtles.

As you might suspect, this is no ordinary muskie. It was built in 1976 and proudly (and accurately) claims to be the World's Largest Fiberglass Structure. Inside is a collection of artifacts related to the sport. A stairway ascends to the fish's gaping mouth, where you and 19 friends can stand on the observation deck and view the rest of the museum complex. Six couples have been married up here. On your way back down, keep your eyes peeled for Herman the Worm, the World's Largest Nightcrawler; he's in there, (a real worm!) . . . but long since dead. Herman once appeared on *The Tonight Show*, where he shot baskets and rolled over on his master's command.

Outside, on the grounds of the shrine, are even more large fiberglass models. Several are outfitted with poles and fishing line for gag photos and unbelievable fish stories. A large building houses the bulk of the Hall of Fame's collection of 6,000-plus lures, 350 outboard motors, Polaroids of record holders, rods and reels, and a couple of Bigfoot-like statues of early fishermen. There's also an exhibit of poor taxidermy. Even if you have no interest in fishing, you'll enjoy this place.

10360 Hall of Fame Dr., PO Box 690, Hayward, WI 54843

Phone: (715) 634-4440

Hours: April–May and September–October, daily 9:30 AM–4 PM; June–August, daily 9:30 AM–4:30 PM

Cost: Adults $6.50, kids (11–17) $4, kids (10 and under) $3

Website: www.freshwater-fishing.org

Directions: At the intersection of Rte. 27 and County Rd. B.

You're not visitors—you're bait. Photo by author, courtesy of the Freshwater Fishing Hall of Fame

HAYWARD

➡ The town of Hayward hosts the **Lumberjack World Championships** (www.lumberjackworldchampionships.com) each July with competitions in ax throwing, log rolling, chainsaw carving, and other woodcutter events. If you can't make it, come anytime in summer to **Fred Sheer's Lumberjack Demo Show** (15638 W. County Rd. B, (715) 634-6923, http://sheerslumberjackshow.com).

SOMETHING'S BIG AND FISHY

OK, so the megamuskie at the Hall of Fame is the biggest fiberglass fish on the planet. Are there other impressive finned creations to be found in Wisconsin? You betcha!

Sunny, the World's Largest Sunfish

700 N. Rte. 35, Onalaska, (608) 781-9530, www.cityofonalaska.com

A 20-foot-long, 12-foot-tall sunfish—Sunny—sits on a Route 35 wayside in Onalaska, overlooking the Mississippi River, a body of water where it might even fit. Onalaska celebrates Sunfish Days each May.

World's Largest Bluegill

Rte. 48 and Vance St., Birchwood, (800) 236-2252, www.birchwoodwi.com

In northern Wisconsin along a chain of lakes, Birchwood is an ideal location to catch bluegill. Maybe not as large as the one looming over a local park (about 14 feet from nose to tail and mounted atop a giant pole) but certainly big enough to eat.

Largemouth Bass

Hudbuck's, 1114 W. Lake Shore Dr., Ashland, (715) 682-2323, www.hudbucks.com

This 15-foot brown largemouth bass is longer than the empty boat on the ground just below it. Nevertheless, it's been snagged by an enormous lure pulled by an unseen angler. Hope somebody has an appetite!

Two-Tailed Walleye

Rte. 83 and Fifth Ave., Shell Lake, (715) 468-7679, http://reporterjessica.wix.com/shelllake

The eight-foot walleye on the town sign in the center of Shell Lake looks normal enough, until you view it from the front. This fish has two tails! Some say it's to make the sign readable from either direction, while others claim it is a radioactive mutation. Believe who you want.

Trout and Mermaid

Beaver Springs Fishing Park, 600 Trout Rd., PO Box 1, Wisconsin Dells, (608) 254-2735, www.beaverspringsfun.com

If you don't catch a fish at this, the Midwest's largest fishing park, you can always pose with the 15-foot fiberglass trout outside. Or, with a bit of creative perspective, you can be photographed with the mermaid that sits on a treasure chest atop the office roof.

Hazelhurst
Hunter-Hunting Deer

Hollywood has been warning us for years about the impending rise of apes. And sure, those primates may have a banana to pick with humans for forcing them to wear funny outfits and ride tricycles in circuses. But how many chimpanzees ever suffer this indignity? Is it really worth conquering the planet over?

Deer, on the other hand, have every reason to be angry. Humans gun them down and run them down in alarming numbers. Is it any wonder that some have chosen to fight back? Just take the buck outside a Hazelhurst taxidermy studio. He sports an orange vest so that some nearsighted or drunk hunter doesn't mistake him for a deer—the perfect camouflage!—and cradles a gun in his outstretched hooves. Once he figures out how to pull the trigger, we'll all be in trouble.

North Country Taxidermy, 6851 US Hwy. 51, #A, Hazelhurst, WI 54531

Phone: (715) 356-4273

Hours: Always visible

Cost: Free

Directions: One mile south of town.

Holcombe
The Holcombe Indian

You might think that tacky roadside attractions like the ones found in this book have only been around as long as there have been roads. Not true—they've been around *longer*. Take, for example, the Holcombe Indian. Carved in 1876 by Luke Lyons, this impressive statue was erected to overlook the Little Falls Dam and was long known to sightseeing lumberjacks sluicing logs down the Chippewa River. The eight-foot-tall brave was washed away in an 1881 flood, but he was pulled from the river near Jim Falls, returned to Holcombe, repaired, and reinstalled. Years later, when a hydroelectric dam was built at the rapids, the Holcombe Indian was moved to its present location: inside a glass case in the town park. He still holds a tomahawk in one hand and a decorated spear in the other, looking none the worse for wear after almost a century and a half on this planet.

Main St. and Spooner Ave., Holcombe, WI 54745

No phone

Hours: Always visible

Cost: Free

Directions: In the park at 275th St. (Main St.) and 262th Ave. (Spooner Ave.).

Hurley
World's Largest Corkscrew

Sometimes, size isn't everything. While this 15-foot corkscrew is impressive, where would anyone ever find a 40-foot wine bottle to open with it? Certainly not at the liquor store that bears its name. You couldn't fit the corkscrew inside it, much less the bottle. But even without a bottle, this is a good place to stop for a gag photo. If you're limber enough to stand within the spiral cork-puller, you can tell all your friends, "I went to Hurley and was totally screwed!"

You're probably wondering *why* this corkscrew was erected in Hurley. The town's namesake, Daniel J. Hurley, was awarded US Patent 372,266 for a "cork-puller" in 1887. His device looks nothing like the World's Largest Corkscrew, but it's the drunken thought that counts.

Corkscrew Liquors, 5819 W. Rte. 2, Hurley, WI 54534

Phone: (715) 561-5645

Hours: Always visible

Cost: Free

Directions: North of town, just west of the intersection of Rtes. 51 and 2.

Screw this!

Jim Falls
Old Abe

Old Abe didn't start out old. As an eaglet, he was traded by a band of Chippewa for some food from the McCann farm in Jim Falls. A few years later, Dan McCann (who was crippled) offered the bald eagle in his place when the Eighth Wisconsin Infantry, Company C, was organized in Eau Claire to fight the Confederates. The company dubbed its mascot Old Abe after the president, and off they went.

Old Abe saw action in 42 battles and barely lost a feather. Soldiers recalled that he would squawk wildly when the shooting began. They took this as his encouragement to fight on, not that he was freaked out by the gunfire. At the end of the war, Old Abe was presented to the state of Wisconsin, and he was given a roost of honor in a special room at the State Capitol building (page 205). Old Abe met General Grant when he came through Madison but died shortly thereafter in a fire on March 28, 1881.

Jim Falls has honored its former citizen with a 10½-foot fiberglass statue at the north end of town, erected in 1990. And as long as they were erecting a monument, they added historical plaques to the pedestal noting Jim Falls's other two claims to fame: Wisconsin's Largest Hydro-Electric Plant and Wisconsin's Largest Cheese Manufacturing Plant.

County Rds. Y and S, Jim Falls, WI 54748
No phone
Hours: Always visible
Cost: Free
Directions: Just east of the river bridge.

Lake Nebagamon
Big Ball of Twine

It started on April 3, 1975: James Frank Kotera—"the real JFK"—quit drinking and, with the help of God, turned his compulsive energy toward a more creative endeavor. Using scraps of baling twine donated by his neighbor, Kotera set out to make the world's largest twine ball. Thirty-eight years later, he's still at it. By day he runs the nearby Highland dump, but whenever he's got free time, and the forest's not hip-deep in snow, he's out under the canopy that protects his 19,920-pound baby from the elements, twisting away.

Around and around he goes . . .

Kotera's creation deserves a close inspection. Not content to simply wrap twine around and around in a circle (how boring!), he takes each string and weaves it in, out, and around the pieces already on the ball. Because the twine scraps are red, yellow, green, and blue, they look more like veins on the surface of a brain than strings on a yarn ball. What's more, the ball is sort of shaped like a brain. And go up and touch it—it's *squishy*, like a brain.

Kotera continues to twist away, and judging from the bagfuls of twine sitting nearby, he'll be at it for many years to come. Let's certainly hope so!

8009 S. Oakdale Rd., Lake Nebagamon, WI 54849

Phone: (715) 374-3518

Hours: Always visible

Cost: Free

Directions: On the south side of the lake, at the intersection with Minnesuing Rd.

Laona
World's Largest Soup Kettle

If the thought of sharing cooking utensils with strangers freaks you out, you might want to take a pass on Laona's annual "Community Soup." Every August since the 1920s, the locals bring their bowls for a taste of soup cooked up in the World's Largest Soup Kettle. The crock is about seven feet in diameter and three feet deep—enough for everyone!

Now, a kettle this big can't fit in most cupboards, so during the rest of the year it hangs on a tripod next to the municipal building. Should an unfortunate critter fall in and not be able to scale its smooth walls, well, that's just more vittles for next year.

Beach St. and Mill Rd., Laona, WI 54541

No phone

Hours: Always visible

Cost: Free

Website: www.laonahistory.com/LaonaCommunitySoupPage.html

Directions: Along Rte. 8 as it jogs in the middle of town.

La Pointe
Tom's Burned Down Cafe

Where have all the hippies gone? In La Pointe, you can find them at Tom's Burned Down Cafe, and many locals are none too happy about it.

Shortly after buying Leona's Bar in 1992, Tom Nelson's investment went up in flames. He had long dreamed of opening a restaurant and bar, so rather than call it quits, he opened the Phoenix Gallery in the ashes of the former structure. The gallery transformed into Tom's Burned Down Cafe, sometimes called the Bar Tent, a combination of eatery, concert hall, and gallery for local artists.

Because it's one of the few places on this oh-so-quaint island to deviate from the prevailing Midwestern-Maine decorating theme, some people got upset. *It's an eyesore!* True. *It attracts bikers, old hippies, and other weirdoes!* True. *The bands are too loud!* True, too. It also siphons off all the fun people from the rest of Madeline Island, which, barring Tom's Burned Down Cafe, isn't worth the time or ferry fare to get to. If you must go, proceed directly to the primary eyesore off Main Street (not counting the T-shirt shops), and you're at Tom's. Odds are you can find somebody in the ruins who will proudly tell you they were at Woodstock, even if they weren't, and ramble on about how things have changed, man.

234 Middle Rd., La Pointe, WI 54850

Phone: (715) 747-6100

Hours: Call ahead; it varies, dude

Cost: Free

Website: www.tomsburneddowncafe.com

Manitowish Waters and Lac du Flambeau
Dillinger Is Almost Nabbed!

In April 1934, the FBI was tipped off: John Dillinger and his gang, which then included "Baby Face" Nelson and Homer Van Meter, were hiding out in the North Woods at Wisconsin's Little Star Lake. J. Edgar Hoover put Melvin Purvis on the case, and a swarm of agents descended on the Little Bohemia Lodge. The feds made hasty attack plans at the nearby Voss Birchwood Lodge (311 Voss Rd., (715) 543-8441, www.vossbl.com). What happened next became the 1930s equivalent of Waco; despite (or because of) overwhelming numbers on the side of the feds, things went horribly wrong.

On April 22, soon-to-be-innocent victim Eugene Boiseneau and two Civilian Conversation Corps (CCC) coworkers were leaving the resort after a chicken dinner, and their car was ambushed. Trigger-happy G-men riddled the car with bullets, killing Boiseneau and injuring the others. Dillinger's gang heard the shots and dove out of the lodge's second-story window, escaping north along the lake. Nelson fired at agents from his cabin next to the main building and then fled south along the shore. During the battle, the FBI riddled Little Bohemia with machine gun fire but didn't hit Nelson or anyone else from the already-departed gang.

Nelson eventually circled back and attacked three agents in a car. He jumped on their running board and fired his machine gun into the cab, killing agent W. Carter Baum and wounding two more. They ran off and Nelson fled in their vehicle.

The walls of Little Bohemia still bear the holes. Shattered windows were left in place with new panes placed over them. Personal items Dillinger forgot in his hasty retreat are now on display, including his clothes, underwear, toothpaste, and laxatives. At one time Dillinger's father operated a museum in the adjoining cabin where Nelson stayed. Also, part of the Johnny Depp film *Public Enemies* was shot here on the shootout's anniversary in 2008.

Little Bohemia is still a working restaurant and bar that brags "Dillinger only left because he had to." Be sure to ask your server about the

$700,000 in securities supposedly buried 500 yards north of the lodge next to two pine trees and an oak. Nobody's found them yet.

Little Bohemia Restaurant, 142 Rte. 51 South, PO Box 443, Manitowish Waters, WI 54545

Phone: (715) 543-8800

Hours: Museum, daily 9 AM–3 PM; breakfast and lunch, Friday–Sunday, 9 AM–2 PM; dinner, daily 5–10 PM

Cost: Museum, adults $5, kids free; meals, $7–20

Website: www.littlebohemialodge.com

Directions: Two miles south of town on Rte. 51, southeast of the airport, on Little Star Lake.

Following the shootouts at Little Bohemia, Baby Face Nelson fled as far as he could in the feds' car, but it broke down and he took off on foot. He eventually found the cabin of Ollie Catfish and his family on the Lac du Flambeau Indian reservation. Trouble was, they were still in it. But Nelson had a gun, so the Catfishes welcomed their guest. He stayed two nights before forcing Ollie to walk him to town. There he stole another vehicle and fled, but not before leaving the Catfishes a $75 tip.

Ollie's cabin has survived to this day, though it has been moved from its original location on the north shore of White Sand Lake to Dillman's Bay Resort on the south shore. Today it is known as the Fisherman's Cabin.

Dillman's Bay Resort, Fisherman's Cabin (#5), 13277 Dillman's Way, PO Box 98, Lac du Flambeau, WI 54538

Phone: (715) 588-3143

Hours: Call for reservations

Cost: $205–260 per night

Website: www.dillmans.com/cabins/cabin_05.html

Directions: Take County Rd. D northeast from town, then north on Sand Lake Lodge Ln.

Medford
Chainsaw Gordy's Garden of Saws

Nothing lasts forever, particularly chain saws when you don't regularly oil the chain. But even properly maintained, they're bound to give out sooner or later, and when they do "Chainsaw" Gordy Lekies knows just what to do: plant them. No, not in the ground, but nose-end through one of the 20-something lodgepoles standing along the ditch adjoining his property.

The Wisconsin Chainsaw Masterpiece.

Today there are more than 300 old, rusty models on display, as well as a carving of Chainsaw Gordy himself, made with a chain saw, of course. If you've go a broken saw, toss it in your trunk and bring it on by the garden—there's always room for more.

W 8743 County Rd. M, Medford, WI 54451
Private phone
Hours: Always visible
Cost: Free
Directions: North 10 miles on Rte. 13, then west 8 miles on County Rd. M, on the south side of the road just before Division Dr.

MEDFORD

➡ Astrologer-psychic Jeane Dixon was born in Medford on January 5, 1918. She once claimed a gypsy told her as a child she would go into this line of work.

➡ The world's first Tombstone Pizza was made by the Joe Simek family of Medford in 1962 and was served at their Tombstone Tap.

Mercer
Smokey Bear's Head

It can be a little unsettling to be walking through a museum and find Smokey Bear's head in a box—actually, *anybody's* head in a box—but not to worry. It's just part of an old costume. Before Smokey Bear was an actual flesh-and-blood bear rescued from a New Mexico forest fire, he was just a marketing campaign put together by the US Department of the Interior. The cartoon character existed solely on paper until a costume was unveiled in August 1950 at a fireman's convention in nearby Hurley.

Kids loved the real fake thing . . . at least until an actual bear cub was found up a tree in a charred forest. The real Smokey Bear ended up at the National Zoo, while the Smokey Bear costume made the rounds of schools and Boy Scout jamborees until it was eventually retired. Today its head can be found at the small museum in this local ranger station.

Ranger Station, 5291 N. State House Circle, Mercer, WI 54547
Phone: (715) 476-2240
Hours: Monday–Friday 8 AM–4:30 PM
Cost: Free
Website: http://dnr.wi.gov/topic/Lands/TurtleFlambeau/
Directions: South off Rte. 51 on the east end of town.

World's Third-Largest Loon

Mercer claims to be "Loon Capital of the World," and Claire de Loon is its spokes-loon . . . not that she talks much. Oh, she used to give a three-minute chat about her fellow loons when you pushed a button on her belly. That was back in 1981, when she was installed here by the Chamber of Commerce. Today the 16.5-foot, 1-ton fiberglass bird sits silently beside the highway, bill upturned.

Maybe she knows there are two other larger loons in Minnesota, one of which floats on a lake where any self-respecting loon should be. Could Claire be suffering from loon envy? If she's upset, she's not discussing it.

Mercer Area Chamber of Commerce, 5150 N. Rte. 51, Mercer, WI 54547
Phone: (715) 476-2389
Hours: Always visible
Cost: Free
Website: www.mercercc.com/attractions/claire-d-loon.html
Directions: On Rte. 51 in the center of town.

Claire's loony.

Minocqua and Wisconsin Dells
Eat Like Paul Bunyan

You can work up a powerful hunger from hours of miniature golf, antiquing, and paddle-boating. Take that tall appetite to Paul Bunyan's Cook Shanty, located just behind a 25-foot lumberjack sign in Minocqua. At the Cook

Shanty, they aren't big on formalities. There are no individual tables—just mess hall seating. There are no menus to speak of—just take what they serve you in "home-style" bottomless bowls. And don't expect any peace and quiet, either. Paul Bunyan's is popular with large families who want to avoid the time-consuming process of having the kids decide what to order.

The restaurant is decorated in a North Woods motif in which almost every wall hanging, grizzly bear lamp, or maple-syrup jug has a price tag on it. No, this isn't a typical cook shanty—it's a gift shop that serves meals! Before you know it, you're walking out with a mounted critter head that you won't realize looks goofy over your sofa until you arrive home, but then you're hundreds of miles from being able to return it.

Paul Bunyan's Cook Shanty, 8653 Rte. 51N, Minocqua, WI 54548

Phone: (715) 356-6270

Hours: Check website

Cost: Meals, $8–14

Website: www.paulbunyans.com

Directions: Just south of intersection of Rtes. 70 and 51.

There's a second Cook Shanty location in the Wisconsin Dells, this one guarded by a fiberglass Paul and Babe. But be forewarned—everything's bigger in the Dells, including the crowds.

Paul Bunyan's Cook Shanty, 411 Hwy. 13, Wisconsin Dells, WI 53965

Phone: (608) 254-8717

Hours: Check website

Cost: Meals, $8–14

Directions: On Rte. 13 between I-90/94 and Rte. 12.

Monico

Kovac Planetarium

Everyone's got a hobby—gardening, stamp collecting, or, like Frank Kovac, building a working planetarium. Even though he could step outside most nights and get a view of the universe for free, after a cloudy evening in 1996, Kovac decided to build his own planetarium, one "where the universe revolves around you." It took him about 10 years, and it was not as simple as you might imagine. He had to build a movable wooden sphere 22 feet in diameter, tilt it on a 45-degree angle to match Rhinelander's latitude, and construct an even larger building to house it all. Finally, Kovac had to paint 5,000 stars on the inner surface of the sphere, each in its proper location and luminosity.

So how does it work? The entire star globe spins, driven by a variable-speed motor. As the observer, you sit on a stationary arm inside the sphere while the stars circle above. Kovac can recreate any evening in the northern hemisphere—no clouds, no bitter cold, no bright lights from Rhinelander. And all those friends who called him nuts? Who's laughing now?

2392 Mud Creek Rd., Monico, WI 54501
Phone: (715) 487-4411
Hours: By appointment
Cost: Adults $12, seniors $10, kids (6–12) $8
Website: www.kovacplanetarium.com
Directions: Four miles east of Monico on Rte. 8.

Phillips
Wisconsin Concrete Park

Fred Smith didn't slow down when he retired from lumberjacking. For a while he occupied himself as a one-man band at the bar he owned, the Rock Garden Tavern (today the Stoney Pub), playing the fiddle and jingling bells on his knees as he jumped from table to table. But then he got an idea to honor people, famous and not, with concrete sculptures he made himself. The Concrete Park was born. It was 1950, and he was 65 years old.

His first piece was a barbecue pit with two Indian heads, one for the Cleveland Indians and one for the Boston Braves, both of which had been in the previous year's World Series. Fred made many figures of Indians who he correctly felt had been mistreated by the immigrant population around him. Over the years he built 237 figures—cowboys, "coolies," Indians, soldiers, loggers, brides and grooms, and occasionally the well-known: Ben Hur, Abraham Lincoln, Paul Bunyan, and the Statue of Liberty. His final piece was a life-size Budweiser Clydesdale team pulling a beer wagon.

Smith eventually couldn't continue his work and in 1968 checked into a nursing home; he died in February 1976. Volunteers tried to restore the figures that had fallen prey to the elements, but then on July 4, 1977, a violent windstorm blew down trees and damaged two-thirds of the figures. The Kohler Foundation, which had acquired the site, undertook a full and remarkable restoration. The tavern and Fred's home (with a Rock Gar-

Fred's Friends. Photo by author, courtesy of Friends of Fred Smith

den Room) are now part of the park, which was made a National Historic Landmark in 2006.

Concrete Park, N8236 S. Hwy. 13, Phillips, WI 54555

Friends of Fred Smith, 104 S. Eyder Ave., Room 217, Phillips, WI 54555

Phone: (800) 269-4505 or (715) 339-FOFS (6371)

Hours: Daylight hours

Cost: Free

Website: www.kohlerfoundation.org/smith.html, www.friendsoffredsmith.org

Directions: One half mile south of town on Rte. 13.

Poniatowski
Center of the Northern Half of the Western Hemisphere

There is nothing particularly unique about the community of Poniatowski, save for the fact that it's located at the exact center point of the northern half of the Western Hemisphere, according to cartographers.

What does that mean? Just northwest of town is a stone marker to indicate you are 90° west of the Greenwich meridian, halfway to the International Date Line, and 45° north of the equator, halfway to the North Pole.

And as you gaze around from this point you'll realize one thing: halfway from all these places is right in the middle of nowhere.

5651 Meridian Rd., Poniatowski, WI 54426

No phone

Hours: Always visible

Cost: Free

Directions: Just north and west of the Meridian Rd. (County Rd. U) and Cherry Ln. intersection.

Rhinelander
Dead John Heisman

John Heisman had many football accomplishments. He supposedly invented the term "hike" as well as the snap from the center. Some believe he thought up the forward pass, but don't dare say that around a Knute Rockne fan. He was also part of the greatest blowout in collegiate sports history: the 222–0 victory of Georgia Tech over Cumberland in 1916.

Heisman went on to coach, piling up an impressive 184–67–18 record. To honor his achievements, each year the Downtown Athletic Club in New York City gives college football's highest award, the Heisman Trophy, to the best player at the amateur level.

Coach Heisman died in New York in 1936 and was buried in Rhinelander, his wife's hometown. Cumberland alumni who still hold a grudge are not invited to the gravesite.

Forest Home Cemetery, 650 Washington St., Rhinelander, WI 54501

Phone: (715) 365-4172

Hours: Daily 9 AM–5 PM

Cost: Free

Directions: One block south of Lincoln St. (Rte. 8 Business), eight blocks east of Oneida Ave. (County Rd. G); Block 3, Lot 11, Grave D.

Rib Lake
Psycho Door

Wisconsin has an intimate connection to Alfred Hitchcock's *Psycho*. It was here that Ed Gein committed the unspeakable acts (which are *constantly* spoken of; see page 283) that inspired the novel, written by Milwaukee author Robert Bloch, that the movie was based on. And now the state has a little bit of the movie itself: the front door of the Bates Motel.

The owner of this Rib Lake funeral home purchased the extrawide door in an online auction and had it installed at his business. He claims it matches the period furniture in the home, and it does. But is "period" just a nice way of saying "creepy"?

Dallmann-Kniewel Funeral Home, 933 West St., Rib Lake, WI 54470

Phone: (715) 427-5465

Hours: By appointment

Cost: Free

Directions: North two blocks on McComb Ave. from Rte. 102, jog left onto West St., and it's a half block ahead.

Sayner
World's First Snowmobile

Carl Eliason built the world's first snowmobile in 1924 to putter around Star Lake. The "motor toboggan" was a hit, and Eliason inaugurated the Ski-Doo line of snowmobiles. He applied for a patent in 1927 but later sold it to the FWD Corporation of Clintonville when orders from Finland became more than he could handle.

His original models are still around, and you can find them at the Vilas County Historical Museum, all lined up in a row, among the 48,000-plus other items on display. For true snowmobile nuts, you can visit the museum in the winter on your machine. The museum's window display is adjacent to a local snowmobile path and kept lit at night, so you can zoom by the shrine to see how it all began.

Vilas County Historical Museum, 217 N. Main St., PO Box 217, Sayner, WI 54560

Phone: (715) 542-3388

Hours: June–October, daily 10 AM–4 PM

Cost: Adults $2

Website: www.northern-wisconsin.com/museum/

Directions: On Rte. 155 (Main St.), at Front St.

Eliason's grandson still owns the hardware store in town and has turned part of it into a minimuseum to the snowmobile. You can see a 1924 Model A, a Model D, a Model K1-0, and a Model K-12.

Eliason Lumber and Hardware, 274 Main St., Sayner, WI 54560

Phone: (715) 542-3233

Hours: Monday–Friday 7:30 AM–4:30 PM; Saturday 8 AM–noon

Cost: Free

Website: www.eliason-snowmobile.com

Directions: On Rte. 155 (Main St.), at Front St.

SUPER SNOWMOBILES

True snowmobile fanatics make the trek to Eagle River each January for the **World Championship Snowmobile Derby** (www .derbytrack.com), the North Woods equivalent of the Indy 500. Rather than race through the forests, contestants compete on a permanent oval track. Winners are inducted into the Snowmobile Racing Hall of Fame. The **Snowmobile Hall of Fame and Museum** is located in nearby St. Germain (8481 W. Hwy. 70, (715) 542-4HOF, www.snowmobilehalloffame.com). And in case you're wondering, Wisconsin has more than 25,000 miles worth of snowmobile trails . . . in the winter, of course.

Shell Lake
The Last Supper

Joseph T. Barta took four and a half years to carve this life-size re-creation of Leonardo da Vinci's masterpiece, but he wanted to do it right since, according to him, it had to "outlast [the] delicate painting which is flaking away from the plaster of the wall in Milan, Italy." Each figure is chiseled from glued two-by-fours purchased from a local lumberyard. It is an impressive centerpiece to the Museum of Woodcarving, the world's largest collection of wood carvings by a single individual. Barta created 100-plus life-size figures and 400 miniatures over a 25-year period.

Barta's interest in carving began while attending the School of the Art Institute of Chicago. After viewing his first composition, his instructors told him (according to Joe), "Your carving is perfect. Young man, go out into the world and make a name for yourself!" Joe wandered the United States and beyond, whittling small figures as he went. He eventually settled in Spooner, north of Shell Lake. It was here, in 1947, that he began creating his larger pieces, most having to do with the life of Jesus.

Who'd have thought lumber could be so spooky?
Photo by author, courtesy of the Museum of Woodcarving

But Barta added features to his scenes that weren't always in the New Testament. For example, his crucifixion scene has a horned Devil taunting Jesus as he hangs on the cross. A dwarf stands nearby, giving him the thumbs-down. The face of the lion in Daniel in the Lion's Den is supposed to be Joseph Stalin's. Herod's face is actually that of Adolf Eichmann. Barta claimed he channeled the spirits of the people he carved, which was trouble when he made Judas, hanging from a noose. "I never felt so mean; in fact, it was difficult to live with myself," he confessed.

Barta was not only an artist, but a poet, though it could be said his verse lacks a certain, um, what's the word? Talent? For example, his poem "Our Mom" begins, "Our mom is fat, there is no doubt / She's plenty broad but also stout." Stick to the chisel, Joe.

Museum of Woodcarving, 539 Rte. 63N, Shell Lake, WI 54871
Phone: (715) 468-7100
Hours: May–October, daily 9 AM–6 PM
Cost: Adults $6.50, kids (12 and under) $4.50
Website: http://shelllakeonline.com/library
Directions: One half mile north of town on Rte. 63.

SOMERSET

➡ Somerset claims to be the Inner-Tubing Capital of the World.

Spooner
JFK and Tommy Thompson Were Here

There are places back east that brag about George Washington having once slept there. But the Father of Our Country never made it this far west, so Wisconsinites have to make do with what they've got.

Take the proprietors of Big Dick's Buckhorn Inn. Back on March 18, 1960, senator Jack Kennedy stopped by the bar during a campaign trip around the state. Before leaving, he used the facilities—nobody is sure whether it was number one or number two, but he definitely did use them. Not wanting the auspicious occasion to be lost to history, the owners carved a wooden plaque and hung it on the men's room door. You can still see it today.

Then, on May 3, 1997, Wisconsin governor Tommy Thompson stopped in and did the same, though again nobody is sure whether it was number one or two. It too was commemorated with a plaque. However, since that historic day, the Thompson plaque has been taken down. Are patrons more enamored with the aura of Camelot than Eau de Tommy?

This establishment is worth a visit, even if you don't know its storied history. Stuffed trophies line the walls and hang from the ceiling, including a two-headed calf and a saber-toothed tiger. A sign next to the latter points out that it is a re-creation and was not bagged by a local hunter, since, you know, they've been extinct for about seven million years.

Big Dick's Buckhorn Inn, 105 Walnut St., Spooner, WI 54801

Phone: (715) 635-6008

Hours: Monday–Saturday 11 AM–2 AM

Cost: Free; beers, $1.50 and up

Website: www.bigdicksbuckhorninnspooner.com

Directions: One block east of River St. (Rte. 63), four blocks north of Maple St. (Rte. 70).

If only porcelain could talk.

SIZE BEATS FAME?

Though the urinal at Big Dick's Buckhorn Inn may be more famous, the pisser at the **Glarner Stube Bar & Restaurant** in New Glarus (518 First St., (608) 527-2216, www.glarnerstube .com) is much larger. Some even claim it is the Midwest's largest urinal. The bar even sells postcards of the fixture claiming so. If that isn't enough to get you to stop by, perhaps Buck, the bar's talking deer-head robot, will.

Mel, the Spooner Cowboy

His name is Mel, and he once guarded Mel's 66 Station in town. But that establishment is long gone, and times being what they are, a big guy's gotta take whatever work he can get. Today this 20-foot cowboy in tight blue jeans sporting a big, white Stetson on his disproportionately large skull silently guards a go-kart track and water park north of town. One of his hands is palm up, looking for your ticket, while the other is turned downward, as if to make a fist. Can you blame him?

Bulik's Amusement Center & Mobile Home Park, N5639 Rte. 63, Spooner, WI 54801

Phone: (715) 635-7111

Hours: Always visible

Cost: Free

Directions: At the north end of town on Rte. 63.

MUFFLER MAN MANIA

Like Mel, many of the big-headed fiberglass men dotting the Wisconsin landscape are commonly known as Muffler Men. The first such giant was manufactured in 1962 for the PB Cafe in Flagstaff, Arizona. He looked like Paul Bunyan—PB—and he drew in a ton of customers. Soon the International Fiberglass Company of Venice, California, was cranking out these statues for other eateries as well as for filling stations, repair shops, amusement parks, and more. Built in four pieces that could be interchanged depending on the buyer, the most common configuration was to have its forearms outstretched with its right hand palm up and the left hand palm down. Muffler shops in particular liked to place a complete exhaust system in its hands (hence the nickname), but they've been know to hold axes, rockets, hot dogs, flags, golf clubs, miniature cars—you name it. Here are a few more to check out:

Larry the Logroller

Wabeno Logging Museum, Oconto Ave. and Rte. 32, Wabeno

Larry looks a lot like Paul Bunyan, but don't most lumberjacks? He stands outside a museum crammed with saws and harnesses and other logging tools.

Fasco Man

Fasco Appliances, 3260 Walter St., Oshkosh, (920) 235-4177, www
.fascoapplianceoshkosh.com

If you have a fetish for burly, bearded fix-it men—think the mascot of Brawny paper towels—stop on by Fasco Appliances, where a gigantic dude in a red shirt and blue jeans guards the entrance to the parking lot.

Big Cowboy

150 Gasser Rd., Lake Delton, (608) 254-7300, www.buffalophilsgrille.com

Dressed in a ten-gallon hat with a six-gun in his hands, the Big Cowboy outside Buffalo Phil's lies flat on his back behind the establishment, waiting for repairs. Let's hope he's up and threatening the tourists soon.

SUPERIOR

➡ Arnold Schwarzenegger is a 1979 graduate of the University of Wisconsin–Superior, with a degree in business administration specializing in international marketing of fitness.

Spring Valley
Crystal Cave

From the outside, Crystal Cave seems like a typical, privately-owned cave attraction. A rustic stone building. A gift shop full of geodes. A picnic area. But there's so much more beneath the surface.

Compared to other caves, Crystal Cave is short on stalactites and stalagmites. It makes up for this with bat colonies and goofy tour guides spouting strange tidbits about the cave. Need a little good luck? Walk once, counterclockwise, around a stone pillar in the first room at the bottom of the stairway. Do it twice and your fortune reverses. Over in the corner are the remains of a caved-in room, where early owners tried to excavate beneath a nonrock ceiling.

Step into the Ballroom, the scene of two weddings over the years. Visit the Ghost and Goblin Room, where the frightening faces of Frankenstein, the *Looney Tunes*'s Road Runner, and Ronald Reagan have been spotted in the formations. See where thousands of bats hibernate in the winter and learn about the tons of droppings that were cleaned out before the cave was presentable for visitors. Experience total darkness at the cave's deepest point, 70 feet below the surface, and pray the guide doesn't lose track of the switch. And come prepared with a coin and a secret desire for the Make-a-Wish Room. It is said if you press the coin into the muddy walls and it sticks, your wish will come true.

W965 Rte. 29, Spring Valley, WI 54767

Phone: (800) 236-CAVE or (715) 778-4414

Hours: June–August, daily 9:30 AM–5:30 PM; September–October, daily 10 AM–4:30 PM; April–
    May, Saturday–Sunday 10 AM–4:30 PM

Cost: Adults $12, seniors (65+) $9, teens (13–17) $9, kids (4–12) $7

Website: http://acoolcave.com/

Directions: One mile southwest of town on Rte. 29; follow the signs.

Superior
Bong Memorial

No, not that kind of bong memorial . . .

Richard Bong of Poplar shot down 40 enemy planes—two on his first combat mission—in the South Pacific during World War II, becoming

America's Ace of Aces. For the most part he flew *Marge*, a Lockheed P-38 Lightning named after his loving wife. Bong's skills as a pilot eventually got him transferred stateside to test experimental aircraft in Burbank, California. He died one week before the end of the war on August 6, 1945, while taking off on a test flight in a P-80 Shooting Star. His body was returned to the Poplar Cemetery (Cemetery Rd.) for burial.

Today, a new Richard I. Bong Veterans Historical Center has been erected near his hometown. You can stand on a re-creation of a South Pacific atoll, complete with palm trees, thatched huts, and machine-gun turrets, while you stare out at the icy waters and iron-ore ships of Lake Superior. A restored *Marge* sits nearby—his plane, not his wife.

Richard I. Bong Veterans Historical Center, 305 Harbor View Pkwy., Superior, WI 54880

Phone: (888) 816-9944 or (715) 392-7151

Hours: May–October, Monday–Saturday 9 AM–5 PM, Sunday noon–5 PM; November–April, Tuesday–Saturday 9 AM–5 PM

Cost: Adults $9, seniors (65+) $8, teens (12–17) $8, kids (6–11) $7

Website: www.bvhcenter.org

Directions: At the intersection of Rte. 2 (Lenroot Hwy.) and Rte. 53 (Second St.).

A World of Accordions Museum

It probably wouldn't surprise you that the World of Accordions Museum is the only one of its kind in the world. Hopefully this isn't because it's a dying art form, but because this museum is so awesome nobody wanted to play second concertina to it. There are more than a thousand squeezeboxes and accordion-related artifacts in this collection owned by Helmi Strahl Harrington, and they're all on display.

In addition to the museum, Harrington also repairs accordions on site and gives performances in its Hani Strahl Concert Hall, named for her mother. If you're looking for sheet music for this instrument, she's got that too, in the gift shop. Lots of it.

1401 Belknap St., Superior, WI 54880

Phone: (715) 395-2787

Hours: Monday–Wednesday 10 AM–2 PM

Cost: Adults $10

Website: http://museum.accordionworld.org/

Directions: On Rte. 2 (Belknap St.) at Hammond Ave.

Tigerton
Rocks for Fun Cafe

Don't think rocks are fun? Well then, you *must* make a pilgrimage to Tigerton to visit with Don McClellan, the guru of geological guffaws. Every square inch of his restaurant has been adorned with rock-based art, most of which have puns, gags, or corny jokes printed on them. He's got a Jail House Rock (a rock behind bars), a Training Rock (a young stone on the potty), a Cough-In Rock (a rock in a casket, killed by cigarettes), a Twelve-Foot Rock (with a dozen feet), and on, and on, and on . . . 322 at last count, and another 186 on the drawing board.

According to McClellan, the collection is valued at $2,844,959.82, which seems rather steep, except when you realize he makes these pieces for his and your amusement, not to sell. If you bother asking a rock's price, you'll get an outrageous quote. Still want that Crabby Rock for $1,154.33? But don't you worry—before you leave McClellan will give you a free Lucky Rock, a googly-eyed pebble affixed to a business card printed with twelve keys to happiness.

Ready to rock. Photo by author, courtesy of Don McClellan

If you want to eat—this is a restaurant, after all—Rocks for Fun serves one thing only: Cornish pasties. They have 13 different varieties, each with a smiley face imprinted into the dough. Not only are they tasty, but they're simple to prepare, leaving McClellan time to roam the dining area and play pranks on his customers. Like the name says, this place is *fun*. Rocks and rocks of fun.

N4410 US Hwy. 45, Tigerton, WI 54486
Phone: (715) 535-2008
Hours: Daily 6 AM–5 PM
Cost: Free; pasties, $5.50 each
Website: http://rocksforfun.com, http://greatpasties.com
Directions: North of town on Rte. 45, northwest of the Beech St. intersection.

Washburn
The Sawdust Factory

There seem to be few communities in northern Wisconsin where someone with a chain saw isn't churning out black bear statues for the disposable-income crowd. The Sawdust Factory (aka the Art Colony) is something unique, however. Their art pieces have personality. Several local artists exhibit their creations in what looks like a New Age commune crossed with an Old Age logging camp.

Most days you can find organizer Bill Vienneaux working on his sculptures outdoors, first with a chain saw and then with a chisel. Most of the pieces on display "a smile south of Washburn" have been made to order and are not for sale, but you're welcome to look through Vienneaux's photo album and commission your own.

1825 W. Bayfield St., PO Box 154, Washburn, WI 54891
Phone: (715) 373-2708
Hours: Call ahead
Cost: Free
Website: http://thesawdustfactory.weebly.com/
Directions: On Rte. 13 south of town.

WINTER

➡ A large, fiberglass black bear stands outside the **Big Bear Lodge** (W1614 County Rd. W, (715) 332-5510, www.bigbearlodgeww.com) in Winter.

Wausau
Wausau Mine Company

The Wausau Mine Company brags about having a working replica of a copper mine, but it's not ore that you find here, but pizza, sandwiches, and beer. For although it looks like a rundown mining shack from the outside, this tilted building houses the Mother Load Eatery and Rusty Nail Saloon.

The restaurant resembles a rock cavern hundreds of feet below the surface, while the bar seems to be the processing operation on the surface. A dummy in a hardhat named Virgil sits bleary-eyed at a table, a drink in his hand, dynamite warnings all around. Customers are encouraged to monitor the canary on a nearby perch, and be sure to punch the time clock when they leave.

3904 W. Stewart Ave., Wausau, WI 54401

Phone: (715) 845-7304

Hours: Monday–Thursday 11 AM–10:30 PM, Friday–Saturday 11 AM–11 PM, Sunday 11 AM–10 PM

Cost: Meals, $7–20

Website: www.wausaumine.com

Directions: Six blocks west of Rte. 51, just north of the Rte. 29 intersection.

Yep, it's a restaurant.

Woodruff
World's Largest Penny

A penny isn't a lot, but don't tell that to Dr. Kate Newcomb, the Angel on Snowshoes. One penny might be worth only one cent, but a million pennies really add up.

Newcomb devised a fundraising effort for the Lakeland Memorial Hospital (today known as the Howard Young Medical Center) called the "Million Penny Parade." It started in 1953 with kids at the Arbor Vitae–Woodruff Grade School and eventually raised $10,000. Her efforts to bring health care to the folks of this region were featured on *This Is Your Life* in 1954, and thousands of pennies flooded in from around the nation. Before it was over, the hospital had received $105,000—that's 10.5 million pennies!

In Newcomb's honor, a huge concrete penny was erected in a local park. That park has since been developed into the One Penny Place senior apartments, but the penny remains at the entrance to the parking lot. It weighs 17,452 pounds and stands 10 feet tall—not exactly able to fit in a gumball machine. Paul Bunyan might be able to use it, but Kate was out of luck.

820 Third Ave., Woodruff, WI 53568

Phone: (715) 358-5541

Hours: Always visible

Cost: Free

Directions: One block west of Rte. 51, two blocks south of Rte. 47, at Hemlock St.

Dr. Kate Pelham Newcomb Museum, 923 S. Second Ave., PO Box 851, Woodruff, WI 53568

Phone: (715) 356-6896

Hours: Monday–Friday 11 AM–3 PM

Cost: Donations encouraged

Website: www.drkatemuseum.org

Directions: At the corner of Second Ave. and Rte. 51.

It ought to buy a pretty big gumball.

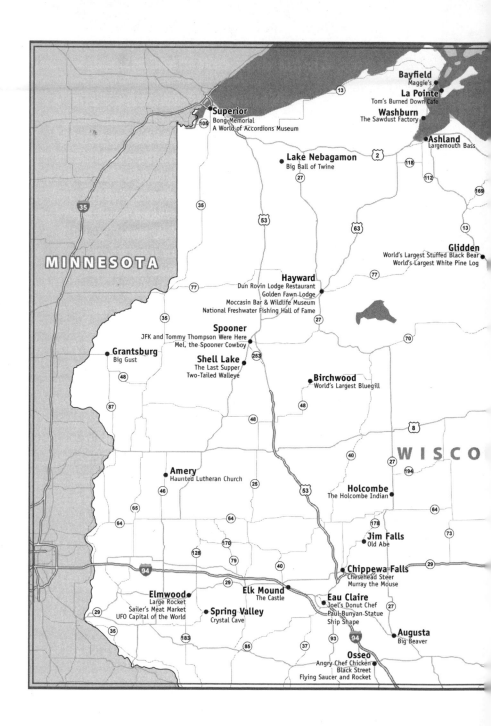

Bayfield
Maggie's

La Pointe
Tom's Burned Down Cafe

Washburn
The Sawdust Factory

Ashland
Largemouth Bass

Superior
Bong Memorial
A World of Accordions Museum

Lake Nebagamon
Big Ball of Twine

Glidden
World's Largest Stuffed Black Bear
World's Largest White Pine Log

MINNESOTA

Hayward
Dun Rovin Lodge Restaurant
Golden Fawn Lodge
Moccasin Bar & Wildlife Museum
National Freshwater Fishing Hall of Fame

Spooner
JFK and Tommy Thompson Were Here
Mel, the Spooner Cowboy

Grantsburg
Big Gust

Shell Lake
The Last Supper
Two-Tailed Walleye

Birchwood
World's Largest Bluegill

WISCO

Amery
Haunted Lutheran Church

Holcombe
The Holcombe Indian

Jim Falls
Old Abe

Chippewa Falls
Cheesehead Steer
Murray the Mouse

Elmwood
Large Rocket
Sailer's Meat Market
UFO Capital of the World

Elk Mound
The Castle

Spring Valley
Crystal Cave

Eau Claire
Joel's Donut Chef
Paul Bunyan Statue
Ship Shape

Augusta
Big Beaver

Osseo
Angry Chef Chicken
Black Street
Flying Saucer and Rocket

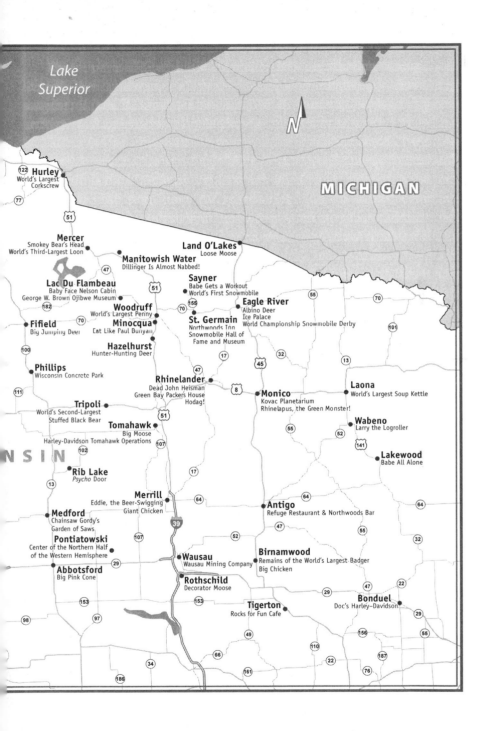

Lake Superior

MICHIGAN

Hurley
World's Largest Corkscrew

Mercer
Smokey Bear's Head
World's Third-Largest Loon

Manitowish Water
Dillinger Is Almost Nabbed!

Land O'Lakes
Loose Moose

Lac Du Flambeau
Baby Face Nelson Cabin
George W. Brown Ojibwe Museum

Sayner
Babe Gets a Workout
World's First Snowmobile

Woodruff
World's Largest Penny

Eagle River
Albino Deer
Ice Palace
World Championship Snowmobile Derby

Fifield
Big Jumping Deer

Minocqua
Cat Like Paul Bunyan

St. Germain
Northwoods Inn
Snowmobile Hall of
Fame and Museum

Hazelhurst
Hunter-Hunting Deer

Phillips
Wisconsin Concrete Park

Rhinelander
Dead John Heisman
Green Bay Packers House
Hodag!

Monico
Kovac Planetarium
Rhinelapus, the Green Monster!

Laona
World's Largest Soup Kettle

Tripoli
World's Second-Largest
Stuffed Black Bear

Tomahawk
Big Moose
Harley-Davidson Tomahawk Operations

Wabeno
Larry the Logroller

Lakewood
Babe All Alone

Rib Lake
Psycho Door

Merrill
Eddie, the Beer-Swigging
Giant Chicken

Antigo
Refuge Restaurant & Northwoods Bar

Medford
Chainsaw Gordy's
Garden of Saws

Pontiatowski
Center of the Northern Half
of the Western Hemisphere

Wausau
Wausau Mining Company

Birnamwood
Remains of the World's Largest Badger
Big Chicken

Abbotsford
Big Pink Cone

Rothschild
Decorator Moose

Tigerton
Rocks for Fun Cafe

Bonduel
Doc's Harley–Davidson

central wisconsin

on't let Door County folks tell you otherwise: central Wisconsin is where the artists are. No, they don't paint shoreline landscapes of Lake Michigan lighthouses, knit cozy and expensive sweaters, or fashion wooden chimes out of teak and mahogany. Central Wisconsin artists use blowtorches and trowels, not paintbrushes and looms. Who needs beeswax and charcoal when you have cement, empty bottles, and junked cars?

And though most of these artists are weekend warriors, their works are not insignificant. On the contrary, they're massive. The Rudolph Grotto and Wonder Cave stretches a fifth of a mile through an artificial mountain of stone. The Prairie Moon Sculpture Gardens and Museum covers an acre of Mississippi flood plain. The Paul and Mathilda Wegner Grotto, the Painted Forest, the J. F. B. Art and Math Museum . . . the list goes on. A few of these artists have even gained recognition and respect during their lifetime, including Clarence Shaler, whose works are scattered all around Waupun, and Clyde Wynia, who's still cranking out dinosaurs in Jurustic Park north of Marshfield.

The funky art would be reason enough to head to the middle part of the state. Throw in a cranberry museum, a motel guarded by a Viking, and a home half-crushed by a boulder, and you've got yourself a road trip!

Appleton
Houdini Historical Center

If you didn't know better, you'd swear that you'd stumbled into an S&M supply house—handcuffs, shackles, leg irons, collars with chains—but these restraints were the instruments of Harry Houdini's trade. The History Museum at the Castle has more than 120 artifacts and 150 photos from

Escape from Appleton!

the life of the world's most renowned escape artist, handed down through Harry's brother, Theodore Hardeen, to fellow magician Sidney Radner.

You'll see the tub where Houdini was submerged in milk, handcuffed and bound, only to emerge unscathed with glowing, supple skin. Check out his early beefcake publicity shots, in which he wears little more than chains and a determined glare. Or see the pair of handcuffs that once held Charles Guiteau, President Garfield's assassin. Houdini escaped from them without any trouble.

Houdini was born Ehrich Weiss in Budapest, Hungary, on March 24, 1874, but he grew up in Wisconsin. Contrary to claims made by his mother, he was *not* born in Appleton on April 6, 1874; she wanted his fans to believe he was American born and chose their family's immigration date as his birthday. Harry's father, Samuel Weiss, was the rabbi for Zion Congregation (320 N. Durkee St.), and the family lived in a storefront apartment on Appleton Street south of College Avenue, which has long since been torn down to make room for a parking lot. Adjacent to the lot is a sculpture entitled *Metamorphosis* by Richard Wolter. The open, unchained box was dedicated by Doug Henning in 1985 and bears the name of the first escape act Houdini ever performed in public. Be sure to pick up the "Houdini Historic Walking Tour" pamphlet at the museum for a stroll past several other Houdini sites downtown.

History Museum at the Castle, 330 E. College Ave., Appleton, WI 54911

Phone: (920) 735-9370

Hours: Tuesday–Sunday 10 AM–5 PM

Cost: Adults $15, seniors (65+) $13.50, kids (5–17) $10

Website: www.myhistorymuseum.org/houdini_harry.html

Directions: At Drew St., four blocks east of Appleton St., one block north of the river.

Joseph McCarthy's Home and Grave

Appleton is one of the few places in the nation where you can still find Joseph McCarthy supporters. It is also the only spot where you can still find Joseph McCarthy—he's buried here! Born in Grand Chute in 1908, the senator was an Appletonian later in life, having a small home here (514 S. Story St.) from 1942 to his death fifteen years later.

McCarthy's life and legacy was built on a mountain of lies. He claimed he earned the nickname "Tail Gunner Joe" during his service in the South Pacific during World War II. True, but his fellow GIs gave him the moniker after he fired 47,000 rounds of ammo at a coconut grove, just for fun. And that limp he supposedly sustained in combat? McCarthy actually injured his leg in a drunken fall from a ladder during a shipboard equator-crossing party.

McCarthy was a circuit judge before being elected an unremarkable US senator. To attract attention and improve his standing with the GOP, in 1950 he came up with the idea of hunting Communists wherever he didn't quite find them. Trouble was, he could never keep his numbers straight. How many "subversives" were there in the US State Department? The number changed each time he wagged his folded laundry list: 205, 57, 81, 10, 116, 121. Nevertheless, conservative writer William F. Buckley Jr. praised McCarthy for "a movement around which men of good will and stern morality can close ranks." But within two years, following the disastrous Army Hearings, the US Senate "condemned" him in a 67-to-22 vote on December 2, 1954. President Eisenhower joked, "Did you hear the latest? McCarthyism is now McCarthywasm."

Joe then crawled into a bottle. Just before his death he confided in a friend, "No matter where I go they look on me with contempt. I can't take it any more." Turns out, he didn't have to. Joe died of liver failure on May 2, 1957, at Bethesda Naval Hospital in Maryland. During his final days, he had detox hallucinations that snakes were after him.

So what's left of McCarthy? "McCarthyism" is in *Merriam-Webster's Collegiate Dictionary*, and Joe's tombstone overlooks the Fox River. Every year on the anniversary of his birth, November 14, members of the John Birch Society (www.jbs.org), today based in Appleton, hold a vigil at the grave of this twisted, misguided bully. They reaffirm their commitment to Commie-hunting, thinly veiled bigotry, and all-around mean-spiritedness. It is a thankfully small gathering.

McCarthy's Grave, Cemetery of St. Mary's Roman Catholic Church, 2121 W. Prospect Ave., Appleton, WI 54914

Phone: (920) 734-3259

Hours: Daily 9 AM–5 PM

Cost: Free

Website: http://stmaryparish.org/cemetery.html

Directions: East from Rte. 47, on County Rd. BB, the first street north of the river.

World's First Electrically Lighted House

Who would have thought this small Midwestern city could be the starting point of the greatest technological revolution in the modern world? Still, it's true. The Hearthstone, built by Henry J. Rogers and powered by the nearby Vulcan Street Plant (600 Vulcan St., since demolished), was the world's first electrically lighted house. The plant began generating hydroelectric power on September 30, 1882, and supplied enough electricity to illuminate 250 50-watt bulbs.

Four years later, on August 16, 1886, the Appleton Electric Street Railway Company (807 S. Oneida St.) began operation, connecting the previously unilluminated towns of Appleton, Kaukauna, Neenah, and Menasha. It was the nation's first electric trolley system.

The Hearthstone is open to the public and still has its original Edison switches and chandeliers. Luckily, historians have kept the rehabbers' hands off this old house.

625 W. Prospect Ave., Appleton, WI 54911

Phone: (920) 730-8204

Hours: Thursday–Friday 10 AM–4 PM, Saturday 11 AM–4 PM, Sunday 1–4 PM

Cost: Adults $7, seniors $5, kids (5–17) $4

Website: www.focol.org/hearthstone/

Directions: At the corner of Prospect Ave. and Memorial Dr. (Rte. 47), at the river.

Black Creek
J. F. B. Art and Math Museum

How long is an inch? One-twelfth of a foot? Is this a trick question? If you ask James Franklin Brunette, it's been a trick all along—what we refer to as an inch isn't an inch at all, but $15/16$ of what it was originally intended. To make his case, he placed dozens of hand-painted signs and exhibits all over his property explaining his reasoning, as well as a mini-Stonehenge if the signs aren't clear enough. Take a look around and ruminate on his wisdom and determination to set the world straight.

Brunette obviously knows his stuff. How else would he have gained the title Magnifico the Math Master, Arithmetician Extraodinaire? OK, so he gave himself that title . . . but only because so few people are qualified to bestow such an honor. Everyone else seems content using their defective rulers to keep humankind in the dark.

5107 Hwy. 47, Black Creek, WI 54106
Phone: (920) 739-0733
Hours: By appointment
Cost: Free
Directions: South of town on Rte. 47.

Black River Falls
Big Orange Moose

There must be something in the Black River Falls water—it's turned two moose bright orange! You can find them both at the Black River Crossing Oasis: one on the shore of a manmade pond in Gebhardt Memorial Park, the other silently guarding semis and minivans around the pumps.

These fiberglass creatures are great for kid photos while Mom or Dad is filling up the gas tank. The Oasis also has a fairly typical fiberglass deer jumping through the air and a fairly adorable fiberglass mouse in a sailor suit. For years the town planned to erect another statue (this one designed for the parents): the World's Largest Beer Stein. That idea has been shelved for now.

Best Western Arrowhead Lodge & Suites, Black River Crossing Oasis, 600 Oasis Rd., Black River Falls, WI 54615
Phone: (715) 284-9471
Hours: Always visible

Cost: Free

Website: www.bwarrowheadlodge.com

Directions: Behind the Perkins Restaurant on the east side of I-94 at the Rte. 54 exit.

MORE MEGA-MEESE

While none of these fiberglass wonders is as large—or as orange—as the Black River Falls moose, they are impressive nonetheless.

Loose Moose

Big Rob's Loose Moose Pub & Grill, 5810 US Hwy. 45, Land O' Lakes, (715) 547-8500

Big Rob may have set this moose loose, but it didn't go very far—it still stands out front.

Big Moose

Big Moose Supper Club, N8796 Business Hwy. S, Tomahawk, (715) 453-6667, www.bigmoosesupperclub.com

What else would you expect to find outside the Big Moose Supper Club—a big elk? This creature stands 15 feet tall and guards the parking lot.

Northwoods Moose

Papa Bear's Northwoods Store, S3949 Business Hwy. 12, Baraboo, (608) 355-9488, www.papabearsnorthwoods.com

So popular is the life-size moose outside this home-furnishings store that at least one couple chose to have their wedding photos staged beside it. This has only happened once, but it's a start.

Horny Moose

Moosejaw Pizza & Brewing Company, 110 Wisconsin Dells Pkwy. S,
Wisconsin Dells, (608) 254-1122, www.dellsmoosejaw.com

There are two moose statues at this log-cabin-style restaurant,
but only one is behaving itself. The larger of the two stands
among some trees atop the eatery's sign, but the other sprawls
atop the pizza-delivery vehicle, appearing to mate with the
unfortunate PT Cruiser.

Decorator Moose

Stoney Creek Inn, 1100 Imperial Ave., Rothschild, (715) 335-6858,
www.stoneycreekinn.com

This place's North Woods decor is only enhanced by the large
moose guarding the place. Expect more meese indoors, but in
pieces—heads on the walls and antlers in the chandeliers.

Wisconsin Death Trip

No oddball trip through Wisconsin would be complete without mention of
Wisconsin Death Trip, a classic of Cheese State weirdness. First published
in 1973, the book by Michael Lesy is a collection of real newspaper stories
from the 1890s that Lesy found in the *Badger State Banner*. Most are brief
and disturbing accounts of turn-of-the-century life. There are tales of disease, mental illness, suicide, murder, and death, all told in the matter-of-fact tone of the era. Clearly the "good ol' days" weren't all good.

Lesy supplemented the text with period photos found in local archives.
Most are pictures of grim-faced immigrants, stern farmers, and deceased
infants lying in coffins, though there are occasional humorous shots, like
a Victorian woman draped in live snakes and laughing like a maniac. Lesy
found most of these photos in the Van Schaick collection of the Jackson
County Historical Society in Black River Falls. The museum has an exhibit
about its relationship to the book.

Jackson County Historical Society, 13 S. First St., PO Box 37, Black River Falls, WI 54615
Phone: (715) 284-5314

Hours: June–August, Thursday–Saturday 10 AM–3 PM; September–May, Wednesday–Friday 10 AM–3 PM, or by appointment

Cost: Free

Website: www.blackriverfalls.com/area/areahistory

Directions: One block west of Water St. (Rte. 12), at Main St. (Rte. 54).

Buffalo City
Big Viking

The large Viking statue outside the Viking Motel in Buffalo City was not originally built for this establishment; it spent most of its early life selling "Kitchen Carpets by Viking." The company's slogan is still emblazoned on his shield. The 15-foot horny Scandinavian was fabricated in 1963, and when he retired he was shipped to this sleepy resort community along the Mississippi. To keep him from falling over, washing away in a flood, or being nabbed by rowdy teens, his feet were encased in cement. It gives the impression he ticked off a mob boss.

Where are my feet?

Viking Motel, 675 N. River Rd., Buffalo City, WI 54622

Phone: (608) 248-2590

Hours: Always visible

Cost: Free

Directions: At the intersection of River Rd. and 22nd St.

Cataract
Paul & Mathilda Wegner Grotto, aka a Landscape for Peace on Earth

In 1929 Paul and Matilda Wegner saw the Dickeyville Grotto (page 143) and were inspired to build one for themselves—and perhaps raise a little money, too. Admission to the Wegners' attraction was free, but photographs were not permitted. This allowed them to make money from picture postcards, as well as concession sales of sodas and food.

As part of their gardens, the Wegners chose to make a statement about the growing religious intolerance in Europe and elsewhere during the 1920s and '30s, so they built the Glass Church. The Glass Church depicts 11 different houses of worship on its outside walls, each from a different religion, and has a Star of David over the front entrance.

And there was more they wished to commemorate. They constructed a 12-foot model of the *Breman*, the steamship that carried the Wegners to America in 1885. For their 50th anniversary, the Wegners "baked" a stone wedding cake. And after Paul died in 1937, Matilda made a headstone for him and one for herself at the nearby Cataract Cemetery. (Matilda died in 1942.) The site was restored by the Kohler Foundation in 1986–87.

Contact: Monroe County Local History Room, 200 W. Main St., Sparta, WI 54656

Phone: (608) 269-8680

Hours: Daily, sunlight hours

Cost: Free

Website: www.monroecountyhistory.org/wegnergrotto.php

Directions: Just west of Rte. 27 on Rte. 71, 1.5 miles south of Cataract.

Clintonville
Four-Wheel Drive Museum and the Great Wall of China Rock

What would Wisconsin be without four-wheel-drive trucks? Probably just a bunch of drunk guys standing around in bright orange hunting suits. And a lot of happy deer.

But thanks to Otto Zachow and William Besserdich, the deer are on the run. In 1908 the pair designed the first vehicle powered by all four wheels. They dubbed it "The Battleship" because it would go anywhere, and over anything, they chose. A year later they founded the Badger Four-Wheel Drive Auto Company, which was later shortened to the FWD Corporation by Walter Olen, a businessman who saved the young company from bankruptcy.

Zachow and Besserdich's vehicles were widely used by the military, leaving other car companies to supply bubbas, and eventually today's urban professionals, with the off-road vehicles they so desperately need. The Four-Wheel Drive Museum is one of the few locations where these folk find common ground.

Though the museum is only open by appointment, the park grounds surrounding it are always open, and it's here you'll find something found almost nowhere else: a hunk of the Great Wall of China. In the 1920s president Sun Yat-Sen donated the four-by-four-foot section to Walter Olen in thanks for the trucks that plowed his country into the 19th century.

Walter Olen Park, 11th St. and Memorial Circle, Clintonville, WI 54929

Phone: (715) 823-2141

Hours: By appointment

Cost: Donations encouraged

Directions: One block east of Main St. (Rte. 22), just north of the river.

Cochrane
The Prairie Moon Sculpture Gardens & Museum

The Prairie Moon Museum was opened in 1955 by 71-year-old farmer Herman Rusch to put his tools on display and as a "good way to kill old-age boredom." He housed his collection in the old Prairie Moon Dance Pavilion and added other fantastic finds, such as a goat-powered washing machine and a tree that had grown around a scythe.

"A good way to kill old-age boredom." Photo by author, courtesy of the Town of Milton

Three years into the project, he decided the surrounding landscape needed something more, and he began building one of 45 different sculptures that eventually made up the Prairie Moon Sculpture Gardens. In the gardens are a Hindu temple, animal sculptures, dinosaurs, a giant jug, two obelisks, an Indian on horseback, and a 260-foot wagon-wheel fence running the length of the property. In addition, Rusch preserved and planted many rare, native species of flowers.

When Rusch decided to hang it up, the place was sold and used as a dog kennel. The sculptures began to fall apart and lost their painted finishes. Then, in 1992, it was rescued and restored by the Kohler Foundation, which then donated it to the Town of Milton. The museum is long gone, but the sculptures have been repaired and repainted. Rusch's old dance hall has been converted to an interpretive center, and today houses a collection of twelve models of Cochrane buildings made by Fred "Fritz" Schlosstein.

Town of Milton, S2921 County Rd. G, Fountain City, WI 54629

Phone: (608) 687-9874

Hours: Garden, daily 9 AM–6 PM; museum, Sunday noon–3 PM

Cost: Free

Website: www.kohlerfoundation.org/rusch.html

Directions: Two miles south of Cochrane on Prairie Moon Rd. (County Rd. OO), just off Rte. 35.

Elk Creek
World's Largest Roasted Chicken

Unlike some establishments we could mention, the Elk Creek Inn believes in truth in advertising. Other restaurants have erected cute fiberglass chickens in chef's hats or swigging mugs of beer, as if you're going to sit down with Charlie Clucker for a brew.

Not here. Chicken is to be plucked, gutted, and *roasted* . . . not unlike the gigantic, succulent dinner sitting on a platter on the roof of this eatery. The portions they serve aren't quite as generous, but honestly, could you fit a phone-booth-size doggie bag in your car if they did?

Elk Creek Inn, N40351 State Rd. 93, Elk Creek, WI 54747

Phone: (715) 985-3304

Hours: Always visible; restaurant, daily 10 AM–2 PM

Cost: Free

Directions: On the north end of town.

Must be hot on that roof.

Fountain City

Elmer's Auto and Toy Museum

Elmer Duellman loves automobiles—always has. So when he started collecting cars, he didn't restrict himself to just the kind that you drive on a road. As you'll see in this five-building museum, he's amassed thousands of toy vehicles—more than 600 pedal cars and 100 pedal tractors and more than 100 classic antique and muscle cars. They cover the floors and are stacked up along the walls of his barn and other outbuildings, with some parked out along the driveway. There are so many that it's hard to take them all in.

Bernadette Duellman, Elmer's wife, has also caught the collecting bug, but her specialty is dolls, the spooky, antique kind. They're all standing at attention in one building, a thousand glassy eyes staring at you when you enter, looking like an invading army from *The Bad Seed*.

W903 Elmers Rd., Fountain City, WI 54629

Phone: (608) 687-7221

Hours: Check website; hours vary by day and month

Cost: Adults $8, seniors (65+) $7, kids (6–17) $4

Website: www.elmersautoandtoymuseum.com

Directions: Rte. 95 east to County Rd. G, north to Elmers Rd., then left.

Rock in the House

At 11:38 AM on April 24, 1995, Maxine Anderson was working in her home at the bottom of a Mississippi River bluff when a 55-ton boulder shaped like a Ding Dong snack cake rolled in her back door. Or, more accurately, *through* her back door . . . and everything else. Surprisingly, the boulder stopped midway through the building and didn't end up on the highway or in the river on the other side.

Unable to live there, Maxine and her husband Dwight sold their home to Fran and John Burt of Fountain City. The Burts ran the numbers and found it would be cheaper to open the house as a tourist attraction at one dollar a head than to pay somebody to remove the rock. Rock in the House was born. The Burts left the house in the same condition as it was the day the rock arrived. The TV is still on, and you're welcome to have a seat on the living-room couch. The structure is stable, and you wouldn't know there was a problem when viewing it from the outside. The gaping rock-filled hole is more impressive from the inside.

Look through this hole and admire the awesome strength of Mother Nature. Recall how others have not been as lucky as the Andersons, like a certain Mrs. Dubler who was squished by a tumbling boulder in 1901 . . . in the home next door. Realize there are plenty of other rocks just itching to fall from the same bluff, through those trees. Then get in your car and get the hell out of the way!

440 N. Shore Dr., Fountain City, WI 54629

Phone: (608) 687-6106

Hours: Daily 10 AM–6 PM

Cost: $1

Directions: On Rte. 35 (Shore Dr.) at the north end of town; watch for the signs—you won't see the rock.

It could have been worse. Photo by author, courtesy of Rock in the House

Galesville
The Garden of Eden?

For years, Reverend David O. Van Slyke would tell anyone who would listen that he had discovered the true location of the Garden of Eden: Galesville, Wisconsin. Just read your Bible. Van Slyke had . . . 25 times. Four rivers, honey, apples, and snakes—they're all here! And he documents his proof in an 1886 pamphlet, *Found at Last*.

Today, Galesville honors its most famous booster with a life-size bronze made by local sculptor Elmer Petersen. The Methodist preacher stands in a flower garden, his knee-length coat flapping in the wind, a Bible in one hand and an apple in the other. The choice, of course, is all yours.

High Cliff Park, Main St. and Mill Rd., Galesville, WI 54630

Phone: (608) 582-2868

Hours: Always visible

Cost: Free

Website: www.galesvillewi.com, www.gardenofedenpreservationsociety.org

Directions: On the east side of Rte. 53 (Main St.) just north of the river bridge.

The choice is yours, sinner.

La Crosse
Big Hiawatha

The 25-foot Hiawatha statue outside the La Crosse Area Convention & Visitors Bureau in Riverside Park once greeted travelers with a pre-sensitive plaque reading, ME WELCOME YOU TO VISITOR CENTER. Today there is no sign and you're left to imagine what he would say. The concrete chief was built in 1962 by Anthony Zimmerhakl, assisted by his sons Don, David, and Stephan. It weighs 25 tons, which, if you're calculating, is a ton per foot.

Hiawatha is there to remind visitors of a vision the famous Native American once had: no tragedy would ever come to the spot where the three rivers meet. Since the Mississippi, La Crosse, and Black Rivers converge in La Crosse, people sleep soundly at night.

La Crosse Area Convention & Visitor's Bureau, Riverside Park, 410 E. Veterans Memorial Dr., La Crosse, WI 54601

Phone: (800) 658-9424 or (608) 782-2366

Hours: Statue, always visible; information center, June–August, daily 10 AM–5 PM

Cost: Free

Website: www.explorelacrosse.com

Directions: Where the La Crosse River meets the Mississippi River, at the end of State St.

Keep Up the Good Work . . . Just in Case

The Franciscan Sisters of Perpetual Adoration have been praying for world peace since 11 AM on August 1, 1878. Praying hard. Twenty-four-hours-a-day hard, seven days a week, 365 days a year (and more on leap years). Two sisters are always at the altar and are relieved in shifts, like a tag-team match. That's how their order earned its name.

Does it matter that during the last 120-plus years, the world has seen two World Wars, hundreds of civil conflicts, and more senseless destruction than anyone cares to remember? No, because it isn't fair to judge these nuns by what *has* happened, only by what *hasn't*, and that's difficult to gauge. God only knows how much more could have gone wrong had these women not been on the case.

St. Rose of Viterbo Convent, 912 Market St., La Crosse, WI 54601

Phone: (608) 782-5610

Hours: Tours, Monday–Saturday 9–10:45 AM, 1–3 PM; Sunday 1–3:30 PM

Cost: Free

Website: www.fspa.org/Prayer/perpetualadoration.html

Directions: At Market and Ninth Sts., just north of Rte. 33.

World's Largest Golf Bag

For those golfers who can't really decide on a club, Northland Golf & Ski has a bag for you—you can bring every club you own, and then some! It stands about 10 feet tall and is painted University of Wisconsin red, which makes it look like a London phone booth. The only drawback to this bag is that you need a very big caddy or an even larger cart to use it. Does Hummer make a golf cart?

Northland Golf & Ski, 2137 George St., La Crosse, WI 54603

Phone: (608) 784-8333

Hours: Always visible

Cost: Free

Directions: On Rte. 35 (George St.) at Hayes St.

World's Largest Six-Pack

Since 1969 this alcoholic monument has graced the south end of La Crosse. These six tanks were made to hold up to 22,000 gallons of beer for the Heileman Old Style Brewery—7,340,796 regular cans (or 688,200 barrels)

Not Old Style, but close.

worth, to be exact. If you drank a six-pack a day, it would have taken you 3,351 years to finish it all off. The World's Largest Six-Pack was the crowning jewel on the Old Style Brewery Tour, unique in the industry for serving samples *before* you were escorted through the plant. They knew their customers!

But then Stroh's bought the brewery in 1999 and stopped the tours. The six-pack was painted over, and there was even talk of demolishing them. But the brewery must have had a guardian angel, perhaps the spirit of King Gambrinus. (A 15-foot statue of the lager-soaked royal guards the World's Largest Six-Pack from across the street.) Today the City Brewery operates the plant, and the cans have been given a facelift—they now sport La Crosse Lager labels. All hail King Gambrinus!

City Brewery, 1111 S. Third St., La Crosse, WI 54602

Phone: (608) 785-4200

Hours: Always visible

Cost: Free

Website: www.citybrewery.com

Directions: At Jackson St. (Rte. 33) and Third St. (Rte. 14/61).

WORLD'S LARGEST THREE-PACK

If you drive eastward on Washington Avenue into downtown Manitowoc, you end at Seventh Street and the **World's Largest Three-Pack**—three 60-foot silos painted to look like bottles of Budweiser. And while the bottles are definitely taller than the La Crosse cans, they can't disguise the fact that somebody snagged half the six-pack.

Markesan

Happy Tales Books

Calling all bibliophiles: your Camelot awaits on the south side of Green Lake. Lloyd and Leonore Dickmann have turned a slurry tank on their property into Castle Arkdale, home to thousands of books, and they're all for sale. With a drawbridge and a moat, the structure looks like it belongs in *Mister Rogers' Neighborhood*, but this place isn't make-believe. The books inside are piled on tables, crammed in shelves, and stacked on the floor. Because the castle won't fit the more than one-hundred thousand titles for sale, more can be found in the adjoining lodge. There's a sort of rough order to it all, but expect to dig. . . . Isn't that the best kind of bookstore experience anyway?

W1778 County Rd. K, Markesan, WI 53946

Phone: (920) 398-3375

Hours: Summer, Saturday 9 AM–3 PM

Cost: Free

Directions: Eight miles north of town; Rte. 44 north to County Rd. H, east to County Rd. O, north to County Rd. K, then east.

Marshfield
Chevy on a Silo

No, a tornado didn't pass just south of Marshfield. The car you see on top of that silo is there for a reason. In addition to being a working farm, this place warehouses cars for local residents. The one on the silo is a 1967 Chevy, and it's been up there since 1983. Owner Curt Evans hoisted it up with a crane. It's hard to beat the advertising value of a severely misparked vehicle.

When Evans isn't plowing his fields or stranding automobiles forty feet in the air, he tries his hand at chain saw art. A small roadside gallery houses sculptures of black bears standing around, rearing on their hind legs, and rowing cute little canoes.

8627 S. Rte. 13, Marshfield, WI 54449

Phone: (715) 676-3659

Hours: Always visible

Cost: Free

Directions: Five miles south of town on Rte. 13.

Jurustic Park

Something strange is going on in McMillan Marsh. Artist-paleontologist Clyde Wynia has been extracting extinct creatures that have been trapped in the mud since the Iron Age. Or at least that's what he tells you. Some of

Dragon from the Iron Age. Photo by author, courtesy of Jurustic Park

these critters look suspiciously industrial, not biological. Take, for example, the dragon with the massive, spinning helicopter blade on its back. Dinosaurs' heads appear to have been fashioned out of oil pans. Storks and cranes have springy necks and claws that resemble gardening tools. What's going on here?

Ask Clyde's wife, Nancy. She'll tell you he's a retired lawyer, a part-time welder, and a full-time jokester. Hundreds of creatures inhabit his Jurustic Park, tucked between the trees along the Little Eau Plaine River. Dragons dangle from branches, huge spiders creep along paths, and birds with bell bodies clang when the wind kicks up. Jurustic Park is best appreciated when taking a tour with Wynia, but only if you've sharpened your wit.

Be sure to visit the Hobbit House, Nancy Wynia's studio inside the park. She's an accomplished glass sculptor and natural-fiber worker. Her work includes marbles, glass fish, eyes for Clyde's sculptures, knit sweaters, and full-size soft sculptures of friends and family.

M222 Sugar Bush Ln., Marshfield, WI 54449

Phone: (715) 387-1653

Hours: "Most days" 10 AM–4:30 PM

Cost: Free

Website: www.jurustic.com

Directions: North of town on County Rd. E, then left on Sugar Bush Ln. just north of Marsh Rd.

A DRAGON GETS LOOSE

Not all of the creatures unearthed from McMillan Marsh are corralled in Jurustic Park. Case in point: an **enormous rusty dragon** has escaped and now stands on a traffic island in the middle of East Veterans Parkway at North Vine Avenue in Marshfield. Thanks a lot, Clyde!

Montello
The Boy Who Would Not Tell a Lie

In 1850, Mr. and Mrs. Samuel Norton, foster parents of orphan Emmanuel Dannan, murdered a traveling peddler on their farm southeast of Montello and then stole his horse. Yet they made the mistake of allowing Emmanuel to witness the deed. When law enforcement officials became suspicious, the Nortons tried to coach Emmanuel to substantiate their alibis.

But Emmanuel had been taught to tell the truth by his deceased English parents. The Nortons tortured the eight-year-old until he perished on November 30, 1851; then they buried him on the farm. The police never had enough evidence to charge the couple with the peddler's murder, but they were able to convict them of first-degree manslaughter in the boy's death.

Emmanuel's body was moved to Greenwood Cemetery in 1858. Early efforts to erect a monument fell through when the man hired to raise funds for the honest child ran off with the donations. Not until 1954 was a granite marker placed over the grave of "The Boy Who Would Not Tell a Lie." It was dedicated on all-to-seldom-celebrated "Truth Day," September 14.

Greenwood Cemetery, County Rd. B, Montello, WI 53949

No phone

Hours: Daily 8 AM–6 PM

Cost: Free

Directions: South on Rte. 22, east on County Rd. B to 18th Rd.

Wisconsin's Largest Tree

There are many different ways to measure a tree. You could measure its height, its width, or count the number of leaves on its branches. But the easiest method is to measure the circumference of its trunk at the base. Using that method, the enormous cottonwood on the courthouse lawn in Montello is Wisconsin's largest at 23.2 feet.

That's what it measured in 1978 when a plaque was erected to celebrate the tree's unique status. At the time it was 138 feet tall with a 132-foot crown, but it has no doubt grown since then. To see if it retains the title, bring a tape measure, record its new dimensions, and then compare it to every other tree in the state.

77 W. Park St., Montello, WI 53949

No phone

Hours: Always visible

Cost: Free

Website: www.montellowi.com

Directions: On the courthouse lawn, one block east of Rte. 23, at the lake.

MONTELLO

➡ The granite for Grant's Tomb was quarried in 1897 near Montello.

Necedah
Virgin Mary Apparitions

Mary Ann Van Hoof began having religious visions on November 12, 1949, and didn't stop until she died in 1984. She would see the Nativity on the Friday before every Christmas. She witnessed the Passion of Christ each Easter. She saw Jesus open the Iron Gates of the Soviet Union 18 years before Mikhail Gorbachev got around to it. In 1951 and 1952 the wounds from a crown of thorns appeared on her forehead during Lent. Mother Cabrini showed up in 1975 and promised to "go with us" if we drove 55 mph, and not over 60, before the national speed limit became law. And, strangest of all, she told her follower that a spaceship piloted by an old guy named Alex would take them all to the center of the hollow earth when the Apocalypse came . . . which would be soon.

Not surprisingly, the local Catholic bishop did not approve of Van Hoof's actions and ordered her to stop. But how could one stop a vision? They kept coming, and Van Hoof kept warning her followers, bishop be damned. Then she suggested 30,000 US priests were Soviet agents. The church excommunicated Van Hoof and her followers in 1975, but they never went away.

The present-day Necedah Shrine (its full name is Queen of the Holy Rosary Mediatrix Between God and Man Shrine) is filled with dioramas, statues, and minigrottos, most based on holy visions and proclamations channeled from on high. The Last Supper, Joan of Arc, George Washington, Abe Lincoln—they're all here! The most interesting is the Crucifixion Shrine. During Lent 1955, Van Hoof was instructed to find a white crucifix and red and purple crayons. A week later, another vision guided her as she marked up the corpus with colorful wounds. Mary Ann had a field day. Sculptors translated her marked-up vision into one of the most horrific, bloody, gouged, and battered crucifixions you're ever likely to see.

The best days to visit the shrine are the anniversaries of Van Hoof's major visions: April 7; May 28, 29, and 30; June 4 and 16; August 15; October 7; and November 12. You're welcome anytime, but if you come, you are asked to dress modestly, not to wear shorts, and if you're a woman, not to wear slacks, either. Wraparound skirts are available to hide your immodest 21st-century attire. As the entrance sign says, "As the women go, so goes the nation!"

Queen of the Holy Rosary Mediatrix Between God and Man Shrine, W5703 Shrine Rd., Necedah, WI 54646

Phone: (608) 565-2617

Hours: Open 24 hours; information center, daily 10 AM–4 PM

Cost: Free

Website: www.queenoftheholyrosaryshrine.com

Directions: A half mile east of Rte. 80 (Main St.) on Rte. 21 (Third St.), then follow the signs south.

MARY DOWN THE DRAIN

Images of the Virgin Mary can be fleeting. Julie Ganser of Sun
Prairie knows this all too well—she spotted the Madonna with
child in her shower . . . in a clump of hair on the tile wall, to be
exact. Ganser had the good sense to photograph this appari-
tion before it washed off and clogged her pipes.

Neenah
Bergstrom-Mahler Museum

Neenah is one of the Great Lakes' biggest paper-producing towns, so it
seems only logical that it would have one of the world's largest collections
of paperweights, too. Remember the rock you painted for your father's
birthday when you were strapped for cash as a child? Well, you won't find
that type of crud here. The 1,800-plus paperweights at this museum are far
too dazzling to hold down a pile of unpaid bills.

The Bergstrom-Mahler's focus is on Germanic Glass, under which
small designs, like flowers, are magnified by the rounded contour of the
spherical weight. Each paperweight is displayed in a lighted case to get the
full effect of the pattern and to keep out of the hands of the little ones. If
you want to see how they're created, come in the summer when artisans
braze weights while you watch.

165 N. Park Ave., Neenah, WI 54956

Phone: (920) 751-4658

Hours: Tuesday–Saturday 10 AM–4:30 PM, Sunday 1–4:30 PM

Cost: Free, donations accepted

Website: http://bergstrom-mahlermuseum.com

Directions: Main St. east to Wisconsin Ave. and Riverside Park, then north on Park Ave.

Neillsville
Chatty Belle, the World's Largest Talking Cow

Wisconsin's reputation as the Cheese State is well deserved . . . just ask Chatty Belle, the World's Largest Talking Cow. She just might be the world's *only* talking Holstein. This 20-foot-long, 16-foot-tall mother shamelessly plugs the local cheese-based economy and tries to dispel all those nasty rumors that the stuff is chock-full of cholesterol.

Is that all you can talk about? Cheese?!?

If Chatty were a real cow, she would produce 270 pounds of milk each day, and at that rate it would take 40 months to deliver the 170,000 quarts necessary to produce the World's Largest Cheese, which was once on display in a semitrailer "cheesemobile" parked beside her. Sadly, that 16-wheel piece of Wisconsin history is just that—history—having gone in 2005 to that great truck stop in the sky. You can, however, still find a Wisconsin-shaped rock, "exactly [that] shape when it was dug out of the ground," at the adjoining Wisconsin Pavilion. The funky building is a remnant of the 1964 World's Fair but now serves as a radio station and gift shop selling—you guessed it—cheese!

Pavilion Cheese & Gifts, 1201 E. Division St., Neillsville, WI 54456

Phone: (715) 743-3333

Hours: Always visible; Pavilion, Monday–Friday 8 AM–5 PM; Saturday 10 AM–3 PM

Cost: Free

Website: www.cwbradio.com/cheesegifts/

Directions: On Rte. 10 near WCCN studios, east of Rte. 73.

COW-A-BUNGA!

Wisconsin's Dean of Dairy, William Dempster Hoard, said it best: "To him who loveth the cow, to him all other things be added—feed, ensilage, butter, more grasses, more prosperity, happier homes, and greater wealth." Residents of the state undoubtedly agree, which is why the cow is Wisconsin's official domesticated animal. Currently there are about 1.3 million dairy cows in the state, which is about 23 cows per square mile. Slightly less dense are the fiberglass members of the species. Here's where to find them:

Antoinette

12 S. Milwaukee St., Plymouth, (888) 693-8263, www.plymouthwisconsin.com

When the city of Plymouth celebrated its centennial in 1977, it erected a statue of a black-and-white Holstein. Her name is Antoinette, and she's 20-feet long and weighs half a ton. A commemorative plaque points out that Plymouth was once home to the Wisconsin Cheese Exchange, starting in 1882.

Cookie

Schopf's Dairy View, 5169 County Rd. I, Sturgeon Bay, (920) 743-9779, www.dairyview.com

Schopf's is a truth-in-advertising establishment, an ice cream and cheese shop where you can watch cows being milked through the glass behind the counter. The whole operation is guarded by Cookie, a huge, lovable Holstein who stands next to the tall flagpole out front.

Bernice

Cedar Crest Ice Cream, 2000 S. Tenth St., Manitowoc, (920) 682-5577, www.cedarcresticecream.com

A jumbo Jersey, Bernice, stands watch over an ice cream factory on the south side of Manitowoc. Cedar Crest has an adjacent malt shop that's open every day of the week. You can almost imagine the milk being squeezed from the cow as you lick your cone and gaze out at her. Or perhaps those thoughts are best ignored until you're finished.

Bessie

Arby's, 3333 Milton Ave., Janesville, (608) 754-0020

For years Bessie stood outside Janesville's Oasis Restaurant, Motel, and Cheese Shop, but that establishment is long gone. Thankfully Arby's, the new owners of the land, kept this Janesville landmark around and even gave this Guernsey a fresh coat of tan-and-white paint. But do they have an ulterior motive, perhaps keeping her as backup should they run low on roast beef?

Sissy

Ehlenbach's Cheese Chalet, 4879 County Rd. V, DeForest, (800) 949-4791, www.ehlenbachscheese.com

Sissy looks a lot like tan-and-white Bessie (maybe they were cast from the same fiberglass mold), but Sissy is black and white—a Holstein! She's about 20 feet long and greets customers at this dairy-based emporium.

Gertrude Basse

Golden Guernsey Dairy Co-op, 2101 Delafield St., Waukesha, (262) 312-5000, www.foremostfarms.com

This sixteen-foot-tall Guernsey named Gertrude Basse was installed outside a Waukesha dairy in 1970. She was hit by a car in 1977, and two of her legs were broken, but thankfully she didn't have to be put down. Apparently fiberglass is easier to heal than flesh and blood.

Cow Flasher

Crazy Cow Saloon, Belmont Travel Center, 102 W. Mound View Ave., Belmont, (608) 762-6250, www.belmonttravelcenter.com/crazy.asp

Have you ever been flashed by a cow? Well, stop on by the Crazy Cow Saloon, where a clearly inebriated Holstein has lifted her apron to flash you her teats. Another cow looks on approvingly from atop a pile of rocks.

Yoap's Cow

Yoap's Blue Ribbon Auction Farm, 11232 Ledge Ln., Coleman, (920) 897-3536

The big fiberglass cow outside this dairy auction is about the only critter these folks won't sell off to the highest bidder.

Cow Couple

Carr Valley Cheese Company, I-94 and Rte. 82, Mauston, (608) 847-4891, www.carrvalleycheese.com

The two cows guarding this Mauston cheese store are life-size, but they look smaller than normal because they're dwarfed by an enormous fiberglass mouse at the same location.

Cow Family

Colonial Cheese House, 230 W. Main St., Omro, (920) 685-6570, www.omrocheesehouse.com

Two regular-size Holstein cows stand near the street at this Omro cheese emporium, while two others hang out by the picnic tables out back.

Big Bull

Farm Crest Auto & Storage, N5635 Frontage Rd., Plymouth, (920) 892-2277

An unnamed red-and-white Hereford bull advertises a used-car dealership/self-storage facility on the east side of Plymouth. Is he aware that poor, lonely Antoinette is just down the road?

Big Steer

Frontier Motor Cars, 5150 S. 27th St., Milwaukee, (414) 282-7100, www.frontiermotorcars.net

Cast off from a Black Angus restaurant, this giant fiberglass steer is owned by Frontier Motor Cars, a used-car lot on Milwaukee's southwest side. It has been repainted dark brown.

Silvercryst Steer

The Silvercryst, W7105 Hwy. 21 E., Wautoma, (800) 358-9663, www.silvercryst.com

This Black Angus is somewhat obscured by this restaurant's sign, but once you pull in you'll see how large it is. Hint: it's very big.

Cheesehead Steer

Heckel's Big Steer Restaurant, 2621 S. Prairie View Rd., Chippewa Falls, (715) 723-0844

Let's hear it for Packers Pride! This gargantuan Black Angus, a recent transplant from Eau Claire, sports an enormous cheesehead wedge atop his oversize noggin. Another steer, smaller and on a flatbed trailer, is parked nearby, wearing nothing.

Black Steer

Moe's Diner, 12701 Tenth St., Osseo, (715) 597-3912

Moe's brags on its sign that it's "Almost World Famous," and the sign is topped with a life-size Black Angus bull. Perhaps they might be world famous if they stepped it up a little and bought a *larger-than-life-size* bull.

Arthur's Steer

Arthur's Supper Club, E4885 US Hwy. 14/23, Spring Green, (608) 588-2521, www.foodspot.com/arthurs

The steer atop the sign at this supper club is not black but tan. In other words, it's a Hereford.

Nelson
Warner Brothers in Cement

Richard Hanson had what many people rightly feel was the ideal retirement. He built a home for himself off a quiet road near the Mississippi River and spent a good part of each day reading old dime westerns and doing odd jobs around the property. The *oddest* job he did, however, was build a new concrete statue every year. He started in 1986 and amassed a nice collection of people and cartoon critters, all standing in his front yard.

Closest to the road are several pieces with Native American themes. Indians on horseback. Indians around a campfire. An Indian teaching his son to shoot a bow and arrow. A very large Indian doing nothing in particular. And one lone cowboy with a sheriff's badge to whom the Indians pay no mind. Back farther, closer to the house, are Bugs Bunny, Yosemite Sam, the Road Runner, and Wile E. Coyote, as well as traditional kid favorites like Little Red Riding Hood and the Big Bad Wolf.

Watch for falling rocks.

Sadly, Hanson passed away in 2002, but his concrete legacy remains for passersby to admire today.

S1509 Mill Rd., Nelson, WI 54756

No phone

Hours: Private property; view from road

Cost: Free

Directions: One mile north of town on Mill Rd., just east of the intersection of Rtes. 25 and 35.

Oshkosh
Apostles on Parade

German immigrant Mathias Kitz was a furniture maker by trade, but the Great Oshkosh Fire of 1875 put an end to his shop and the rest of the town's business district. Everything gone, Kitz turned to making cigar boxes and tinkering with clocks in his spare time. He had a vision of an elaborate, mechanical cuckoo clock incorporating Jesus and the twelve apostles. He started in 1889, and six years later the Apostles Clock was completed.

Every hour on the hour, Jesus throws open the central doors (where the cuckoo is normally located), and the twelve apostles march out in a circular route. As each figure passes directly in front of the Messiah, he turns toward Jesus and bows his head—with one exception. Judas, the last in the parade, turns his back when he gets to the front so you can see the sack of coins in his hand. Jesus lifts his arms toward his betrayer, but when Judas doesn't respond, Jesus's head drops.

You can catch this Biblical steeplechase at the Oshkosh Public Museum, a place with even more to offer than this remarkable timepiece. But a visit would not be complete without witnessing this holy cuckoo drama, so plan accordingly. Hour after hour, year after year, decade after decade, Judas never learns.

Oshkosh Public Museum, 1331 Algoma Blvd., Oshkosh, WI 54901

Phone: (920) 236-5799

Hours: Tuesday–Saturday 10 AM–4:30 PM, Sunday 1–4:30 PM

Cost: Adults $7, seniors (62+) $5, kids (6–17) $3.50

Website: www.oshkoshmuseum.org

Directions: Just south of Congress Ave. (Rte. 21).

The EAA AirVenture Museum

This place was formerly called the Experimental Aircraft Museum, but today goes by the name AirVenture. The enormous aircraft collection is equally split between well-known, popular planes and experimental, one-of-a-kind models. The homemade craft are the heart and soul of the museum—planes like the *Aerocar I*, a prototype of an all-purpose land-and-air vehicle, or the Stits *Skybaby* biplane with three-foot-long wings. How did these things ever get into the air? Others look airworthy but strange nonetheless, like the Crosley *Flying Flea* dubbed La Cucaracha by its creator, the JM-2 Formula Racer *Pushy Galore*, and the Rutan Varieze *Very Easy*. AirVenture has dozens of these funky fliers filling its hangar berths.

And then they've got the planes you all know and love. See replicas of the Wright brothers' Kitty Hawk flyer, a working *Spirit of St. Louis* reproduction winging over a diorama of nighttime Paris, and a *Voyager* cockpit poured in the same mold as the original that flew nonstop around the world in 1986. They also have the *Double Eagle V* gondola, the first hot-air balloon to cross the Pacific.

In the adjoining Eagle Hangar, there's a salute to World War II aircraft featuring planes from both sides of the conflict. Inside the "Classified Area," you'll see where engineers are dissecting Axis aircraft beside a replica of the Fat Man atomic bomb. Part of an aircraft carrier's flight deck has smashed through a wall in the US Navy display, yet the department-store mannequins on its balconies seem unconcerned. The Hangar X exhibit contains the military's prototype F22 and a Podracer from *Star Wars Episode I*—that's really in the experimental stage! Outside the buildings are more planes, including barnstormers and craft too large to park inside.

If you come during the late-July AirVenture Fly-In, you'll see even more. The Oshkosh Airport becomes the world's busiest, with 15,000 planes from around the globe. Many are experimental, or built from kits by hobbyists, so keep watching the sky for something strange to happen.

EAA Aviation Center, Whittman Airfield, 3000 Poberezny Rd., Oshkosh, WI 54902

Phone: (800) 564-6322 or (920) 426-4800

Hours: Monday–Saturday 8:30 AM–5 PM, Sunday 10 AM–5 PM

Cost: Adults $12.50, seniors (62+) $10.50, kids (6–17) $9.50

Website: www.airventuremuseum.org, www.eaa.org; Fly-In: www.airventure.org

Directions: Eastbound off Rte. 41 on Rte. 44 (Knapp St.), first right on Koeller St., and first right on Poberezny Rd.

Nativity Collection

Years ago Mildred Turner, a kindergarten teacher from Omro, was saddened by the death of her mother. But she pledged, "I will not be blue at Christmas," and to that end she started collecting nativity scenes, big and small, expensive and cheap, from all corners of the globe. She even found odd nativities, like those making up a set of dominoes or another made from marshmallows. The largest stands five feet tall, while the smallest is the size of a thimble.

Turner collected more than 1,000 sets, and today they're on display in the basement of this Oshkosh church. Visitors are welcome whenever the building is open. All they ask is that you not arrive like the Magi bearing a new nativity gift for the museum—this was Mildred Turner's collection, and it's going to stay that way. Plus, the basement's full, like the Bethlehem Holiday Inn.

Algoma Boulevard United Methodist Church, 1174 Algoma Blvd., Oshkosh, WI 54901

Phone: (920) 231-2800

Hours: Monday–Thursday 8:30 AM–2:30 PM; Friday 8:30 AM–1:30 PM; Sunday 8:30 AM–noon

Cost: Free

Website: www.abumc.org/nativity-collection

Directions: One block south of Rte. 21 (Oshkosh Ave.), two blocks east of the river.

Northern State Hospital for the Insane

While it can be safely said that we still have a long way to go in our treatment of the mentally ill, at least we can say this: we're no longer barbaric. Walking through the 10-room collection of the Julaine Farrow Museum at the former Northern State Hospital for the Insane (today the Winnebago Mental Health Institute), you'll learn just how far we've come in the last century.

Farrow was a registered nurse who worked at the facility for 36 years and tirelessly documented the institution's history, bad and good. In addition to the patient archives, you'll see tools of the trade, including an electroshock machine and a collection of items swallowed by patients—26 spoons by one man alone.

Julaine Farrow Museum, 4150 Sherman Rd., Oshkosh, WI 54901

Phone: (920) 235-4910

Hours: February–October, Thursday 1–3:30 PM

Cost: Free

Website: www.dhs.wisconsin.gov/mh_winnebago/wmhi_museum.htm

Directions: Take Snell Rd. east to the lake, then south on Sherman Rd.

Schettl's Menagerie

I don't know where old roadside attractions go to die, but I do know where they go to be *adopted*: Schettl's. This salvage and resale operation has the requisite closeout kitchen cabinets and boat docks, but it is best known for its oversize statuary, weird artifacts, and architectural remnants . . . and they're almost all for sale!

Looking for a 30-foot tall King Kong to mount on your roof? Got it. A steampunk mechanical dinosaur sculpture? That, too. A fiberglass hip-

Need one of these? Schettl's has it. Photo by author, courtesy of Schettl's

popotamus, a Cinderella carriage, or a skeleton dressed in World War II fatigues? Yep, uh-huh, sure thing. Of course, there's no guarantee that you'll find exactly what you're looking for on this four-acre spread (or its new overflow location), but you will find plenty that you didn't expect but want anyway. Now all you have to do is figure out how to strap that eight-foot-tall chipmunk to the roof of your car. No worries—Schettl's also sells trailers.

Original location: 5105 County Rd. S., Oshkosh, WI 54904

Phone: (920) 426-1681

Hours: Monday–Friday 9 AM–5:30 PM, Saturday 9 AM–5 PM, Sunday 11 AM–4 PM

Cost: Free

Website: www.mschettl.com

Directions: Exit County Rd. T (Ryf Rd.) from Rte. 45, heading west, then take County Rd. S
north at the first intersection.

Second location: 5851 Green Valley Rd., Oshkosh, WI 54901

Phone: (920) 966-9900

Hours: Monday–Saturday 9 AM–5:30 PM

Cost: Free

Directions: Exit Rte. 46 northbound from Rte. 41, then take Green Valley Rd. northeast at the
first intersection.

Pepin
Little House in the Big Woods

Before there was the *Little House on the Prairie*, there was the *Little House in the Big Woods*, the home in which author Laura Ingalls Wilder was born on February 7, 1867. Within three years of her birth, the Ingalls family would move from their cabin in Wisconsin and start to bounce around the upper Midwest. Laura wrote a book about every last place they lived, starting with the Big Woods, though she didn't write her first story until she was 65 years old. It was published in 1932.

The original cabin Pa built is long gone, as are most of the Big Woods. You have to use your imagination to cover the rolling farmland with trees around this reconstructed cabin. You also have to picture the place without picnic tables and modern pit toilets.

In town, at the Pepin Historical Museum, are Ingalls family artifacts: a family quilt and a letter written by Laura, as well as common household items and farm implements from her era. Each September the town throws a festival for their famous native daughter.

Ingalls Cabin, County Rd. CC, Pepin, WI 54759
No phone
Hours: Daily 8 AM–5 PM
Cost: Free
Directions: Seven miles north of town on County Rd. CC.

Laura Ingalls Wilder Museum, 306 Third St., Pepin, WI 54759
Phone: (715) 442-2142
Hours: May–October, daily 10 AM–5 PM
Cost: Donations encouraged
Website: www.lauraingallspepin.com
Directions: At the intersection of Count Rd. N and Rte. 35 (Third St.).

Plover
Get Out, You Drunks!

When the Mulderink family converted historic Sherman House to a restaurant in the early 1980s, the former owners were not happy. But how were the Mulderinks to know? The former owners were long dead.

The Mulderinks found out just the same. It all began when the wine glasses began exploding. Doors and windows would open and close by themselves, and there were footsteps in the halls. Why were the spirits upset? Apparently the original owners were staunch teetotalers, and when the Mulderinks converted the master bedroom into a bar, it was too much for the spirits to stay silent about.

Eventually the Mulderinks sold the business; whether the ghosts had anything to do with it is anyone's guess. Today it's known as the Cottage Cafe. You can still have a glass of wine here . . . but be sure to wear your safety goggles.

The Cottage Cafe, 2900 Post Rd., Plover, WI 54467

Phone: (715) 544-0370

Hours: Wednesday–Saturday, 5–10 PM

Cost: Meals, $8–15

Website: www.facebook.com/TheCottageCafePlover

Directions: On Rte. 51 Business (Post Rd.), just north of Rte. 54.

Princeton
Big Rosary

Was Paul Bunyan Catholic? If so, he might find this roadside shrine helpful—it's an enormous rosary. Each of the beads on this long chain is made from a bowling ball, and a hubcap joins the main loop of mysteries to the dangling crucifix.

The rosary was made by Ken Soda, who has also made a Dr. Seuss–like tree out of colored bowling balls at the entrance to his driveway. Ken's wife, Eunice, has also gotten into the "big religion" business by collecting more than 1,200 statues of the Virgin Mary. These, however, are not open to the public.

Hail Mary, VERY FULL of grace . . .

W928 County Rd. J, Princeton, WI 54968

Private phone

Hours: Always visible

Cost: Free

Directions: Five miles west of town, west of the County Rd. N intersection.

Reedsburg
Norman Rockwell Exhibit

When the Norman Rockwell Museum went belly-up a few years back, all was not lost. In fact, none of it was—it was just moved into the hallways of this Dells-area motel and restaurant. And you're the beneficiary of the museum's downfall—now you can see it all for free!

There are hundreds of original covers and illustrations from Rockwell's career on display, floor to ceiling, though no original art is here. Best known for his work on the *Saturday Evening Post*, Rockwell also did illustrations for *Collier's*, *Boys' Life*, *Leslie's*, *The Literary Digest*, *The Country Gentleman*, *Red Cross Magazine*, and Ma Bell phone books. He even painted several album covers for Pure Prairie League and a portrait of the First Lady used on the sheet music for "Lady Bird Cha Cha Cha."

Framed magazine covers might seem a poor substitute for art lovers, but in many cases, they're the best anyone has of Rockwell's work. Originals are hard to come by because he used cheap materials that quickly deteriorated. These prints are often in better shape than the originals.

Voyageur Inn, 200 Viking Dr., Reedsburg, WI 53959
Phone: (800) 444-4493 or (608) 524-6431
Hours: Daily 9 AM–5 PM
Cost: Free
Website: http://voyageurinn.net/
Directions: On County Rd. H (Viking Dr.), one block north of Main St. (Rte. 23/33).

Ripon
Birthplace of the Republican Party

When a group of seventeen Ripon citizens gathered on March 20, 1854, at the Little White School House (then standing at the corner of Fond du Lac and Thorne Streets), they had an admirable goal: to oppose the newly-passed Kansas-Nebraska Act that allowed slavery to be extended north through the territories from its southern stronghold all the way to the Canadian border. Fifty-four locals—mostly Whigs and Free-Soilers but a few Democrats, too—formed a new local party. They called themselves Republicans. They were led by Ripon attorney Alvan Earle Bovay, a Democrat, who had the ear of Horace Greeley. Bovay and Greeley had been tossing around the idea of a Republican Party for a few years.

Greeley, editor of the *New York Tribune*, encouraged others to join in the fledgling movement. The first Republican State Convention was held in Jackson, Michigan, on July 6, 1854. And the first Republican National Convention was convened in Pittsburgh on February 22, 1856. Four years later, Abraham Lincoln was elected president of the United States. So far, so good.

The GOP's newest recruit.

Though you'll never hear it recalled at this museum, Wisconsin's GOP history has slipped some since its founding. On the one-hundredth anniversary year of the Ripon get-together, another Wisconsin Republican was condemned by the US Senate for the tactic that still bears his name: McCarthyism. That had to put a damper on the centennial celebrations!

The Little White Schoolhouse was moved three times; its current location is in front of Ripon's 1857 Republican House. Until recently it was a Chinese restaurant; today it's a museum.

Little White Schoolhouse, 303 Blackburn St., PO Box 305, Ripon, WI 54971

Phone: (920) 748-6764

Hours: June–August, daily 10 AM–4 PM; May, September–October, Saturday–Sunday 10 AM–4 PM

Cost: Adults $2, kids (12 and under) free

Website: www.littlewhiteschoolhouse.com

Directions: On Rte. 23/49, in the middle of the two-block "jog" downtown.

Rudolph
Rudolph Grotto and Wonder Cave

Unlike the redemption killjoys who seem to populate the shrine-building community, those who constructed the Rudolph Grotto intended it to be fun, even if it was a holy place. While training to be a priest in Europe, Father Philip Wagner was injured in an athletic accident. As many of the faithful did in 1912, he journeyed to Lourdes for the healing waters. Here he cut a deal with the Virgin Mary: if he was healed, he'd build her a shrine.

Mary came through, and so did Wagner. When he was transferred to the Rudolph parish (St. Philomena's) in 1917, he started working on his promise. First, he built a sledding hill for the Catholic school. This made a big impression on student Edmund Rybicki, who ended up doing most of the heavy lifting for Wagner in later years.

In 1918, construction started on a new church. A year later, in an old potato field directly behind it, Wagner began planting trees for the shrine. In 1927, the Rudolph Grotto started going up. Not everyone, however, was enamored by Father Wagner's extracurricular efforts. His bishop ordered Wagner to stop the project in 1949, angry that the parish church had not been finished "while the most elaborate developments are going on in this series of caves which are to me perfectly nonsensical." Thankfully, Wagner returned to his nonsensical work after completing the chapel.

The Wonder Cave stretches one-fifth of a mile through a fake rock hill. Recorded organ music is pumped into the cave to add an air of holiness as you contemplate the "needlepoint virtue" lessons along the path. Each lesson is a large tin sheet punctured thousands of times with a nail, spelling out a Bible verse or depicting a narrative scene. All are backlit with colored bulbs, giving the sense you're viewing a Holy Lite-Brite. There are 26 shrines inside the cave, each more astounding than the previous. At the center of it all is a two-story grotto of Christ in the Garden of Gethsemane.

Whether you're religious or not, you'll believe the Wonder Cave is a miracle. To honor Wagner, the parish was rechristened St. Philip's in 1961.

Rudolph Grotto Gardens, 6957 Grotto Ave., Rudolph, WI 54475

Phone: (715) 435-3120

Hours: Gardens, daylight hours; gift shop and cave, June–mid-September, daily 10 AM–5 PM

Cost: Gardens, free; cave, adults $2.50, teens (12–17) $1.25, kids (6–11) 25¢

Website: www.rudolphgrotto.org

Directions: Behind St. Philip the Apostle Church, off Second St.

SAUK CITY

➡ Sauk City brags that it is the "Cow Chip Throwing Capital" and holds a contest and festival every Labor Day weekend to determine a champ (www.wiscowchip.com).

Sparta
Ben Bikin and the Elroy–Sparta State Bike Trail

Sparta claims to be "America's Biking Capital," and it has the pedal power to prove it. First, check out its statue of Ben Bikin, a Victorian chap who's riding the World's Largest High-Wheeler Bicycle, on the south side of town. If you want to see a real "penny farthing" up close, stop on by Sparta's Deke Slayton Memorial Space & Bicycle Museum (below). It has plenty of bicycles on display.

But if you'd rather ride than reflect, take off on a trip along the Elroy–Sparta State Bike Trail. This 32-mile bicycle park starts in Sparta and runs southeast through the communities of Norwalk, Wilton, and Kendall before it ends in Elroy. The trail follows the decommissioned tracks of the Chicago & North Western Railroad, and along the route passes through three tunnels, the longest of which is ¾ mile. On a hot summer outing, it's the best place to stop for a breather, unless you're worried about getting run over in the dark.

Ben Bikin, Water and Wisconsin Sts., Sparta, WI 54656
Phone: (608) 463-7109
Hours: May–October, daylight hours
Cost: Adults trail pass (16 and older) $4, kids free
Website: www.elroy-sparta-trail.com
Directions: Trail begins at the corner of Water and Milwaukee Sts. on the south end of town.

Deke Slayton Memorial Space & Bicycle Museum and Sacred Objects of Secret Societies

You have to hand it to the Monroe County Historical Society. While most small towns have a hard-enough time making one museum interesting, this place has *three* great collections under the same roof. That roof is Sparta's old Masonic Hall, and what better place to exhibit its Sacred Objects of Secret Societies collection? Well, they're blowing the lid off all the clandestine activities of the Masons, the Oddfellows, the Modern Woodmen of America, and more. See their ceremonial robes, their swords and secret artifacts, and the stuffed goat on wheels that MWA initiates had to ride to get into the club (page 93).

And that's just on the ground floor! Upstairs (technically a different museum) see the world's largest collection of Deke-abilia. What's that? Astronaut Deke Slayton was born in Sparta on March 1, 1924, and it is here where you can find his personal memorial today. Slayton was chosen for the Mercury program but due to a heart murmur did not fly a mission; his mothballed spacesuit can be found in a display case here. Slayton did, however, serve on the 1975 Apollo-Soyuz mission, and the museum has some artifacts from that flight. And though he never went to the moon, he was given a moon rock, which is also here.

Finally, because Sparta is the America's Biking Capital (page 90), half for the second floor is reserved for hundreds of bikes, old and new, penny farthings and recumbent, single and tandem—if it's human-powered, they've got it.

200 W. Main St., Sparta, WI 54656

Phone: (608) 269-8580 and (608) 269-0033

Hours: May–October, Monday–Saturday 10 AM–4:30 PM; November–April, Monday–
Saturday 10 AM–4 PM

Cost: Monroe County Museum, free; Deke Slayton Museum, adults $3, kids (6–15) $1

Website: www.monroecountyhistory.org, www.dekeslaytonmuseum.com

Directions: Downtown, at Court St.

F.A.S.T. Corporation

Few American corporations have done as much for the road-tripping public as F.A.S.T. If you've ever putted around a miniature golf course, locked up your brakes at the sight of a hot-dog-shaped wiener stand, licked ice cream beneath an enormous fiberglass cone, or stolen a Big Boy statue as a senior prank, chances are you were dealing with a F.A.S.T. product.

F.A.S.T. stands for Fiberglass Animals, Shapes & Trademarks and they're the nation's largest producer of outdoor sculpture. Marble dissolves. Granite is too hard and heavy. But fiberglass makes roadside wonders affordable. F.A.S.T. is responsible for many of the giant roadside attractions listed in this book, including Hayward's Giant Muskie and Delavan's Circus Elephant.

Because these sculptures are formed in molds, the fields around this production facility are littered with the detritus of hundreds of former projects. Come see where your local taco stand was born. It can be creepy

Land sharks! Photo by author, courtesy of F.A.S.T.

running across the Jolly Green Giant broken into a dozen body parts, but you're likely to do just that. If you want to look around, ask a worker for permission before wandering off.

This facility is a working factory, so you'll see several new sculptures being finished for shipping around the country. If you're interested in something for the person who has everything (but probably not a 25-foot gorilla), ask for their current price list. A Chicken Swing will set you back $8,900, a Pirate (in a tub) $7,300, a Mexican Bandito Concession Stand $24,200. And that Big Boy? Only $5,000. Relatively speaking, he sounds like a bargain.

F.A.S.T. Corporation, 14177 County Rd. Q, PO Box 258, Sparta, WI 54656
Phone: (608) 269-7110

Hours: Daylight hours
Cost: Free
Website: www.fastkorp.com
Directions: One half mile east of town on Rte. 21, where it intersects with County Rd. Q.

Tomah
Gasoline Alley

Though cartoonist Frank King was born in nearby Cashton in 1883, he always considered Tomah his home. It was this small Wisconsin community that inspired his world-famous comic strip, *Gasoline Alley*. Several local landmarks, like Humboldt Hill and Fieting's Store appeared in the strip, should anyone question whether these toon folk really lived in Tomah.

Gasoline Alley was an offshoot of a strip King was writing for the *Chicago Tribune*, called *The Rectangle*. It was the first comic to feature a single dad (Walt Wallet finds the infant Skeezix on his front step on Valentine's Day), and the first to age its characters. Unlike Bart Simpson, Skeezix actually grows up. In the jargon of the comic strip world, the aging phenomenon has become known as "King's Law." So, as the readership fattens and sags, so does its favorite characters: Slim and Pudge, Adam and Eve, Joel and Rufus and their donkey, Becky, are someday all headed to that Great Big Strip in the Sky. It's the law!

Greater Tomah Area Chamber of Commerce, 901 Kilbourn Ave., PO Box 625, Tomah, WI 54660
Phone: (800) 94-TOMAH or (608) 372-2166
Hours: Always visible
Cost: Free
Website: www.tomahwisconsin.com
Directions: "Gasoline Alley" is the honorary name for Superior Ave. (Rte. 12/131).

Valton
The Painted Forest

The Painted Forest was built to be the ceremonial meeting space of the Modern Woodmen of America, Camp 6190, a secret society much like the Masons. Its plain white exterior hides the amazing piece of folk art inside. Every square inch of the interior walls is covered in a wraparound woodland mural, which was painted from 1897 to 1899 by Ernest Hüpeden, a wayward artist. He was put up in a local hotel in exchange for his services and managed to drag the job out for two years.

The mural depicts, both literally and figuratively, the initiation rites and benefits of joining this fraternal order. The Woodmen's main purpose was to provide burial fees for its members, but it was also a social club. To join, you were put through a series of wacky rites with great mystical significance. For example, inductees were blindfolded, placed on a mechanical goat, and bucked about in an attempt to knock each rider to the floor. This rite was depicted on the mural by a man with an arm in a sling riding a runaway goat.

The Modern Woodsmen are still around as the Woodmen of the World Life Insurance Company. Thankfully you don't have to ride a goat, robotic or not, to get a policy.

E846 Painted Forest Dr., Valton, WI 53968

Phone: (608) 663-2230

Hours: June–August, Saturday 1–3:30 PM, or by appointment

Cost: Free; donations accepted

Website: http://paintedforest.edgewood.edu

Directions: Off County Rds. EE and G, on Painted Forest Dr. at Sixth St.

Warrens
Wisconsin Cranberry Discovery Center

Wisconsin's biggest fruit export is . . . drum roll . . . cranberries! That's right, and this state has recently surpassed Massachusetts as the nation's largest cranberry producer, which is why it is the official Wisconsin state fruit. The Wisconsin Cranberry Discovery Center is a monument to the farmers who make Thanksgiving tart each year.

You'll learn a lot of interesting facts at Cranberry Expo, the best smelling museum around. Did you know "cranberry" is a bastardization of "craneberry," the name given to the crane-shaped blossom of the flower? Were you aware cranberries are one of only three fruits native to North America, blueberries and Concord grapes being the others? And how many chances is a cranberry given to bounce on a picker board to demonstrate its freshness? Seven bounces, no more, no less.

Cranberry farming is a specialized industry, and as such, the machinery and tools used to plant, grow, and harvest cranberries have to be custom made in Warrens. You'll see vine trimmers, cutting pushers, fruit pickers, berry sorters, and plastic baggers at the museum.

At the end of the tour you'll be given free sample of cranberry ice cream, pie, or jelly beans to entice you to buy cranberry-related items in the gift shop. September is the best time to visit; Warrens holds its Cranberry Festival, and a Cranberry Queen is crowned with a ruby tiara.

204 Main St., Warrens, WI 54666
Phone: (608) 378-4878
Hours: May–July and November–December, Monday–Saturday 10 AM–4 PM; August–October,
    daily 10 AM–4 PM
Cost: Adults $4, seniors (65+) $3.50, kids (6–12) $3
Website: www.discovercranberries.com, www.cranfest.com
Directions: At the intersection of County Rds. O and EW.

Waupun
Sculptureville

Clarence Addison Shaler was an accomplished inventor. Ever repair a tire with a vulcanizer or slip a cover on an umbrella? If so, your life was touched by this creative genius. When Shaler retired at the age of 70, he tried his hand at sculpture. Waupun's public parks display the result.

Today Waupun calls itself the "City of Sculpture." Most of the artwork was done by Shaler, though some were collected by him and donated. The local Chamber of Commerce offers a free map of all the town's pieces. Here are three of the best:

Dawn of Day

Carved by Shaler in 1931, this statue of a nude woman appears to be running toward the entrance to city hall. Is she applying stag for a marriage license? Has she lost all her belongings to high property taxes? Is she just a common streaker? You be the judge.

WAUPACA

➡ Each year on the third weekend in June, the town of Waupaca throws a **Strawberry Festival** (www.waupacaareachamber.com/event/strawberry-fest/). The culminating event is the construction of the World's Longest Strawberry Shortcake.

Do you ever feel you're being watched?

The Citadel

A young woman cries on the steps of the Waupun Historical Museum while a fiendish devil looks over her shoulder. No, she hasn't lost her library card. This 1939 Shaler piece is a commentary on the rise of Fascism. The woman represents Europe. Guess who the devil is?

The End of the Trail

The world-famous sculpture by James Earle Fraser might be the third generation of the masterpiece, but it's the oldest version existing today. The piece shows a Native American slumped over on his horse, both of which have seen better days. It was first created in 1894 at the Art Institute of Chicago; then Fraser recreated it in 1915 for San Francisco's Panama-Pacific Exposition. Both incarnations were made of plaster and were later destroyed. The Waupun statue is bronze.

Dawn of Day, City Hall, 201 E. Main St., Waupun, WI 53963

The Citadel, Waupun Heritage Museum, Madison and Jefferson Sts., Waupun, WI 53963

The End of the Trail, Shaler Park, Madison St., Waupun, WI 53963

Contact: Chamber of Commerce, 324 E. Main St., Suite 200, Waupun, WI 53963

Phone: (920) 324-3491

Hours: Always visible

Cost: Free

Website: www.waupunchamber.com

Directions: *Dawn*, on Rte. 49 (Main), on the north side of the courthouse; *Citadel*, on Rte. 26, on the east side of the museum; *Trail*, on Rte. 26 at the river, in Forest Mound Cemetery.

Westfield
A Lost Wagon Train

The enormous "pioneer" in the parking lot of the Pioneer Motor Inn in Westfield looks both out of place and out of proportion. First of all, with his coonskin cap and long musket, he looks more like a French trapper than a pioneer, and second, he's twice the size of the oxen pulling his covered wagon. And what are those concrete deer doing at his feet, and why aren't those oxen hitched to the wagon? This whole arrangement begs more questions than it answers, which is a good reason you should never draw historical conclusions from a fiberglass commercial display.

Westfield Pioneer Motor Inn, 242 N. Pioneer Park Rd., PO Box 97, Westfield, WI 53964

Phone: (608) 296-2135

Hours: Always visible

Cost: Free

Website: http://pioneermotorinn.com

Directions: Just west of County Rd. J exit from Rte. 51.

Winneconne
Winneconne Secedes

You've no doubt studied the Civil War, but did you know there has been a recent attempt to break away from the Union, or at least the state of Wisconsin?

The trouble began when Winneconne was left off the official Wisconsin highway map in 1967. The outraged citizenry decided that if Wisconsin didn't want them, they didn't want Wisconsin. They drafted a Declaration of Independence and sent it to the governor. On June 22 they seceded and erected a toll bridge on Route 116 over the Wolf River.

These actions got the governor's attention, and soon he issued an order that Winneconne be returned to the state map. Satisfied their demands had been met, Winneconne rescinded its declaration on June 23, and the tollbooth came down. A bloody war pitting brother against brother was avoided. Let this be a cautionary tale to mapmakers everywhere.

Winneconne Area Chamber of Commerce, PO Box 126, Winneconne, WI 54986

Phone: (920) 582-4775

Hours: Always visible

Cost: Free

Website: www.winneconne.org

Directions: The tollbooth sat on the Rte. 116 bridge in the middle of town.

Wonewoc
Spook Hill

Spiritualism doesn't have the following it did in the years after the Civil War, but it still has its adherents. Every summer since 1877 a group of mediums has gathered at 39 small cabins—Camp Wonewoc—to assist those who want to contact the spirit world. Anyone's welcome; just bring $25 and an open mind. Séances, tarot readings, past-life regressions—they're all available for a price.

The mediums at Camp Wonewoc follow the precepts of Andrew Jackson Davis, one of the faith's early leaders. They're a quiet and thoughtful bunch, making no judgments about those who seek their guidance. Still, not everyone is happy about the goings-on here. Some have dubbed the rise on which the camp sits "Spook Hill," which the mediums have good-naturedly taken as their unofficial moniker. In recent years Christian fundamentalists have picketed the camp because, well, that's just what they do to people with whom they disagree.

Wonewoc Spiritualist Camp, 304 Hill St., PO Box 187, Wonewoc, WI 53968

Phone: (608) 464-7770

Hours: June–August, Tuesday–Saturday 9 AM–6 PM, Sunday–Monday 1–5 PM, by appointment

Cost: Readings, $25 for 30 minutes; Friday Circle Reading (séance), $25; Saturday Past Life Regressions, $25

Website: www.campwonewoc.com

Directions: On the east side of town, off Quinn Rd.

WISCONSIN

Neillsville •
Chatty Belle, the World's
Largest Talking Cow

Pepin •
Little House in the Big Woods

Nelson •
Warner Brothers in Cement

Elk Creek •
World's Largest Roasted
Chicken

Black River Falls •
Big Orange Moose
Black River Crossing Oasis
Wisconsin Death Trip

Cochrane •
The Prairie Moon Sculpture Gardens & Museum
Rock in the House

Buffalo City • •
Big Viking

Warrens •
Wisconsin Cranberry
Discovery Center

Fountain City •
Elmer's Auto and Toy Museum

Cataract •
Paul & Mathilda
Wegner Grotto

Galesville •
The Garden of Eden?

Tomah •
Gasoline Alley

Oakdale
Cowboy Mouse

Sparta •
Ben Bikin
Caboose Cabin B&B
Elroy-Sparta State Bike Trail
Deke Slayton Memorial Space
& Bicycle Museum
F.A.S.T. Corporation

Onalaska •
Sunny, the World's Largest Sunfish

La Crosse •
Big Hiawatha
Keep Up the Good Work...Just in Case
World's Largest Golf Bag
World's Largest Six-Pack

Hillsborough •
Grocery Mouse
Guilty Mouse

MINNESOTA

Viroqua •
Viroqua Shortline Inn

IOWA

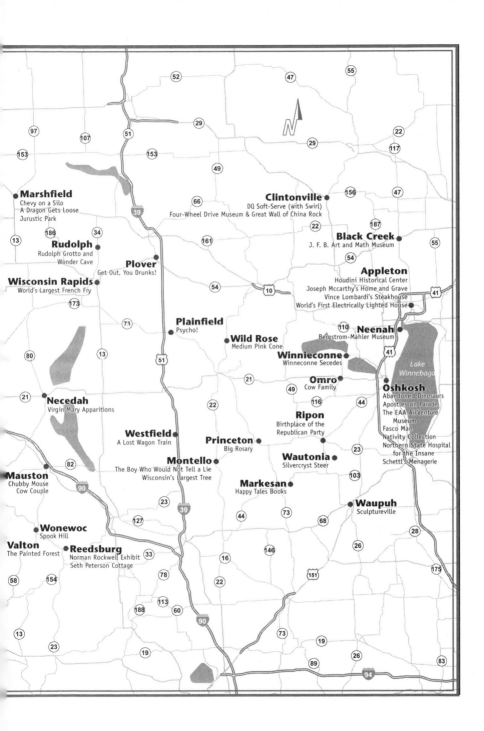

Marshfield
Chevy on a Silo
A Dragon Gets Loose
Jurustic Park

Rudolph
Rudolph Grotto and
Wonder Cave

Plover
Get Out, You Drunks!

Wisconsin Rapids
World's Largest French Fry

Clintonville
DQ Soft-Serve (with Swirl)
Four-Wheel Drive Museum & Great Wall of China Rock

Black Creek
J. F. B. Art and Math Museum

Appleton
Houdini Historical Center
Joseph Mccarthy's Home and Grave
Vince Lombardi's Steakhouse
World's First Electrically Lighted House

Neenah
Bergstrom-Mahler Museum

Plainfield
Psycho!

Wild Rose
Medium Pink Cone

Winnieconne
Winneconne Secedes

Omro
Cow Family

Oshkosh
Abandoned Dinosaurs
Apostles on Parade
The EAA AirVenture
Museum
Fasco Man
Nativity Collection
Northern State Hospital
for the Insane
Schettl's Menagerie

Necedah
Virgin Mary Apparitions

Ripon
Birthplace of the
Republican Party

Westfield
A Lost Wagon Train

Princeton
Big Rosary

Wautonia
Silvercryst Steer

Mauston
Chubby Mouse
Cow Couple

Montello
The Boy Who Would Not Tell a Lie
Wisconsin's Largest Tree

Markesan
Happy Tales Books

Waupuh
Sculptureville

Wonewoc
Spook Hill

Valton
The Painted Forest

Reedsburg
Norman Rockwell Exhibit
Seth Peterson Cottage

Lake Winnebago

THE DELLS

*F*irst, the good news. There is still no town in the Cheese State with a higher concentration of weirdness than the Wisconsin Dells. If you prefer staying in one place on vacation, come to the Dells and crack open the kids' college fund—this type of fun doesn't come cheap. You'll find museums for robots, torture devices, and clowns; water-ski thrill shows and haunted mansions; amphibious troop carriers and bungee towers; and more go-karts, miniature golf courses, and waterslides than you can shake a block of fudge at.

Now for the bad news: the Dells used to be *weirder*. As the region transforms into Wisconsin's version of Orlando, some of the quirkier attractions have met the wrecking ball. A few years ago, sacred fiberglass figures from Biblical Gardens were auctioned off to the highest bidder. Xanadu, the House of the Future, met an even more tragic fate: the bubble-shaped Styrofoam structure was bulldozed to make way for a miniature golf course. Storybook Gardens? This book has come to "The End," though the statues remain in a weed-filled lot. And what about the energy-efficient Sybarite Underground Home? Buried. The Enchanted Forest? Chopped down. Prehistoric Land? It's history. Serpent Safari? Slithered away. The Dungeon of Horrors, the Castle of Terror, Adventures in Time, and Mass Panic? As dead as their exhibits. And the Wonder Spot? Wonder no more—it's gone.

In other words, go see the Dells now, before the resorts finish off the torture museum, sink the water-ski show, and exorcise Wizard Quest. Don't think it'll stay the "old" Dells forever.

Baraboo

Circus World Museum

Years ago, the Ringling brothers lived in Baraboo, where their father was a harness maker. Five of the Ringling brothers decided to organize a circus in 1884. It consisted of a trained goat, Zachary the horse, and a few rabbits and chickens "from Timbuctoo." Some show. But before long they were billing themselves as "The Ringling Brothers Stupendous Consolidation of Seven Monstrous Shows," setting the standard for bombast and buncombe that would put them in the leagues with P. T. Barnum. For example, when they purchased a hyena for their menagerie, its common name was not enough; they dubbed him "The Hideous Hyena *Striata Gigantium*, the Mammoth, Midnight Marauding, Man-Eating Monstrosity."

The Ringling Brothers' circus wintered in Baraboo from 1884 to 1918, and it was here they bought the Barnum and Bailey Circus in 1906 from Bailey's widow for $410,000, forming the Ringling Brothers and Barnum & Bailey Circus we know today. Five other minor circuses also called Baraboo home, which is why the town today calls itself the "Capital of the American Circus" (though most circuses are now based in Florida).

It only makes sense that Baraboo is the location of Circus World Museum. The complex spreads out over 50 acres on the Ringling Brothers' original site. They have more than 200 wagons (more than anywhere else in the world), a big top, magic shows, miniature carnivals, steam calliope concerts, elephant rides, and plenty of clowns to keep the kids in check and the parents creeped out. Best of all, they've got a freak-show tent with a replica of the Cardiff Giant, the Bearded Lady, Jo-Jo the Dog-Faced Boy, and the original Siamese Twins.

Circus World also has the world's largest archive of circus material and famous artifacts from the industry, including Clyde Beatty's lion-taming chair, outfits worn by Gunther Gebel-Williams, a balancing chair from the Flying Wallendas, a human cannon used by Frank "Fearless" Gregg, giant clown hammers, and the tusks of famous elephants who have long since gone to that big center ring in the sky.

550 Water St., Baraboo, WI 53913

Phone: (866) 693-1500 or (608) 356-8341

Hours: May–August (performance season), daily 9 AM–6 PM; September–October, daily 10 AM–4 PM; November–April, Saturday–Sunday 10 AM–4 PM

Cost: Performance season, adults $14.95, seniors (65+) $12.95, kids (5–11) $7.95; fall/winter, adults $7, seniors (65+) $6, kids (5–11) $3.50

Website: www.circusworldmuseum.com

Directions: Five blocks east of Rte. 123 (Broadway St.) on Rte. 113 (Water St.).

International Clown Hall of Fame and Research Center

If you didn't get your fill of clowns at Circus World, you're in luck—stop on by the International Clown Hall of Fame and Research Center, recently relocated from Milwaukee. Rather than being a disturbing memorial to long-dead stars who'd been trampled by rogue elephants, blown out of cannons, or smothered in little cars, it is instead a living tribute to this unique entertainment form. Inductees to its Hall of Fame include Emmett Kelly Sr., Willard Scott (the first Ronald McDonald), Bob Keeshan (Howdy Doody's Clarabell and later Captain Kangaroo), and Red Skelton. Check out the display cases filled with oversize shoes, big noses, and colorful costumes and wigs, including the first Bozo costume.

The museum's research center probably isn't what you'd expect. It doesn't study optimum cream pie or seltzer trajectories, but it archives the history of the pancake-faced arts and preserves the memories of the profession's greatest performers.

102 Fourth Ave., Baraboo, WI 53913

Phone: (608) 355-0321

Hours: Wednesday–Saturday 11 AM–5 PM

Cost: Adults $5, kids (under 12) $4

Website: www.theclownmuseum.com

Directions: Four blocks south of Eighth Ave. (Rte. 33), one block east of Broadway.

International Crane Foundation

Though cranes have suffered greatly at the hands of human development, they've fared better than the passenger pigeon (page 131), though that's not saying much. Much of the thanks for preserving these lanky birds goes to the International Crane Foundation, founded by George Archibald. It has representatives of all 15 crane species, including the endangered whooping crane. These birds come from around the world, not just Wisconsin, and are part of the ICF's breeding and release program.

During hatching season, naturalists are required to "dance" with the females to get them in the mood. These rituals are closed to the public because visitors would distract the cranes while laughing at the staff. Also, when crane chicks are born, handlers limit their contact with the young birds to avoid "imprinting." A chick will imprint the notion that it's a human if allowed to see too many people.

Three tours leave the ICF Center daily, but you're welcome to take a self-guided walk around the grounds. If you do take a tour, ask your guide to show you the mating dance.

E11376 Shady Lane Rd., PO Box 447, Baraboo, WI 53913

Phone: (608) 356-9462

Hours: April–October, daily 9 AM–5 PM; tours 10 AM, 1 PM, and 3 PM

Cost: Adults $9.50, seniors (62+) $8, kids (6–17) $5

Website: www.savingcranes.org

Directions: Off Rte. 12, two roads south of I-90/94, heading east.

A Punctual UFO

Most of the Dells' weirdness can be easily explained, but folks near Baraboo have been sighting the same orange UFO at the same time and place for years. Explain *that*. Weather permitting, it rises from the Baraboo Bluffs and flies off to the southeast between 8:00 and 8:30 AM, just off Route 113.

Nobody has been able to explain the phenomenon, and like the pot of gold at the end of the rainbow, nobody has been able to approach the craft as it sits on the ground. Could it be aliens emerging from a netherworld porthole at Devil's Lake? Perhaps it's Bigfoot being dropped off on its morning commute? Or is it the active imagination of a bunch of bathtub-gin-soaked circus carnies?

Manchester Rd. and Rte. 113, Baraboo, WI 53913

No phone

Hours: Daily 8:00–8:30 AM

Cost: Free

Directions: Southeast of the intersection, over the bluffs.

Lake Delton
Buffalo Phil's Train-Delivered Food

While it might sound inefficient to have meals at a restaurant arrive via train, have no fear—the choo choo here is toy sized. Buffalo Phil's is a big hit with the model-railroad set, which is primarily 6-year-old children and 60-year-old men who spend most of their free time in their basements. If either of those types is in your vacationing party, you're going to have to ask to be seated in the Train Room—otherwise the grub will arrive under human locomotion. And what's so special about that?

150 Gasser Rd., PO Box 298, Lake Delton, WI 53940

Phone: (608) 254-7300

Hours: Sunday–Thursday 11 AM–10 PM, Friday–Saturday 11 AM–10:30 PM

Cost: Meals, $10–20

Website: www.buffalophilsgrille.com

Directions: West on Gasser Rd. from Wisconsin Dells Pkwy., just north of I-90/94 interchange.

Sinclair Dinosaur Station

The Kelly-green Sinclair brontosaurus was once a ubiquitous roadside icon, but today it is as rare as . . . well . . . Sinclair gas stations themselves. But not in Lake Delton, where you can still find that familiar dinosaur statue, and it's life-size. Or half life-size. You see, only the front half exists. It sticks out of the entrance to the station's minimart—you enter between its legs. If the owners had a (second grader's) sense of humor, they'd add the back half to the other side of the building and make it the entrance to the rest rooms.

Gargantuan green gasateria.

1280 Wisconsin Dells Pkwy. S, Lake Delton, WI 53965

Phone: (608) 254-7022

Hours: Always visible

Cost: Free

Directions: Two blocks north of I-90/94 on Rte. 12 (Wisconsin Dells Pkwy.) at Gasser Rd.

ABANDONED DINOSAURS

If *Jurassic Park* taught us anything, it's that you don't leave a world of dinosaurs to their own devices. So why has it been done in two Wisconsin communities? On the north side of Oshkosh you can still see the abandoned **Jurassic Valley Miniature Golf Course** (5850 State Rd. 76), its life-size T. Rex and Apatosaurus still visible above the weeds and trees. A far scarier (and uglier) dinosaur is hiding behind a tree in long-gone and now overgrown **Johnson Park** in Milwaukee (76th St., north of Good Hope Rd.). What happens when these beasts get hungry?

Wisconsin Dells
Downtown Dells

If you make the trip to the Dells, whatever you do, don't spend all your time holed up in some all-inclusive megaresort and fail to explore the miniwonders to the downtown strip. This is where the Dells tourism juggernaut originated with H. H. Bennett (page 112), and it is here where the tackiest traditions continue. Tucked in between the T-shirt shops and fudge-aterias are some real gems. Ripley's Believe It or Not!, Wizard Quest, and the Museum of Historic Torture Devices are covered later in this chapter with their own entries, but here are a few more to get you started.

First, stop outside **Bailey's Landing** gift shop to see the oxymoronic jumbo troll. It might look like a statue, but watch out—it's only napping. When you least expect it, the troll will come to life to sing songs that you expect even less, like "What a Wonderful World" and "As Time Goes By."

131 Broadway, Wisconsin Dells, WI 53965

Phone: (608) 254-8721

Hours: May–November, daily 10 AM–10 PM

Cost: Free

Directions: One block east of the river bridge.

Fluorescent freaky fun.

Across the street, King Kong battles a gigantic squid atop the facade of **Wild Fun Zone**. This indoor arcade offers bumper cars, a virtual roller coaster, a fluorescent laser tag cave that looks like a set from *Lost in Space*, and a 3-D Jungle Mini Golf course, also illuminated with black lights. Freaky, man!

310 Broadway, Wisconsin Dells, WI 53965

Phone: (608) 253-0607

Hours: June–September, daily 11 AM–11 PM

Cost: Free

Website: www.wildfunzone.com

Directions: Three blocks east of the river bridge.

If Gram and Gramps have come along on your trip, and they're longing for the days in the old country, stop by the **Bavarian Village & German Glockenspiel**. This "village" is more of a courtyard decorated in a German motif with a large clock that comes alive every half hour. Every 30 minutes, watch the Pied Piper lead off the rats, and then the children, never to be seen again. Then celebrate your newfound freedom with a plate of schnitzel at an adjoining restaurant.

400 Broadway, Wisconsin Dells, WI 53965

Phone: (608) 254-8321

Hours: Always visible

Cost: Free

Directions: Four blocks east of the river bridge.

Though the **Ship-Shaped Gift Shop** is fairly typical inside, the front of the building looks like the prow of a boat jutting out over the sidewalk.

116 Broadway, Wisconsin Dells, WI 53965

No phone

Hours: Always visible

Cost: Free

Directions: One block east of the river bridge.

Want all the class of a Vegas wedding without the airfare? Stop on by the **Dells Bells Wedding Chapel** in this former taxi stand for a 30-minute nuptial ceremony. The miniature church with pew seating for 42 is run by Tara and Scott Joles, who were ordained by the mail-order Universal Life Church. But note: Wisconsin has a five-day waiting period from license to ceremony, so if you're tying the knot, be sure to book a week-long water-slide package, because you'll be here a while.

43 La Crosse St., PO Box 755, Wisconsin Dells, WI 53965

Phone: (608) 393-4228

Hours: By appointment

Cost: $295–1,500, depending on the package and extras

Website: http://dellsbellsweddingchapel.com

Directions: Just south of Broadway, one block east of the river bridge.

The Ducks

Going to the Dells and missing the Ducks is like going to San Francisco and missing the cable cars. A Duck is a World War II army surplus amphibious vehicle, capable of speeds up to 50 mph on land and 15 mph in water. Hop aboard one of these crafts and careen through the woods with your barely-old-enough driver. Is that water you see up ahead? No problem! Hold on to your camera and loved ones as you slam into the river at the trail's end. If you're really lucky, a Duck just might swamp a canoe or capsize a paddle boat!

The second part of your journey is a tour of the Dells' rock formations. You'll view famous Stand Rock, and perhaps witness a dog jumping onto the tall pillar from the shore. It used to be vaulted by a man in an Indian costume, but today only a pooch is allowed to do it. Who knows how long that will last with heightened concern for our furry friends.

There are two outfits that offer Duck rides. And if you're looking for a Duck-like experience with a little more firepower, at Dells Army Ducks you can hop a ride on the *J.F.K. PT-109* for a patrol up the river. "Kids Play Commando on Our 50 Cal. [Machine Gun]" the advertisements scream. *"Brraakkakakakaka!"* How *adorable*!

Original Wisconsin Ducks, 1890 Wisconsin Dells Pkwy., PO Box 117, Wisconsin Dells, WI 53965

Phone: (608) 254-8751

Hours: June–August, daily 8 AM–7 PM; March–April and September–October, daily 9 AM–4 PM

Cost: Adults $18.50, kids (6–17) $8.25

Website: www.wisconsinducktours.com

Directions: On Rte. 12/23 (Wisconsin Dells Pkwy.) just south of County Rd. A.

Dells Army Ducks, 1550 Wisconsin Dells Pkwy., Wisconsin Dells, WI 53965

Phone: (608) 254-6080

Hours: June–August, daily 9 AM–6 PM; April–May and September–November, Saturday–Sunday 10 AM–3 PM

Cost: Adults $25, kids (6–11) $12

Website: www.dellsducks.com

Directions: On Rte. 12/23 (Wisconsin Dells Pkwy.) three blocks south of County Rd. A.

Grave of Belle Boyd, Confederate Spy

Belle Boyd was a hothead, a shameless self-promoter, and a brave defender of unjust causes like slavery and the right of the South to destroy the American union. Nevertheless, she was hailed in her day, but she's being punished in death . . . right here in Wisconsin.

This infamous sneak started her career at 17 when a drunken Union soldier tried to push his way into her family's Martinsburg, Virginia (later West Virginia), home. It was the Fourth of July, 1861, and he wanted to hang the Stars and Stripes from the building's upper window. He never made it—Boyd shot him in the head. Sound vaguely familiar? It should; Margaret Mitchell lifted the story and put it in *Gone with the Wind*.

A Union commander freed Boyd after an interrogation, never questioning her claim that the soldier was there to do worse than hang a flag. Emboldened by the deed, Boyd decided to become a full-time Confederate spy. When Union officers stayed with her family, she'd steal their weapons and hand them over to Johnny Reb. In 1862, when Northern troops were laying a trap for Stonewall Jackson in Front Royal, Virginia, Boyd crossed battle lines to tell Jackson to attack early, before the Union could amass its troops. Jackson won the battle.

This treachery got Boyd in big trouble. She spent some time in a Washington, DC, prison before another officer/sucker released her to head south, threatening to shoot her if she returned. In Richmond she met Confederate president Jefferson Davis, who sent her on a European mission to enlist England's support for the Southern cause. Boyd's ship was captured while trying to run the Southern Blockade. Boyd fell in love with a Union officer on the ship that detained her, coaxed him over to the Rebel cause, and then enlisted his help to flee through Canada to England.

Before she could do any more damage, the South lost. Boyd worked the lecture circuit, spent 10 years on Broadway as an actress, and married three times. While on a tour through Wisconsin in 1900, she fell ill and died on June 11. She is now planted in Yankee territory. As fitting punishment for her work against the Union, her grave is festooned with the Stars and Stripes each Memorial Day. Most days it has a Confederate flag, so if you're planning a visit, bring a real flag—the American flag—to stick into her plot.

Spring Grove Cemetery, Broadway and Weber Ave., Wisconsin Dells, WI 53965

No phone

Hours: Daily 9 AM–5 PM

Cost: Free

Directions: Two blocks east of Rte. 13/16 on Rte. 23 (Broadway), east of downtown.

H. H. Bennett Studio Museum

Wedged between the tacky shops in the downtown Dells is one of the most remarkable historical museums in the state: the H. H. Bennett Studio Museum.

Never heard of the man or his studio? Next to Matthew Brady, H. H. Bennett was arguably one of America's premier photographers, developing new techniques for the medium. The Civil War veteran began taking wilderness photographs in the great frontier, but when he wanted to include human or animal subjects they were required to stand very still while he exposed the plate. This was tough enough with people but even more difficult with wildlife. Because Bennett's hand had been maimed in the war, the process was even more time-consuming. Out of necessity, Bennett invented a fast-shutter camera that operated with rubber bands. With it Bennett snapped the world's first stop-action photo in 1886: a thrill-seeker—Bennett's son Ashley— caught midair, jumping to Standing Rock. Bennett is also credited as the first photojournalist; he did an exposé on Wisconsin lumbermen in 1886 and documented the life of the local Ho Chunk Indians.

The bulk of Bennett's photographs were stereo views of the Dells. When placed in a special device, the images had depth, exactly like View-Masters. You can see many of these images today at the museum housed in his former studio, the oldest continuously operating photography studio in the United States.

Stepping into the museum is like stepping into a Ken Burns documentary. Bennett's images of the Dells have been recreated full-size and positioned in such a way as to re-create the stereo effect, as if you're walking through the images. You'll visit the old portrait studio and the darkroom where he developed negatives and made his prints. An interactive computer system allows you to search through his impressive collection and to experience the 3-D effect with special goggles. The museum-studio still has more than 8,000 of Bennett's original negatives, and they will even make prints for you . . . for a price.

215 Broadway, PO Box 147, Wisconsin Dells, WI 53965

Phone: (608) 253-3523

Hours: May, daily 10 AM–4 PM; June–September, daily 10 AM–8 PM; October, daily 10 AM–4 PM

Cost: Adults $7, seniors (65+) $6, kids (5–17) $3.50

Website: http://hhbennettstudio.wisconsinhistory.org

Directions: Downtown, between Superior and Oak Sts., two blocks east of the bridge.

Mt. Olympus Water & Theme Park

Mt. Olympus is one of those Dells attractions that started out small and then got way out of hand. What was once Big Chief Go-Kart World, a respectable collection of racetracks, dumped its Native American roots for an ancient Greek theme, starting with a 60-foot-tall Trojan horse and three roller coasters: Zeus, Cyclops, and Pegasus. Mt. Olympus was born!

But the park couldn't really consider itself a destination attraction until it added a waterslide or two . . . or 44 (to date), including the Lost City of Atlantis, which looks like a human-size version of the game Mouse Trap. And now they've added three more roller coasters, a wave pool called Poseidon's Rage, a crumbling Coliseum that's the lobby for the Hotel Rome, and about a zillion other amusements to keep you and the little ones from leaving the complex.

1881 Wisconsin Dells Pkwy., Wisconsin Dells, WI 53965

Phone: (800) 800-4997 or (608) 254-9560

Hours: Opens daily 10 AM; check website for closing times

Cost: Adults $39.99, seniors (60+) $31.99, kids (3 and up) $39.99

Website: www.mtolympuspark.com

Directions: On Rte. 12/23 (Wisconsin Dells Pkwy.) just south of County Rd. A.

No Greeks inside—just go-karts.

RESORT RUNDOWN

OK, so you're overwhelmed with choices of where to stay. Since the beds are pretty much the same, you need to pick a motel or resort based on its overall theme, which is often reflected in its waterpark or pool area. Here are a few that stand out in the crowd:

Alakai

1030 Wisconsin Dells Pkwy., Lake Delton, (608) 253-3803, www.alakaihotel.com

The Alakai has a Hawaiian theme—palm trees and tiki heads and parrots surround the pools, though a monkey or two can be found, too. Hawaii has monkeys? In Wisconsin it does!

Atlantis

1570 Wisconsin Dells Pkwy., Wisconsin Dells, (800) 800-6179, www.theatlantishotel.com

It may have disappeared into the Mediterranean years ago, but it has resurfaced in the Dells. The Atlantis has an indoor and outdoor water park (with volcano), and Fantasy Suites—Roman Palace, King Neptune, Volcano, and Mermaid Whirlpool—though they're more stylish than kitschy.

Black Hawk

720 Race St., Wisconsin Dells, (608) 254-7770, www.blackhawkmotel.com

This is the way the Dells used to be—a family-owned motor hotel with low-key kitsch. Just two fiberglass statues guard the pool, a log-toting beaver at the kiddie pool and an Indian in a headdress scanning the far horizon.

Carousel Inn & Suites

1011 Wisconsin Dells Pkwy., Wisconsin Dells, (608) 254-6554, www.carousel-inn.com

Goody goody gumdrops!

The decor at the Carousel Inn will remind you of the Candyland board game—mountains of pink marshmallows sprouting lollipops and candy canes surround the pool. So sweet it'll give you cavities.

Chula Vista Resort

2501 River Rd., Wisconsin Dells, (855) 388-4782, www.chulavistaresort.com

Chula Vista is one of the area's megaresorts, with an 18-hole golf course, spa, and indoor and outdoor water parks. The indoor park has a Central American theme featuring toucans, palm trees, and a "roller coaster" slide called the Flyan Mayan. Outdoors you'll find the Cyclone, a spiraling wet tornado that, at 48 feet tall, is North America's tallest waterslide.

Flamingo Motel

1220 Wisconsin Dells Pkwy., Wisconsin Dells, (608) 253-2911, www.dellsflamingo.com

There's not much to this motel from another era, except for its eye-catching jumbo flamingo sign, one of the gaudiest on the strip and certainly the largest.

Grand Marquis Waterpark Hotel & Suites

840 Wisconsin Dells Pkwy., Wisconsin Dells, (608) 254-4843, www.grandmarquis-dells.com

The Grand Marquis is a leftover from the pre-megaresort days of the Dells, despite what you might gather from its name. The water park here is more of a water patch—dolphin-themed indoor and outdoor pools with small slides and, for some reason, an odd pink stegosaurus.

Great Wolf Lodge

1400 Great Wolf Dr., Lake Delton, (800) 559-9653, www.greatwolf.com/dells/waterpark

You know something's different the moment you enter the lodge's Grand Lobby—an enormous log "clock tower" populated by robotic raccoons, moose, trees, and woodsmen who come to life for a twice-a-day show. There's also a Northern Lights Arcade, where the carnies aren't the least bit scary, and the obligatory indoor water park with a Wyoming theme.

Kalahari Resort

1305 Kalahari Dr., Lake Delton, (877) 525-2427, www.kalahariresorts.com/wi/

The largest indoor water and theme park in the Dells, Kalahari is popular with winter vacationers. It's got climbing walls, go-karts, bowling alleys, amusement-park rides, and a Kenyan jungle. Oh, and dozens of waterslides, both indoor and outdoor. You don't even have to stay here—you can buy a visitor's pass for the day.

The Polynesian

857 N. Frontage Rd., Wisconsin Dells, (800) 272-5642,
www.dellspolynesian.com

Arrrrgh! All aboard the pirate's frigate to the South Seas in the Polynesian's outdoor water park, or visit the Temple of the Black Pearl, site of Blackbeard's Dark Tunnel! Wait a second . . . whaaa?

The Wilderness

511 E. Adams St., Lake Delton, (800) 867-9453, www.wildernessresort.com

Like Mt. Olympus, this behemoth has gobbled up all the land in sight and covered it with every amusement imaginable. Haunted Tombstone Town with a mine-shaft mirror maze, zip lines and bumper boats, minigolf and laser tag. And seven distinct water parks, including the Lost World, Klondike Kavern, and the Wild West.

Wintergreen Resort & Conference Center

60 Gasser Rd., Lake Delton, (800) 648-4765, www.wintergreen-resort.com

What better way to cool off than to spend your vacation with polar bears and penguins? Does it matter that these species live at opposite ends of the planet? Heck no! The motel's outdoor pool is a maze of caves and icebergs, while the indoor pool has an ice-block castle fit for the Snow Miser.

Museum of Historic Torture Devices

Have you had it with all the kids' squabbling at the minigolf range? There's no better way to get those ungrateful brats back in line than a trip to the Museum of Historic Torture Devices. Here the little ones will be treated to more than 40 exhibits on the Chinese death cage, the heretic's fork, the dunking stool, the iron gag, the gibbet, the rack, the piety belt, the skull crusher, and so on. You'll even see a mannequin Joan of Arc, wood piled around her feet, moments from being burned at the stake.

And when you're finally through with all that, you exit through the gift shop to find one last surprise: a charming painting of Walt Disney's Seven Dwarfs. You lean up close, nose to the display case, to realize it was created by John Wayne Gacy. Around it are birthday cards from the serial killer, along with newspaper clippings detailing his horrific hobby.

OK, kiddies—now who wants some ice cream? And no teasing your sister, m-kay?

740 Eddy St., Wisconsin Dells, WI 53965

Phone: (608) 254-2439 or (608) 893-6666

Hours: May–September, daily 11 AM–10 PM

Cost: Adults $6.99, kids (under 12) $5.99

Website: www.dellstorturemuseum.com

Directions: South of Broadway, one block east of the river.

SCARY SITES

Did the Museum of Historical Torture Devices fail to do the trick? Are the kids still bickering? I suspect the tykes have seen too many episodes of *CSI* and have grown desensitized to human misery. Maybe its time to crank up the thumbscrews with these other Dells horror spots.

Count Wolff von Baldazar's Haunted Mansion

112 Broadway, Wisconsin Dells, (608) 254-7513

This spooky establishment bills itself as nine dungeons of terror, though only one of the rooms actually looks like a dungeon. At the first room you'll meet a green-skinned witch and her raven sidekick. These low-budget robots warn you there's no turning back, even though you can see the entrance just behind you. As you proceed, fumbling through the dark, you'll set off electric sensors that trigger a headless man to begin speaking, skeletons to pop out of nowhere, compressed air to blast you in the face, and a woman's head to rot to its skull before your very eyes! Along the way you'll see graveyards and

cobwebs and fluorescent bones. For some reason, Count Balda-
zar doesn't appear until the end of the tour. His queeny ghost
hologram sits up in a coffin, rolls his *r*'s and eyes as he cackles
about the undead. Then he settles back into his mortal body for
the tape to rewind and the next group to come through.

Ghost Out-Post

2233 Wisconsin Dells Pkwy., Wisconsin Dells, (608) 254-2127,
www.ghostoutposthauntedhouse.com

The two skeletons at the entrance warn you about what lies
ahead. Sure enough, just inside you'll watch a hooded dummy
fry in an electric chair, the first of 17 violent vignettes. Watch
a poisoned nuclear plant worker vomit glowing radioactive
waste, or an alien burst forth from an astronaut's body, or a
criminal meet his punishment at the end of a hangman's noose
. . . it's all part of the fun!

Lost Temple

2255 Wisconsin Dells Pkwy., Wisconsin Dells, (608) 254-4548,
www.dellslosttemple.com

The newest addition to the strip, Lost Temple is Indiana Jones
meets David Copperfield. Follow your guide through the Mayan
temple in search of the golden skull. Around every corner is
another illusion or jungle guard with a blow dart.

Noah's Ark

The hottest temperature ever recorded in Wisconsin was at the Wisconsin
Dells on July 13, 1936. That day it hit 114°F. Had Noah's Ark been around
at the time, it might have been bearable.

In a town where every resort seems to have its own water park, it's
quite an accomplishment to draw visitors to pay for the experience at $37
a head. But thousands of folks flood the park every day to toss themselves
down slides on inner tubes. With 51 different slides to choose from, Noah's

Ark claims to be America's largest waterpark. Some are basic, open to the air, while others, like Black Thunder, flush you through a pitch-black tube faster than a White Castle slider with a coffee chaser. Try the Plunge, where you drop 50 feet before skidding out over a pool, or the Kowabunga family slide, where the whole clan rides in one giant raft. The newest slide is the scariest—Scorpion's Tail starts with a six-story drop through a trapdoor and then shoots you up and around a see-through loop.

Sick of slides? There's always the Endless River, where you bob along in a lazy loop, roasting in the sun, or the Big Kahuna wave pool, where rubber rafts are capsized every few minutes by a series of minitsunamis.

1410 Wisconsin Dells Pkwy., Wisconsin Dells, WI 53965

Phone: (608) 254-6351

Hours: June–August, daily 10 AM–8 PM; times can vary, so check website

Cost: All-day pass $36.99, seniors (55+) $29.59

Website: www.noahsarkwaterpark.com

Directions: On the Wisconsin Dells Pkwy. (Rte. 12) north of Lake St.

Ripley's Believe It or Not! Museum

No tourist trap town would be complete without a Ripley's Believe It or Not! Museum. From the street this place looks tame enough—strange but manageable. You can view a full-size, wooden Mercedes Gullwing automobile, built by Livio De Marchi and sailed as a boat, without paying admission, but if you want a peek at the rest, fork over the dough. Just around the corner you'll run into a medieval chastity belt, a Tibetan human-bone rugen and skull bowl, and a genuine shrunken head from the Jivaro Indians of Ecuador. It's part of the new Shrunken Head Alley exhibit.

And that's just the warm up. Weird displays surround a plane that appears to have crashed inside the building. Grasshoppers pulling rickshaws; a tattoo surgically removed and preserved by W. K. Foster of Winnipeg, Canada; a python skeleton squeezing the life out of a monkey skeleton; flattened mice pelts; the head of a four-horned Australian "Geep"; and the conjoined skulls of a two-headed calf.

Animal oddities seem to be this place's specialty. They've got the stuffed carcass of Slim, a six-legged cow from Mineral Point, Wisconsin, and Andy, a footless goose from Hastings, Nebraska, who was outfitted with tennis shoes. And finally, the mummified head of a human animal, Peter Kurten, better known as the Dusseldorf Vampire. This fellow was beheaded in Germany in 1931 after being convicted of killing nine people (he was tried for 68). His noggin was sliced in half (top to bottom, through the nose), cured like jerky, and hung on a meat hook, all in the name of "science." Now you can see it spin in circles in an old icebox . . . believe it or not!

115 Broadway, Wisconsin Dells, WI 53965

Phone: (608) 254-2184

Hours: June–August, daily 9 AM–11 PM; September, Sunday–Thursday 10 AM–8 PM, Friday–Saturday 10 AM–10 PM; October, Sunday–Thursday 10 AM–6 PM, Friday–Saturday 10 AM–8 PM; November–February, Friday–Monday 10 AM–5 PM; March–April, Sunday–Thursday 10 AM–5 PM, Friday–Saturday 10 AM–6 PM; May, Sunday–Thursday 10 AM–5 PM, Friday–Saturday 10 AM–8 PM

Cost: Adults $12.99, kids (5–11) $10.99

Website: www.conceptattractions.com/html/wismain.htm

Directions: Downtown between Eddy and Superior Sts., one block east of the bridge.

Timber Falls Adventure Park

Timber Falls is a survivor, a hodgepodge of attractions with a little bit of what you'll find in larger concentrations elsewhere, but seldom all in the same location. Minigolf? They've got four different 18-hole courses that weave through the trees. Bumper boats? Don't just ram your friends and family; douse them with the onboard squirt guns. Log flume? Theirs has two big vertical drops *and* a volcano that erupts in flame twice an hour. Roller coaster? The Hellcat roars through 90-degree banked turns on one of the fastest tracks in the Dells.

And then there's the Skyscraper. Imagine a 70-mph, 10-story, 2-arm Ferris wheel that pulls 4 Gs at its bottom arc. Then picture yourself strapped in an open carriage that freely spins upside down, regardless of where you're at in the loop. The Skyscraper is not included in the all-day pass and will set you back another $22. And probably a pair of underwear.

1000 Stand Rock Rd., Wisconsin Dells, WI 53965

Phone: (608) 254-8414

Hours: Check website; each ride is different

Cost: Skyscraper $22; roller coaster, bumper boats, log flume $6.50 each; Minigolf (18 holes), adults $7.75, kids (6–12) $5.75; all-day pass, over 46" $19.99, under 46" $14.99

Website: www.timberfallspark.com

Directions: On the north side of Rte. 13 (Stand Rock Rd.) on the west side of the river bridge.

Tommy Bartlett Exploratory

Tommy Bartlett's old Robot World was beginning to look dated. After all, who still believes robots will do our housework, cook our food, and give us baths? Would we trust them? And what would happen if they fell under the control of a computer virus? So Tommy Bartlett, visionary that he was, updated the museum shortly before his death, turning it into the Tommy Bartlett Exploratory. Your visit still begins with a futuristic tour through the remnants of the old Robot World, but later on you find yourself learning a thing or two . . . on vacation, no less!

The tour begins by blasting off to a space station. You're treated to a "cathode ray scanner" before entering the "shuttle," a three-floor elevator. The space station is run by Tattoo and his sidekick who quickly lose track of astronaut Buster Leapyear somewhere in outer space. This bungling becomes a theme. When lights start flashing "Radiation Alert!" a red robot with a Scottish brogue warns you to "move along before the whole place goes up like a roman candle!" *That's* encouraging . . .

You're unceremoniously dumped out into a collection of hands-on exhibits designed to trick your eyes and surprise your senses. Adjacent to the museum is a gyroscope harness, and you can flip yourself silly for an additional fee. It's all preparation for the grand finale: a *MIR* Space Station module!

Bartlett purchased a portion of *MIR* from the cash-strapped Russian government, a module that was never attached to that orbiting junk heap. You're welcomed by Dr. Norman Thagard, a *MIR* astronaut/survivor, via space-age videotape. The module hangs in a large room, at an angle, making you feel unbalanced as you stand inside. Strapped to a wall is a genuine Space Guitar. Now you really *are* starting to feel ill.

560 Wisconsin Dells Pkwy., Wisconsin Dells, WI 53965

Phone: (608) 254-2525

Hours: June–August, daily 9 AM–9 PM; September–May, daily 10 AM–4 PM

Cost: Adults $13, seniors (65+) $10.40, kids (6–11) $10

Website: www.tommybartlett.com/exploratory/

Directions: On the Wisconsin Dells Pkwy. (Rte. 12) north of the Rte. 23 split.

WISCONSIN DELLS

➡ A mysterious cougar has been spotted near the Wisconsin Dells along Route 16 and Route 23.

The Tommy Bartlett Sky, Ski, and Stage Show

Don't let this attraction's shameless promotion campaigns discourage you from visiting—it actually lives up to its own hype. Tommy Bartlett has never allowed his water-ski show to grow stale, not even in death. It is impossible to describe what you will see in any given season since it changes every year. Rest assured, your show will have all the flare of a 1970s TV variety hour with perky musical numbers, comedy skits, magic acts, dance routines, and lots and lots of sequins.

To get a sense of what you might experience, consider Tommy Bartlett's most recent extravaganza, "Livin' the Dream," a salute to Bartlett's 60 years on Lake Delton. The show begins with speedboats pulling skiers waving anniversary banners who are then released so that the *boats* can launch over the wooden jumps. Before long Aqua the Clown (that little scamp!) interrupts the performance in an outboard dinghy, which he soon crashes onto the shore. A circus trainer arrives with a gorilla and, of course, it escapes. The ape chases Aqua down the dock and onto skis, and the two battle it out with rowboat oars at high speeds. As they exit lake left, four

Don't try this at home. Photo by author, courtesy of Tommy Bartlett's

spangled women ski by, tethered only by their ankles. And what's that? A space shuttle? It roars by for a few passes before stopping to open its cargo bay doors. Out pop three astronauts with chrome helmets for a battle of acrobatic ski jumps . . . and this is all still before intermission!

After you've been given ample time to purchase snow cones and hot dogs, the stage show begins. First up, two acrobats perform death-defying tricks on a spinning Sky Pendulum Wheel, well into the splatter-if-you-fall territory. After they cheat the Grim Reaper, a juggler-unicyclist—is there any other kind?—shows up with flaming batons. A family of Filipino gymnasts follows; the father flips his trusting children end over end through the air with his feet, catching them each time. Evening shows are topped off with an Entrancing Waters dancing fountain and Laser-Rama finale!

If you watch this high-spirited hokum for the full two hours and don't walk out of the show smiling, I suggest you check the hole where your soul used to reside. Maybe *nothing* makes you happy.

560 Wisconsin Dells Pkwy., Wisconsin Dells, WI 53965
Phone: (608) 254-2525
Hours: June–August, 4:30 and 8:30 PM
Cost: Adults $21, seniors (65+) $16.80, kids (6–11) $11
Website: www.tommybartlett.com/water-show/
Directions: On the Wisconsin Dells Pkwy. (Rte. 12) north of the Rte. 23 split.

Top Secret

I have a theory about how the creators of this weird attraction came up with the name: *they have no idea what the hell it's about.* Call it Top Secret and nobody else has the security clearance to know! So, for the time being, suspend your disbelief . . .

Top Secret is often called the Upside-Down White House because, from the outside, it looks like the executive mansion has been lifted off its foundation, turned over, and dropped to the ground. The president's limo has crashed nose-down next to the portico, but nobody's around. What happened? Time to go inside.

A guide will take you on a tour through all the historic rooms, offering more jokes than clarification. George Washington stands on the ceiling/floor in the Oval Office, the red "hotline" phone on a nearby desk. All the furniture hangs upside down, over your head, and the drapes hang up—

If you figure it out, call me. Photo by author, courtesy of Top Secret

not even gravity works here. The guide rambles on about aliens and mad scientists while you file down a hallway past a lunatic in a straight jacket to the Red Room, then the Green Room, and finally an underground laboratory where somebody's making a robotic Obama. An earlier model, a mechanical Bill Clinton, looks down from a balcony. He doesn't have hands—"He couldn't keep them to himself!" the guide explains, and for once something makes sense. On it goes, room after room, until you're dumped back in the parking lot without any answers to your top-secret questions.

527 Wisconsin Dells Pkwy., Wisconsin Dells, WI 53965

Phone: (608) 254-6700

Hours: May–September, daily 11 AM–5 PM

Cost: Adults $12, kids (5–12) $10

Website: www.dellstopsecret.com

Directions: Where County Rd. A meets Rte. 12/23 (Wisconsin Dells Pkwy.).

Wizard Quest

Any parent concerned that their children will loose valuable cognitive skills during the summer vacation should put Wizard Quest on their Dells itinerary. What it lacks in waterslides it more than makes up for in problem-solving exercises. Sound like a bummer? No, no, no!

Upon entering, you gather around a caged white owl and learn about your quest. Four wizards are trapped, one in each of the four realms. Your task is to uncover the clues found in those realms, solve the riddles, free the wizards, and earn glimmer points, redeemable later at the exit gift shop. You have 90 minutes. GO!

For the next hour and a half you'll be crawling through dark passageways into secret rooms, bumping down slides, stumbling through mirrored mazes, and encountering some of the most disturbing elfin creatures imaginable. If you think you've solved part of the puzzle, find a computer kiosk, scan the bar code on your ticket, and answer the prompts on the touch screen. If you're really stumped, ask for a hint from the designated teenage helper in the central courtyard.

The world's largest preteen girl's bedroom. Photo by author, courtesy of Wizard Quest

Wizard Quest has come up with a different set of clues for each day of the week, so you can come for seven days in a row if you or the kids really like it. Or if you never find an exit.

527 Wisconsin Dells Pkwy., Wisconsin Dells, WI 53965

Phone: (608) 254-6700

Hours: Times vary; check website

Cost: Adults $12.99, kids (5–11) $10.99

Website: www.wizardquest.net

Directions: Downtown between Eddy and Superior Sts., one block east of the bridge.

SOUTHERN WISCONSIN

Y es, all of Wisconsin is the Cheese State, but Southern Wisconsin supports the biggest wedge of the industry. Cheese fanatics are everywhere you turn: the Historic Cheese Museum in Monroe, the Dairy Shrine in Ft. Atkinson, the Swiss Historical Village in New Glarus. Businesses are guarded by animals who have expanded to dangerous proportions after feasting for years on the yellow stuff, like Igor the Mouse in Fennimore and Bessie the Cow in Janesville.

This singular dairy focus has had an eclipsing effect on the rest of the tourist industry. Monuments to cheese get so much attention that other roadside attractions are almost overshadowed. Did you know the Lost City of Atlantis . . . or something close to it . . . has been found in Lake Mills? Have you visited the Kewpee Restaurant, the World's Largest Can of Chili Beans, or the Birthplace of the Gideon Bible? Probably not—you're sitting on the couch eating cheese, aren't you? Time to work off that orange spare tire.

Arena

Concretion Museum

What's a concretion? Think of it as a kidney stone for a lake. Over hundreds of years, mineral deposits form on the outside of a piece of clay, layer after layer after layer, slowly growing into a globule of indeterminate shape. In the Great Lakes, these concretions are found mostly on the southwest shore of Lake Superior.

Enter Byron Buckeridge. For years he hiked the lake's shore, picking up concretions whenever he found them. Over time he amassed a 50,000-piece collection. Buckeridge would then stare at his finds like a daydreaming kid watching the clouds, and in some he would see famous individuals—Miss America, Buddha, and characters from Shakespeare. And he might have been onto something; the Bad River Chippewa have long claimed that these stones have souls.

But in 1995, the Chippewa declared that these special stones belong to the tribe. Because of this, Buckeridge no longer collects concretions, but the ones he does have are on display today at the construction business owned by his son. See if you can guess the famous figures before reading their display cards.

Buckeridge Construction, 409 Dalogasa Dr., Arena, WI 53503

Phone: (608) 753-9117

Hours: By appointment

Cost: Free

Directions: Two blocks north of Rte. 14, east of Village Edge Dr.

Argyle
Toy Train Barn

Hey, all you train lovers—ever heard of the Argyle & Eastern Railroad? Probably not, because it's very small and doesn't really go anywhere—just around and around in loops on this 18-acre spread near Argyle. The miniature railroad was built by Buck Guthrie in 2002, the tracks laid out over a truss bridge, across a driveway grade, and through cuts in hills on his farm. He's even got a roundhouse to turn around his homemade locomotive.

Wisconsin winters being what they are, the A&ER doesn't operate year-round, though this attraction does. Inside the Guthries' barn are a number of model train layouts in various gauges. And it isn't just the trains on these layouts that move. See the cows plod around their holding pens, marvel as a hot-air balloon soars overhead, and watch firefighters attack a blaze. Some of the layouts even have buttons to allow you to control the action.

W9141 Hwy. 81, Argyle, WI 53504

Phone: (608) 966-1464

Hours: Daily 10 AM–5 PM

Cost: Adults $5, kids (under 10) $3

Website: www.whrc-wi.org/trainbarn/

Directions: Just west of the Rte. 78 intersection.

Ashippun
Honey of a Museum

Don't know much about the birds and the bees? Honey Acres might be able to assist you . . . at least halfway. This working apiary has been run by the

Diehnelt family since 1852, and they know their bees. (The museum has only been here for a few decades.) Were you aware these stinging insects were originally brought to North America by settlers, and were known as the "white man's fly"? See—you're learning already!

Peer through a glass-enclosed beehive to see them in action. Read displays on pollination and beeswax. Taste honey directly from taps. Check out the 20-minute slide show on Wisconsin's state insect—the bee, of course! And scold Mr. Black Bear, dreaded enemy of nature's pollinator.

Honey Acres, N1557 Rte. 67, PO Box 346, Ashippun, WI 53003

Phone: (800) 558-7745 or (920) 474-4411

Hours: November–May, Monday–Friday 9 AM–3:30 PM; May–October, Monday–Friday 9 AM–3:30 PM, Saturday–Sunday noon–4 PM

Cost: Free

Website: www.honeyacres.com

Directions: On Rte. 67, two miles north of town.

Bagley
Good-bye, Passenger Pigeons!

There was a time when swarms of passenger pigeons blackened the skies of North America, and Wisconsin was a main stop on the species' annual migration. In 1871, a flock of 136 million descended on Jackson County in the center of the state, blanketing 850 square miles of land. It was a mess—a natural mess, but still a mess.

Overwhelmed settlers felt something had to be done. The pigeons were oblivious to their human predators and were easy targets, and because each nesting pair laid only one egg each year, they couldn't replenish their quickly diminishing population. In less than thirty years, they were extinct in the wild.

Conservationists have erected a small monument to the birds in Wyalusing State Park along the birds' former flyway. It is "dedicated to the last Wisconsin Passenger Pigeon, shot at Babcock, September 1899. This species became extinct through the avarice and thoughtlessness of man." And howdy.

Though Babcock (in central Wisconsin) claims to be "Where the Last Passenger Pigeon Was Killed," records indicate the last bird was picked off in Pikes County, Ohio, on March 24, 1900. Some birds remained in captivity, but the final one perished at a Cincinnati zoo in 1914.

Wyalusing State Park, 13081 State Park Ln., Bagley, WI 53801

Phone: (608) 996-2261

Hours: Daily 6 AM–11 PM

Cost: One-hour pass $5, daily sticker $7

Website: http://dnr.wi.gov/org/land/parks/specific/wyalusing/ and www.wyalusing.org

Directions: County Rd. C west of Rte. 18/35; plaque is located at the Green Cloud picnic area.

Beloit
Angel Museum

First things first. According to its literature, the Angel Museum "refrains from promoting religion or a theology of angels." That's a tough sell. It's kind of like collecting stamps without promoting the postal service.

This museum started with the private collection of Joyce Berg. Over many years she amassed more than 12,000 angel figurines, mostly at garage and estate sales, and was about to give some away (to make room for more) when she learned a former Catholic church was about to be demolished. Why not start a museum and use her collection as the "seed"?

The angel-loving public responded with open wings. Berg's museum can display only 6,000 of its collection at any one time, so it's constantly rotating in new cherubs. Oprah donated 570 African American angels she received after asking on her talk show why there weren't any black angels. Apparently there were.

Berg has porcelain angels, Hummel angels, crystal angels, wooden angels, raw spaghetti angels . . . you name it, somebody's glued wings to it . . . including Joyce Berg. That's right, sometimes she dons a pair of flapping wings, silver robe, and halo to greet her visitors as if they were passing through the Pearly Gates. Perhaps that's the wrong outfit to meet a tour bus full of senior citizens, but they don't seem to mind.

656 Pleasant St., PO Box 816, Beloit, WI 53511

Phone: (877) 412-6435 or (608) 362-9099

Hours: Tuesday–Saturday 10 AM–4 PM, Sunday call ahead

Cost: Adults $7, seniors (62+) $5, kids (5–12) $4

Website: www.angelmuseum.org

Directions: On Rte. 51 (Pleasant St.), three blocks north of Rte. 81, on the river.

World's Largest Can of Chili Beans

One of the first sights visitors see when entering Wisconsin from Illinois on I-90 is a gigantic can of Hormel Chili with Beans. Could it be cookout garbage left behind by Paul Bunyan? Is it part of the nation's strategic reserve of natural gas? Or is it what it seems, an external holding tank at the Hormel plant, painted as a giant advertisement?

The more you eat, the more you toot.

Strike the first theory. Paul Bunyan was long dead before canned chili or the can opener was invented. The second scenario seems unlikely, too. Wouldn't a gas supply like this be stored in a more secure location? That leaves the third option, which seems all too obvious.

But that's maybe what somebody wants us to believe . . .

Hormel Plant, 3000 Kennedy Dr., Beloit, WI 53511

Phone: (608) 365-9501

Hours: Always visible

Cost: Free

Directions: On the west side of I-90, just south of the Rte. 43 Exit.

BETTER THAN BEANS?

Another Wisconsin business, the Stark Candy Company in the Milwaukee suburb of Pewaukee (700 Hickory St.), has painted its factory tower with a different motif: a **gigantic stack of Necco Wafers** (www.necco.com).

Blue Mounds
Cave of the Mounds

Cave of the Mounds was discovered on August 4, 1939, on the farm of Ebinezer Bringham when workers blasting limestone inadvertently opened what is now the entrance to the cave. Realizing tourism was more lucrative than limestone, Bringham developed this hole in the ground into an attraction.

Early visitors had to hike down a wooden stairway, but the steps have long since been replaced with concrete. Down below you'll see impressive stalactites and stalagmites, uncommon in small caves like Blue Mounds because they grow at the rate of one inch every 200 years. You do the math. Your guide will also point out a cephalopod fossil found in the cave. The tour takes about an hour, and during it they'll turn out the lights for the experience of total darkness. Don't worry; they'll turn the lights back on before the kids (or you) start crying.

Due to its long operating history, Cave of the Mounds has been honored as a National Natural Landmark. The temperature down below is 50°F year-round, so if you come in the summer, bring a light jacket, and if you come in the winter, leave the snowmobile suit behind or you'll work up a sweat.

Bringham Farm, Cave of the Mounds Rd., PO Box 148, Blue Mounds, WI 53517

Phone: (608) 437-3038

Tour hours: March–May, Monday–Friday 10 AM–5 PM, Saturday–Sunday 9 AM–6 PM; June–August, daily 9 AM–7 PM; September–November, Monday–Friday 10 AM–5 PM, Saturday–Sunday 9 AM–6 PM; December–February, Saturday-Sunday 10 AM–5 PM

Cost: Adults $15, kids (4–12) $7.50

Website: www.caveofthemounds.com

Directions: One mile east of town off County Rd. ID.

WHO LET THE ELVES LOOSE?

Just down the road from Cave of the Mounds is *Nissedahle*, Norwegian for "Valley of the Elves." These little elves have been busy, reconstructing a *Stavkirke* (a 12th-century Norwegian church) originally built for Chicago's 1893 Columbian Exposition, as well as a sod house and a *Stabbur* (a storage house on stilts). It's all part of **Little Norway** (3576 Rte. JG North, (608) 437-8211, www.littlenorway.com), a little bit of Scandinavia in the heart of cheese country.

Blue River
Death Row Totem Poles

Rod Pasold had many fine years on his motorcycle, out on the open road. And occasionally, he had some not-so-fine moments skidding off, scraping along, and tumbling end-over-end on some of those same roads. To commemorate those memories, and to remind himself how lucky he is to still be alive, he erected a collection of "totem poles" made from crutches, wrecked bikes, cracked helmets, and other mangled objects.

The Death Row Totem Poles have attracted many bikers over the years, and some come bearing their own contributions to the artwork. Pasold adds the crumpled items to his property-line fence, making passersby wonder just how many wrecks this guy has been in, and how to avoid him when he's out on the open road.

2643 Rte. 133, Blue River, WI 53518
Private phone
Hours: Always visible
Cost: Free
Directions: On Rte. 133 on the way to Muscoda.

Boscobel
The First Gideon Bible

On September 4, 1898, traveling salesmen John Nicholson and Samuel Hill arrived at the Central House Hotel looking for a room. The place was packed, and just one room was left. According to their recollections, the place was filled with "drummers and hang-abouts playing cards shaking dice, smoking, laughing, cursing, yelling, and singing with clinking of glasses and men drunk and asleep in chairs." Neither man felt comfortable in *that* crowd, and though they had never met before that night, they shared a bed in Room 19. Hill and Nicholson spent a good part of the night talking, and decided they had to come up with a plan to make hotels more welcoming to guys like them. You know, Christian folk.

They began in 1899 by organizing the Christian Commercial Travelers' Association, better known as the Gideons. It took nine years, but in 1907 the first Gideon Bibles were placed in a Montana hotel. Millions of trees and a hundred years later, it's hard to find a room that doesn't have one in a bedside drawer.

The Gideons' name comes from the Book of Judges, and contrary to the Eighth Commandment, you are *encouraged* to steal their Bible from your room. But if you do, they would like you to confess your sin to the management so it may be replaced.

Today's Hotel Boscobel (the former Central House Hotel) has been the scene of other historic events as well. Candidate John F. Kennedy stayed here for a few hours with Jackie on March 25 during the 1960 Wisconsin presidential primary. Some believe John-John was conceived in Room 19.

Hotel Boscobel, 1005 Wisconsin Ave., Boscobel, WI 53805

Phone: (608) 375-4714

Hours: Daily 10 AM–2 PM; bar, daily 11 AM–2 PM; restaurant, lunch 11 AM–2:30 PM, dinner 5–9 PM

Cost: Lunch $5–10, dinner $9–15

Website: www.boscobelwisconsin.com/hotel.html

Directions: Three blocks east of Rte. 61, south of Bluff St.

Burlington
Angels in the Belfries

God may work in mysterious ways, but one of the strangest ways is as a building inspector. Back in July 1970, parishioners at St. Mary's Catholic Church began to notice a strange glow in the middle of the church's steeple. Was it a swarm of fireflies? Static electricity? Or a message from on high?

Take a guess. That's right, hundred of the faithful flocked to the church to stand around the intersection and gawk up at the spire, night after night. Sometimes the light was blue, sometimes it was orange, yet it was never Packers' green and gold.

Then, as quickly as it appeared, it vanished. Some doubting Thomases decided to check out the steeple from the inside and discovered the builders had miswired its lightning rod. Had the cross on the top been hit by a bolt, the entire structure could have been lit up . . . by flames!

Some interpreted these series of events as a warning from God to save the church. We'll know if lights reappear just before the floorboards are infested with termites or the basement floods.

St. Mary's Catholic Church, 108 McHenry St., Burlington, WI 53105

Phone: (262) 763-1504

Hours: Always visible

Cost: Free

King James's Death Site

Shortly after prophet Joseph Smith was murdered in an Illinois jail in 1844, the head of a Mormon settlement near Burlington, James Jesse Strang, produced a letter from Smith (of questionable veracity) ordaining Strang as the Mormons' new leader. It also claimed that at the new settlement "people shall wax fat and pleasant in the presence of their enemies." The community was Voree, the "Garden of Peace," and at its peak had 2,000 inhabitants.

To further bolster his questionable claims, Strang unearthed his own copper plates—three in all—from the Hill of Promise, along the Racine /Walworth county line at the White River. When Brigham Young took the majority of the Latter-Day Saints westward, Strang headed east with his followers to Beaver Island in Lake Michigan. And then he got stranger.

On July 8, 1850, Strang proclaimed himself King James. He started wearing a secondhand Shakespearean robe and a tin crown. He issued bizarre edicts, first banning tea and coffee, but later mandating that all women must dress in bloomers. The husband of one woman who did not comply was horsewhipped. That man later shot Strang in the back on June 16, 1856, and then pummeled him with the butt of his gun. And thus ended the so-called Kingdom of God on Earth.

Before Strang died, he returned with his five wives to Wisconsin, where he passed away on July 9, 1856, in his parents' home. His grave is located in the Burlington Cemetery.

Death Site, 4325 Mormon Rd., Burlington, WI 53105
No phone
Hours: Always visible
Cost: Free
Website: www.strangite.org/Tour.htm
Directions: North on Mormon Rd. off Rte. 36 (State St.) on the west side of town.

Sci-Fi Café and Earth Mysteries Museum

More than one-third of Americans believe that the earth has been visited by aliens from outer space, so the pool of potential customers for

Take us to your lunch counter! Photo by author, courtesy of the Sci-Fi Café

this restaurant should be huge. However, the place is rather quiet. Perhaps not everyone wants to dine while big-eyed aliens stare at them from every corner and UFOs hover overhead. But if you're OK with the surroundings, it's just more room for you!

Owners Brad and Mary Sutherland are true believers. Mary even once spotted a triangular UFO—that usually does it. You can see a model of what she saw in the café. The adjoining museum and bookstore is usually only open if you ask them to unlock it, which you should most definitely do. It's crammed with self-published UFO books and tapes, New Age trinkets, and miniature stuffed animals.

532 N. Pine St., Burlington, WI 53105

Phone: (262) 767-1116

Hours: Daily 6 AM–8 PM

Cost: Free; meals, $4–7

Website: www.burlingtonnews.net/scificafe

Directions: Just south of the intersection with Rte. 36 (Milwaukee Ave.).

HAVE THE ALIENS ALREADY LANDED?

According to *The W-Files* (Wisconsin Trails, 1997) by Jay Rath, Martians made contact with Dean T. Anderson near Fish Creek in Door County's Peninsula State Park (9462 Shore Rd., (920)

868-3258, http://dnr.wi.gov/topic/parks/name/peninsula/) on six different occasions from 1975 to 1976. At first Anderson only spotted UFOs, but then he began making physical contact, usually in the early morning hours. A Martian couple introduced themselves as Sunar and Treena, and corrected Anderson's term for their home planet. It's not Mars, but Muton.

Spinning Top Exploratory Museum

Judith Schulz may very well forget her own name one of these days. Why? More people call her the Top Lady than refer to her as Judith. But don't think she doesn't appreciate the moniker—it's better then Yo-Yo Mama, though folks call her that, too.

Schulz has been collecting spinning tops since she was a child, and to date has amassed a collection of more than 2,000. Her hands-on museum has "snake" tops, dreidels, gyroscopes, rev tops, casting tops, doodle tops, bracket tops, sonic satellites, diabolos, a five-pound Malaysian top, and returning tops, better know by their common name: yo-yos. She has tops that blow bubbles, dance like ballerinas, and spin up to seven days without stopping! You can only see these twirling toys if you sign up for one of her two-hour presentations, which are well worth the time and money.

Schulz is handy with her yo-yos and will perform a variety of tricks during your visit. She has the classics, like gravity grippers, sleepers, walk the dog, forwards, and breakaways, but also string tricks like an ice cream cone, a Confederate flag, and the Eiffel Tower. She performed that last one in front of the Eiffel Tower a while ago.

For her grand finale Schulz brings out the Chinese Poison Top, a movie prop from *My Summer Story*, the sequel to *A Christmas Story*, for which she acted as a Top Consultant and performer. Whenever a top appeared from off-screen it had been cast by ever-accurate Schulz. When Disney is dropping thousands of dollars an hour for production, they aren't going to trust the tough jobs to Macaulay Culkin's brother. That's a job for . . . drum roll . . . the Top Lady!

533 Milwaukee Ave., Burlington, WI 53105
Phone: (262) 763-3946

Hours: By appointment only

Cost: $15

Website: www.topmuseum.org

Directions: At the intersection of Rtes. 11 (Pine St.) and 36 (Milwaukee Ave.).

YO!

During the 1950s and '60s the Duncan Yo-Yo company (www. yo-yo.com) was located in the northern Wisconsin town of Luck. It has since been bought out by an Ohio consortium and has left town.

Town Full of Liars

How strange it seems that a town should celebrate the fact that many of its prominent citizens are certified, card-carrying liars. In fact, they actually *compete* to see who can come up with the most outrageous falsehood. But that's just what they do in Burlington, home of the Burlington Liars' Club, founded in 1929 by two local reporters, Manuel Hahn and Otis Hulett. They wrote a fake story about a nonexistent contest between the city's police and fire departments as to who could tell the best lie. The chief of police won when he claimed he had never told a lie in his life.

The only thing worse than being accused of telling a lie is to not get the satisfaction of actually telling it. So a year later, when the issue of the contest came up again, the contest really took place. Contestants were charged a dime for each fib and a winner was crowned for the most outlandish statement. Some of the best lies over the years have been commemorated on plaques placed around the city's main business district—the Tall Tales Trail—such as the one from Tacoma resident John Zelenak outside the May's Insurance Agency (500 N. Pine St.): "My wife is so lazy that she feeds the chicken popcorn so that the eggs will turn themselves when she fries them." For a walking tour of the infamous lies, pick up a map at city hall or the chamber of commerce.

The Burlington Liars' Club still hosts the World Lying Championships on New Year's Eve each year, or at least that's what they say. To enter, send in your fib and a buck. If you don't hear back, you've either lost or been had.

Burlington Liars' Club, 113 E. Chestnut St., PO Box 156, Burlington, WI 53105

Phone: (262) 763-6044

Hours: Plaques, always visible; contest, New Year's Eve

Cost: Free; lies $1

Website: www.burlingtonliarsclub.com

Directions: All around downtown; follow map provided by the chamber of commerce (at address above).

Clinton
A Truck in a Tree

Luke Madsen probably knew that when he asked his dad to build him a tree house, it wouldn't look like anything his friends had. His father, Mark "Mad Man" Madson, was known for making strange vehicles—the Little Limestone Stunt Car (it belches fire!), the topless Cadillac Packer Mobile, and the Cadillac Boat Car that can be "driven" across a lake.

But the elder Madson took an "upside-down and backward"

Parallel-to-the-ground parking.

approach to the project, using a prefabricated structure for the job. Well, not so much a prefab structure as a 1959 Chevy Fleetside pickup truck. He hoisted the vehicle up 50 feet and jammed it between the crooks of two trees, and it's been there ever since. Drivers along I-43 can see the blue-and-white pickup on the north side of the highway to this day.

8729 E. Little Ln., Clinton, WI 53525
Phone: (608) 676-5166
Hours: Always visible
Cost: Free
Website: http://truckinthetree.com or www.harleyheartbeat.com or http://markmadson.com
Directions: On the north side of I-43, just west of the Rte. 140 exit.

Columbus
Christopher Columbus Museum

Tucked away on the top floor of an enormous antique mall in Columbus is a private museum dedicated to the town's namesake, Christopher Columbus. Most of the 2,000-plus items on display are souvenirs from Chicago's 1893 Columbian Exposition. Statues, glassware, posters, maps, trinkets, needlework, tickets, models, and books document the World's Fair better than anything you'll ever see in Chicago. But because the exhibits wrap around shelves filled with stuff that's for sale, it can be difficult to determine where the museum stops and the store starts.

For true Columbus nuts, visit the fiberglass statue of Chris before leaving town. It was created in 1988 by David Oswald and dedicated on Columbus Day of that year. It stands at the intersection of Routes 151 and 16 on the northwest side of town. The work is titled *Columbus Taking Possession*, a characterization many might take issue with.

Columbus Antique Mall, 239 Whitney St., PO Box 151, Columbus, WI 53925
Phone: (920) 623-1992
Hours: Daily 8:30 AM–4 PM
Cost: Adults $2
Website: www.columbusantiquemall.com
Directions: One block east of Rte. 151 Business, two blocks north of Rte. 16.

Delavan
A Giant, Clown-Stomping Elephant

If you dislike clowns, check out the monument in downtown Delavan. A 10-foot, 6-inch replica of Romeo, the infamous rogue elephant, raised up and poised to stomp the life out of a clown in this quiet little park. Yet he never does. Not that he couldn't—the real Romeo trampled or gored no less than five unfortunate handlers over a 15-year period. (There's also a giraffe statue in the park, but that critter never killed anyone.)

The park in which Romeo's statue stands has its own dark history. In 1874, circus balloonist Rodley Palmer took off from this spot, ran into the cornice of the nearby Park Hotel (117 Park Place), and plunged to his death.

Delavan has a long history with the circus, which is why it calls itself the Circus City. Baraboo be damned! Twenty-six different circuses have operated out of Delavan, and it was here that the P. T. Barnum show was organized in 1871. Over the years the town has been home to two of the Ringling Brothers and a 12-year-old runaway named Harry Houdini. Seventy-something performers and carnies, strong men and bearded ladies, geeks and dog-faced boys, are buried in the local Spring Grove and St. Andrews Cemeteries, both at the north end of Seventh Street.

Tower Park, 100 E. Walworth Ave., Delavan, WI 53115

Phone: (262) 728-5095

Hours: Always visible

Cost: Free

Website: www.delavanwi.org

Directions: On Rte. 11 (Walworth Ave.), three blocks west of County Rd. O.

Dickeyville
Dickeyville Grotto

Father Mathias Wernerus had big plans when he was assigned to Dickeyville's Holy Ghost Parish in 1918: he would build a shrine to God and Country. It was originally intended to honor three local men killed in the Great War, but it soon became much more than that. He got the idea from the Grotto of the Redemption in West Bend, Iowa.

Officially called Grotto of Christ the King and Mary His Mother, it took five years to build, beginning in 1925. The grotto's foundation was excavated by hand by the parish schoolchildren who received 10¢, a cookie, and a glass of wine for their day's labor. Most of the work after that was done by Wernerus himself, embedding glass, stones, petrified sea creatures, and crystals into the cement structure. His flock would bring broken glassware that he would melt into brazed chunks and affix somewhere.

The result is a collection of monuments including the Patriotism in Stone shrine to Lincoln, Washington, and Columbus; Holy Ghost Park

Built with wine, cookies, and a lot of cement.

adjoining the parish cemetery; and the grand grotto itself. From the front, the grotto resembles a giant ogre whose mouth is the entrance and whose eyes glare out toward the road. On its left is a papal flag and on the right an American one.

But now the final question: *Why?* Father Wernerus once gave a cryptic explanation: "Many reasons urged me to put up 'Religion in Stone' and 'Patriotism in Stone.' The main reason it was done I could not reveal. The Last Day will tell you more about that." Uh-oh . . .

The Dickeyville Grotto had an enormous impact on folk art in Wisconsin, inspiring the Rudolph Grotto (page 88), the Wegner Grotto (page 58), the Prairie Moon Sculpture Gardens (page 60), and Fred Smith's Wisconsin Concrete Park (page 33). There is even some evidence that Simon Rodia, creator of the Watts Towers in Los Angeles, worked as a laborer for Wernerus on his way west. Rodia complained that the priest never paid him, and he resented it.

Holy Ghost Church, 305 W. Main St., Dickeyville, WI 53808

Phone: (608) 568-3119

Hours: Always visible; gift shop, April–May, daily 9:30 AM–3:30 PM, June–October, daily 9 AM–
   4 PM, November–December, Saturday–Sunday 11 AM–2 PM

Cost: $1 donation encouraged

Website: http://dickeyvillegrotto.com

Directions: On Rte. 61 (W. Main St.), one block west of the Rte. 151 intersection.

Dodgeville

Don Q Inn

The Plaza? The Waldorf Astoria? Forget about 'em! At Dodgeville's Don Q Inn, every room has a theme *and* a 300-gallon copper cheese-vat hot tub! It's the ideal place to spice up a marriage, or escape from one.

The names of several of the suites are self-explanatory: Jungle Safari, the Cave, Geisha Garden, the Treehouse, Caesar's Court, Space Odyssey, Northern Lights, Sherwood Forest, and Glasshouse. But others need some explaining. At Tranquility Base you'll sleep in a moon lander. In Up, Up and Away your bed is a balloon gondola. Deer trophies line the walls in Shotgun and the Swinger's bed is suspended with chains. (Actually, 16 rooms have swinging beds—they're very popular.) The largest suite is an old steeple from a Methodist church. But the most-asked-for suite, Mid-Evil, has shackles on the bed and riding crops for the naughty guests.

There's more at the Don Q than kinky rooms, though. Parked out front is a Boeing C-97 Stratofreighter transport signed by Farrah Fawcett. Inside the motel, a creepy tunnel connects the two wings of the building. And spend some time hanging out in the lobby—every seat is a barber's chair.

The Don Q was the brainchild Ron Dentinger, who no longer owns the place. On Saturdays and Sundays at 3 PM, the staff at the Don Q conducts free tours during which you can view any of the rooms that are not in use.

3656 Hwy. 23 N, Dodgeville, WI 53533
Phone: (800) 666-7848 or (608) 935-2321
Hours: Tours, Saturday–Sunday 3 PM; check-in 4 PM
Cost: Tour free; rooms $99 and up, depending on the day and suite
Website: www.donqinn.net
Directions: On Rte. 23, north of town.

Elkhorn

Stevie Ray Vaughn Death Site

Otis Redding wasn't the only rock legend to be killed by the miserable Wisconsin weather. On August 27, 1990, guitarist Stevie Ray Vaughn and Eric Clapton had just finished playing a concert at the Alpine Valley Music Theater (W2699 County Rd. D, (262) 642-4400, www.alpinevalleymusic. com), and Vaughan and three members of Clapton's band hopped into a helicopter headed for Chicago's Midway Airport. Clapton and his entourage took another chopper, but when they emerged from the haze, Vaughn's craft was nowhere to be seen. About a mile southeast from where they took off, Vaughn's helicopter had slammed into a ski slope near the top of the main lift in a heavy fog. All aboard were killed. Vaughn now holds the dubious distinction of failing to clear one of the few mountains in a relatively flat state.

Alpine Valley Resort, W2501 County Rd. D, PO Box 615, Elkhorn, WI 53121

Phone: (800) 227-9395 or (262) 642-7374

Hours: Always visible

Cost: Free

Website: www.alpinevalleyresort.com

Directions: Take a lift to the top of Mohawk run, on the left near the top.

Watson's Wild West Museum

The promotional flier promises, "You don't have to go to South Dakota to enjoy the Old West." Truth is, you don't even have to go as far west as Beloit! Tucked away in what looks like a typical Midwestern barn (with a covered wagon in front) is a time portal to the 1880s. Step into Watson's Wild West Museum and you're transported to Deadwood or Tombstone or Dodge City. Doug Watson, decked out in cowboy garb, is your host and head honcho. Rather than let you wander aimlessly through his recreated General Store and Tumbleweed Mine, Watson offers background information, recites cowboy poetry, tells goofy jokes, gives some of his family's history in the region, and quizzes you on western lore minutiae. If you come up with an answer, you just might win a cold bottle of sarsaparilla that he'll slide to you down the old-timey bar.

The walls of this cavernous space are filled with authentic general merchandise from the era, including cracker barrels, chewing tobacco, tools, coffee and tea, horse tack, lard, and some 42-year-old pickles. He's also got collections of Lincoln Logs, Big Little Books, Raggedy Ann dolls, guns, elk trophies, and more than 2,000 branding irons. Try your hand at panning gold in the mine. Keep what real gold you find, but please return all the fool's gold for the next visitors. Watson wanted to showcase his collection in the famous Bird Cage Theater in Tombstone, but despite protracted negotiations, no deal was cut.

Arizona's loss is Wisconsin's gain. Watson is even planning to expand on this site, as well as the offerings at the bar; lard sandwiches will be on sale soon. If you've got a large posse (more than 40), ask about Watson's private parties where the whole spread can be rented out for a gen-u-ine ho-down. They'll rustle you up some grub, line dancers, and western singers!

W4865 Potter Rd., Elkhorn, WI 53121

Phone: (262) 723-7505

Hours: May–October, Monday–Saturday 10 AM–5 PM, Sunday 1–5 PM

Cost: Adults $5, kids (4–10) $3.75

Website: www.watsonswildwestmuseum.com

Directions: Just east of Rte. 12/67 on Potter Rd., just north of the Rte. 67 intersection.

Fennimore
Fennimore Doll and Toy Museum

If you're wondering what to do with the doll collection you inherited from your great aunt, perhaps you should consider donating it to this place. Most of the collection is from the late local residents Dorothy White and Mildred "Millie" Rudersdorf and current Disney-Pixar animator Jeff Pidgeon, who have brought their lifelong hobbies to the general public.

Collectors of today's action figures are unlikely to admit they have a doll fixation, but the Fennimore Doll and Toy Museum doesn't dwell on the distinction. Gathered together are Barbies and *Toy Story* figurines, Mrs. Beasley and John Wayne, Raggedy Ann and Jack from *The Nightmare Before Christmas*. And they've got plenty of stuff you probably never thought existed or, if it did, are amazed anyone kept. Do you remember 1970s dolls of *Welcome Back Kotter*'s Horshack and Epstein, *Police Woman*'s Sgt. "Pepper" Anderson, or the Six Million Dollar Man and Bigfoot?

Of course, they have a large Barbie display. Maybe its a Barbie Fashion Show or a Barbie at the Beach diorama with Sun-Lovin' Malibu Ken. You never know what you'll find at the Fennimore Doll Museum because every January they rotate in new displays from their collection of more than 6,000 dolls. Next year could have a case filled with Dionne Quintuplets or *Star Wars* action figures—you'll just have to visit to find out.

1135 Sixth St., Fennimore, WI 53809

Phone: (608) 822-4100

Hours: May–October, daily 10 AM–4 PM

Cost: Adults $3, kids (6–18) $1.50

Website: www.dollandtoymuseum.com

Directions: At Lincoln Ave. (Rte. 18/61).

BARBIE WAS A CHEESEHEAD?

According to Mattel, Barbie Millicent Roberts—the Barbie doll (www.barbie.com)—hailed from Willows, Wisconsin, born to George and Margaret Roberts. She attended Willows High School, though also spent some time at Manhattan International High School, in New York, presumably.

Igor the Mouse

It might seem strange to use a rodent to attract customers, but if it worked for Walt Disney, it could work for the Fennimore Cheese Factory.

Igor the Mouse is 12 feet tall and sits on a flatbed trailer in front of the building—perfect for photos. (Why "Igor"? The composer Igor Stravinsky died the same day the statue arrived in Fennimore—April 6, 1971.) Your Facebook friends will gasp and think, "Geeez, look at the vermin at that place!" Reassure them the entire cheesemaking process is clean and open to public inspection through bubble-shaped windows on a self-guided tour. The "tour" is actually more of a walk around the outlet store, but it's still interesting.

If you're looking for a Styrofoam cheesehead hat, a cheese tie, a set of cheese coasters, or a cheese postcard, this is the place to visit. And they've got plenty of real cheese for sale too, much of it pressed into interesting shapes and coated with wax, such as cows, mice, pigs, and the great state of Wisconsin.

Carr Valley Cheese Company, 1675 Lincoln Ave., Fennimore, WI 53809

Phone: (608) 822-3777

Hours: Always visible; store, Monday–Saturday 9 AM–5 PM, Sundays 10 AM–4 PM

Cost: Free; cheese extra

Website: www.fennimorecheese.com

Directions: At the south end of town on Rte. 61 (Lincoln Ave.), at 16th St.

FOOTVILLE

➡ Francis Wiggins Ford of Footville wrote *The Little Engine That Could* in 1912.

RODENT INFESTATION

If you've had mice, you know that once you have them, they're tough to get rid of. The same goes for fiberglass mice, too, apparently:

Murray

Red Zone Sports Bar, 2071 S. Prairie View Rd., Chippewa Falls, (715) 726-3030

Cast from the same fiberglass mold as Igor the Mouse, the oversize rodent outside this drinking establishment sports a neon green T-shirt and has forsaken its cheese for a giant beach ball. His name is Murray.

Grocery Mouse

County Market, E18590 Hwy. 31, Hillsboro, (608) 489-2423

Another Igor-style mouse can be seen bagging groceries outside this Hillsboro store. Clearly he doesn't have a retirement portfolio that allows him to lounge about in cabana wear like Murray.

Mouse House Cheese House

4494 Lake Circle, Windsor, (800) 52-MOUSE, www.mousehousecheese.com

As this establishment's name suggests, the mouse is in charge here. It's big, so that's understandable. The megamouse sits atop a massive wedge over the main entrance, nibbling away on another hunk that is also enormous.

Dells Mouse

Market Square Cheese, 1150 Wisconsin Dells Pkwy. S, Lake Delton, (608) 254-8388, www.humbirdcheese.com

Another very large mouse holds an even larger wedge of cheese at the entrance to this Dells cheese outlet, and because it's at ground level it's perfect for photos.

Jimbo

Jim's Cheese Pantry, 410 Portland Rd., Waterloo, (800) 345-3571,
www.jimscheesepantry.com

Jimbo resembles the Dells Mouse but wears more stylish overalls. He stands guard over a wedge of cheddar outside Jim's
Cheese Pantry.

Mouse from Mars

Mars Cheese Castle, 2800 W. Frontage Rd., Kenosha, (800) 655-6147,
www.marscheese.com

You can find the large mouse at the Mars Cheese Castle *inside*,
where the cheese is. Until they buy a larger fiberglass cat, it
will probably remain in the store.

Chubby Mouse

Carr Valley Cheese Company, I-94 and Rte. 82, Mauston, (608) 847-4891,
www.carrvalleycheese.com

Whether the name of this town and the weight of this mouse
have anything to do with each other is unknown, but one thing
is not: this critter is *fat*. And no wonder—it has a wedge of
cheese in one paw and an enormous summer sausage in the
other.

Another Chubby Mouse

Arena Cheese, 300 Hwy. 14, Arena, (608) 753-2501, www.arenacheese.com

Another big-eared butterball can be found near the parking lot
at this factory-outlet cheese emporium. It also holds a cheese
wedge and a summer sausage.

Tyrolean Climbing Mouse

Ehlenbach's Cheese Chalet, 4879 County Rd. V, DeForest, (800) 949-4791,
www.ehlenbachscheese.com

He wears a pair of red lederhosen and a cute Tyrolean cap as he scurries up the sign outside this Madison-area cheese store. His goal is clear: CHEESE. It's the only word found on the sign.

Farmer Mouse

The Cheese Maker, 1050 Watcher Ave., Plain, (877) WI-CHEESE, www.cheesemaker.com

Holding a platter of samples and wearing a pair of bib overalls, this farmer mouse is the perfect host for the Cheese Maker, a small store in a not-much-larger town near the Dells.

Cowboy Mouse

Road Ranger, 102 C. Woody Dr., Oakdale, (815) 209-9040, www.roadrangerusa.com

He wears a cowboy hat and boots and stands on a sign reading "Welcome to Wisconsin," which is a little odd—by the time anyone gets to Oakdale they've been in the state for a while. But are you going to argue with him? He's 20 feet tall!

Happy Mouse

Ron's Wisconsin Cheese, 124 Main St., Luxemburg, (920) 845-9423, www.ronscheese.com

What he lacks in height he more than makes up for in personality. This smiling mouse stands on a cheese wheel holding a wedge in one front paw while pointing to where he snagged the loot with the other.

Guilty Mouse

Cheese Store & More, 186 Madison St., Hillsboro, (608) 489-2651, www.cheesestoreandmore.com

The fiberglass mouse atop this large cheese wedge isn't feasting on it just yet, but the guilty expression on its face suggests you may have happened by just before it started.

Fontana

Concrete Frog

The Concrete Frog in Fontana has seen better days, but since it is made of concrete instead of fiberglass, nobody's planning to bulldoze it just yet. The frog is painted in Packers green and gold, some of which is flaking off. Its eyes are empty electrical sockets, the bulbs long since bashed out. Over the years it has served as a fireworks stand and a putter-hut for the adjacent miniature golf course. Today, the frog is padlocked and the firecrackers are sold from a shack next door, a sad present from a glorious, hip-hoppety past.

543 Valley View Dr., Fontana, WI 53125

No phone

Hours: Always visible

Cost: Free

Directions: Just north of Fontana Outdoor Sports on Rte. 67 (Valley View Dr.), south of the Fontana Blvd. intersection.

Kermit in concrete.

Fort Atkinson
Dairy Shrine

For those milk lovers who want to show their respect to "America's Dairyland," homage can be paid at the Dairy Shrine, a wing of the Hoard Historical Museum in Fort Atkinson. It's got artifacts from the dairy industry, both past and present, as well as photos of men and women who made Wisconsin the milk, butter, and cheese powerhouse it is today. The journey begins on a multimedia extravaganza that traces the history of the dairy industry. Exhibits highlights include goat- and dog-powered butter churns, a parachute used for artificial insemination, and a royal blanket that covered Elsie, the Borden cow, at the 1939 World's Fair.

The shrine is only part of the larger Hoard Historical Museum, named for former Wisconsin governor William Hoard, who once advised, "Speak to a cow as you would a lady." The museum covers every aspect of local history and a few things farther afield. For example, they have a mitt used by Billy Sullivan to catch three baseballs dropped 555 feet from the top of the Washington Monument in 1911, and one of the baseballs, too.

And keep your eyes peeled for the Hoard's rotating exhibits. On a recent visit there was a tribute to Fort Atkinson butcher Ernie Hausen, who won the 1922 National Chicken Picking Championship by denuding a clucker of its feather in six seconds flat. In 1935 he set a world record at 3.5 seconds!

Hoard Historical Museum, 401 Whitewater Ave., Fort Atkinson, WI 53538

Phone: (920) 563-7769

Hours: Tuesday–Saturday 9:30 AM–4:30 PM

Cost: Free, but $5 suggested donation

Website: www.hoardmuseum.org

Directions: On Rte. 12 (Whitewater Ave.) at Fourth St., four blocks south of Rte. 106 and the river.

The Panther Intaglio

A Native American intaglio is the reverse of an effigy mound in which, instead of piling soil up in the shape of an animal, a cookie-cutter hole is excavated. There is only one known existing intaglio in the United States, and that is the Panther Intaglio.

How Increase Lapham ever recognized the panther shape of this unremarkable earthen depression when he discovered it in 1850 is anyone's guess, but he did. Archeologists believe the Panther Intaglio was created around 1000 AD by the Effigy Mound Culture which lived in the area at the time. They used the hole for religious ceremonies.

Soil sampling reveals there were once 11 intaglios near this site; two were bears and the rest were panthers. The tail of this sole survivor has been filled in by a driveway, but the rest of the shape is faintly visible.

1236 Riverside Dr., Fort Atkinson, WI 53538
No phone
Hours: Always visible
Cost: Free
Directions: On the west end of town on Rte. 106 (Riverside Dr.).

Hollandale

Grandview

Nick Engelbert was a world traveler. Born Engelbert Kolethick in Austria, he sailed from Europe to North and South America as a ship's engineer; then he worked on farms from California to Kansas. But when he met his future bride, Swiss immigrant Katherine Thoni, in Chicago, he decided to settle down. After they were married he went to work with her brother making cheese in Hollandale.

But Engelbert never lost his memories of far-off places. Starting in 1937 and continuing into the 1950s, he built statues to embellish his rural home. With concrete, semiprecious stones, and broken glass he created Snow White and the Seven Dwarfs, Uncle Sam driving a donkey/elephant team, a Viking on the prow of the boat, Paul Bunyan, the founders of the Swiss Republic, a "monkey tree" with a drunken man at its base, Neptune, a mermaid, an organ grinder, a stork delivering a baby, and Blarney Castle.

By the time he hung up his trowel, there were more than 40 sculptures, and he named his private hilltop park Grandview. When he could no longer sculpt, he took up painting. He rendered scenes from his life and travels in oil on canvas and masonite. Only his death in 1962 stopped Engelbert's creative output.

Grandview deteriorated through the 1970s and '80s and weeds grew up around the crumbling figures. The Kohler Foundation rescued Engelbert's paintings, and in the early 1990s his Hollandale home. Today you can see the restored environment, returned to the way it looked when Engelbert was alive. When the museum is open, you can come inside and view his paintings.

7351 State Hwy. 39, Hollandale, WI 53544

Contact: PEC Foundation, PO Box 95, Blanchardville, WI 53516

Phone: (608) 967-2322 or (608) 967-2122

Hours: Grounds, daily 9 AM–5 PM; home, June–August, Thursday–Sunday 1–4 PM

Cost: Donations encouraged

Website: www.nicksgrandview.com

Directions: One mile west of town on Rte. 39.

Hubertus
Holy Hill

Scenes from my life. Photo by author, courtesy of PEC Foundation

A French hermit praying at a wooden cross atop this hill in 1855 was miraculously cured of paralysis. Believing the hermit had experienced a true miracle, the Discalced Carmelite Order of Friars built a church on the site and moved the healing cross to the vestibule. Today, there's no reason you shouldn't expect the same consideration. At least that has been the hope of thousands of pilgrims every year.

This place is officially known as the National Shrine of Mary, Help of Christians, which is longhand for Holy Hill. The Shrine Chapel, to the right of the main altar, houses hundreds of crutches and walkers the faithful have tossed aside after receiving miraculous cures. It's safe to assume most of them made it back down the hill, but there's no word on how many were walking and how many were tumbling.

If the shrine isn't special enough, visit the well-stocked gift shop, the outdoor Way of the Cross, or hike the 178 heart-stopping steps to the top of the observation tower from which you can see all the way to Milwaukee.

1525 Carmel Rd., Hubertus, WI 53033

Phone: (262) 628-1838 or (262) 628-4735

Hours: Daily 6 AM–5 PM

Cost: Free

Website: www.holyhill.com

Directions: Four miles west of town, off Rte. 167.

Janesville
Lyons Mechanical Man

Fans of the Japanese cult classic *Johnny Sokko and His Flying Robot* will no doubt see a resemblance between the oversize man atop this Janesville building and the flying robot from the TV series, yet the similarity is strictly coincidental. This box-headed mechanical man was created by Lyons Mechanical Contractors, not the secret spy agency Unicorn. He does not shoot missiles out of his fingertips, either. All he has is an enormous pipe wrench in his right hand, which won't do much good fighting off Gargoyle, should it plan to attack Wisconsin.

Lyons Mechanical Contractors, 2020 Center Ave., Janesville, WI 53546

Phone: (608) 756-0368

Hours: Always visible

Cost: Free

Directions: Just south of Kellogg Ave. on Rte. 51 (Center Ave.).

White Buffalo Calf Woman

Many centuries ago a white buffalo calf appeared to two Lakota hunters, one bad and one good. While they watched, the calf turned into White Buffalo Calf Woman. She floated above the ground and burned the flesh off the bad warrior and then told the good warrior to tell his tribe to expect a message in four days. Among the many prophecies she revealed, she announced that the birth of a white buffalo calf would signal a time of worldwide peace, followed by her return. She left the tribe a sacred peace pipe and told them to keep it until she came back.

Jump ahead 2,000 or so years to August 20, 1994, on the farm of Dave and Valerie Heider. A female white calf was born, and unlike an albino, had dark eyes and a black nose. The Heiders named her Miracle. When word got around, everyone flocked to Janesville. Ted Nugent wanted to buy Miracle because of his song "Great White Buffalo," but the Heiders declined.

For White Buffalo Calf Woman's prophecy to come true, Miracle had to turn every color of the human race. Sure enough, Miracle turned black in January 1995, red in June, yellow in November, and finally brown. Sadly, she died shortly after her tenth birthday on September 19, 2004. That doesn't mean you can't still see her, though—she's been stuffed and is on display in the new gift shop and museum.

Heider Farm, 2739 S. River Rd., Janesville, WI 53546

Phone: (608) 752-2224

Hours: Monday–Saturday 10 AM–4 PM

Cost: Free

Website: http://whitebuffalomiracle.homestead.com/

Directions: On the east side of the river, off Avalon Rd. (Rte. 351), northeast of the airport.

Kenosha
Franks Diner

Most diners look like they've been around a long time, but only one can be the oldest continuously operating diner in the United States, and that record-setter is Franks. How old? When Anthony Franks bought it in 1926 for $7,500, the Jerry O'Mahoney company of New Jersey shipped it to Wisconsin by rail and Franks had to have it towed here by a team of horses.

Franks expanded the joint in 1935, adding a larger dining room in 1935 and a bigger kitchen in the 1940s. It has hosted such luminaries as Liberace, Duke Ellington, Bela Lugosi, Lawrence Welk, and the Three Stooges. The Franks family eventually sold the diner in 2001, and today the place is owned and operated by Julie Rittmiller and Kevin Ervin. It looks pretty much the same way it has for decades.

508 58th St., Kenosha, WI 53140

Phone: (262) 657-1017

Hours: Monday–Friday 6 AM–1:30 PM, Saturday 7 AM–1:30 PM, Sunday 7 AM–12:30 PM

Cost: Meals, $5–10

Website: www.franksdinerkenosha.com

Directions: Four blocks east of Sheridan Rd. (Rte. 32) at Fifth Ave.

Mike Bjorn's Fine Clothing and Museum

Every town should have a Mike Bjorn, a tireless advocate for shopping locally, an enemy of the Big Boxes. That doesn't mean his downtown menswear store has a fraction of the selection at twice the price of a chain outlet. Just the contrary—he's got more tuxedos than any place in Wisconsin, and none of them will set you back more than $99. To *buy* them. If you can't

He's been up there a while. Photo by author, courtesy of Mike Bjorn

find what you're looking for upstairs, visit the basement, which has miles and miles of jackets to choose from.

Even better than the prices and selection, this store/museum is fun, fun, fun. Kitschy crap, from Pee-Wee Herman dolls to ship models to unicycle-riding skeletons hang from the pressed-tin ceiling. Weird lithographs and newspapers announcing famous events cover the walls, and the shelves are topped with old taxidermy. All the dressing rooms have themes, such as the Diana—very British—and the Over 18, a salute to presidential infidelities. Almost makes a person want to dress up.

5614 Sixth Ave., Kenosha, WI 53140

Phone: (262) 652-0648

Hours: Monday–Friday 10 AM–5 PM, Saturday 10 AM–2 PM

Cost: Free

Website: www.tux-a-rama.com

Directions: Three blocks east of Rte. 32 (Sheridan Rd.) at 56th St.

Orson Welles's Birthplace

Orson Welles never had kind words for his birthplace, Kenosha. His family moved away when he was only four years old, so it is hard to imagine where he developed his strong, negative opinions.

Welles was the son of Richard, the inventor of a new car jack, and Beatrice, chairman of the local board of education and an accomplished pianist. He was born on May 6, 1915, in a small house at what was then 463½ Park Ave. (later renamed Seventh Ave.). He was reportedly named after stockbroker Orson Wells, life partner of humorist George Ade, whom Richard and Beatrice had met on a cruise to Rio de Janeiro. Welles claimed he was conceived at that South American port of call, an embarkation point that sounded more romantic to him than Kenosha.

By all accounts, Orson was a precocious child, even before his family left for Chicago. According to family lore, at eighteen months he is said to have told his pediatrician, "The desire to take medicine is one of the greatest features which distinguishes men from animals." Though debatable on substance, the proclamation demonstrated the verbal authority that would become his trademark.

6114–16 Seventh Ave., Kenosha, WI 53143

Private phone

Hours: Private property; view from street

Cost: Free

Directions: On Seventh Ave., just south of Library Park south of 61st St.

THE STARS OF KENOSHA

Orson Welles wasn't the only Hollywood star to come from Kenosha, though he was perhaps the biggest. Four Italian-American actors grew up in roughly the same neighborhood on the south side of town. **Don Ameche** was born here on May 31, 1908, and lived at 5714 22nd Avenue. **Al "Happy Days" Molinaro** lived at 2417 53rd Street after greeting the world on June 24, 1919. **Daniel J. Travanti**, born in Kenosha on March 7, 1940, grew up at 5129 30th Avenue. He graduated from Kenosha's Mary D. Bradford High School (3700 Washington Rd., (262) 359-6200, http://bradford.kusd.edu/) in 1958 where he took second place in the Elk's Leadership Contest. And finally, **Mark Ruffalo** was born on November 22, 1967, in—you guessed it—Kenosha.

Lake Geneva
Andy Gump Statue

When *Andy Gump* premiered in the *Chicago Tribune* in 1917, it was the first daily comic strip the paper had ever published. Gump was the type of commoner who would have been unwelcome by the upper crust of Lake Geneva, but his creator, cartoonist Sidney Smith, was accepted with open arms. Smith built an estate here in 1922, Trudehurst, and in 1924 the *Tribune* gave him a plaster statue of Gump as a housewarming gift. That same year, Gump ran for president of the United States.

Smith died in an automobile crash in 1935, and the Gump statue sat idle until being donated to the town by executor Robert Twyman in 1947. The plaster didn't hold up very well in the harsh Wisconsin elements, but it was a Fourth of July riot in 1967 that finally did it in—thousands of teenagers overran the town and smashed Gump with a park bench.

A new statue was quickly commissioned, this one made of bronze, but it was unceremoniously decapitated in 1981. Repaired, the whole thing was stolen in 1988, probably melted down for scrap. And though the current third statue looks like bronze, it's just fiberglass.

Flat Iron Park, 205 Wrigley Dr., Lake Geneva, WI 53147

No phone

Hours: Always visible

Cost: Free

Website: www.lakegenevawi.com

Directions: Just south of the Chamber of Commerce Building, on Wrigley Dr. (Rte. 120), one block south of Main St. (Rte. 50).

End of the Line

You may have long dreamed of riding the rails in a caboose—tootin' that steam whistle, wavin' at cars at crossings, chasin' hobos out of the boxcars. But when the railroads stopped using cabooses, your dream died. However, you do have options. In Lake Geneva, you can have the next best thing: spending the night in an old caboose.

The End of the Line opened in 1986 on the old Chicago and North Western tracks running to Lake Geneva. Five cabooses were converted for guests, each decorated with a unique theme and outfitted with a bathroom. Within a few years the motel was expanded to 33 units, seven of which were doubles, and one triple. Owners built a lobby out of three boxcars and filled the space with railroad memorabilia and toy trains.

Get it in the caboose. Photo by author, courtesy of End of the Line

The End of the Line has attracted high-profile guests like Oprah Winfrey and low-profile guests like Michael *"Family Ties"* Gross. It has also changed much over the years. The cabooses were sold off as condos in the 1990s when the original owner retired. Twenty of these cabooses are currently available for rent. Most new owners did away with the themes and modernized their cars, making them at least as modern as an extinct piece of railroad equipment can be.

301 E. Townline Rd., Lake Geneva, WI 53147

Phone: (262) 248-7245 or (800) 747-RAIL

Hours: May–October, reservations required

Cost: $59 (Standard, off-peak) to $139 (Villa, peak)

Directions: County Rd. H south of Rte. 50, east on Townline to the railroad tracks.

THREE LONELY CABEESE

If solitude and caboosing is your thing, you might want to try the **Caboose Cabin B&B** in Sparta (1102 S. Water St., PO Box 414, (608) 269-0444, www.caboosecabins.com). Here, a single 1968 SOO Line caboose stands beside a small pond, ready for guests. Similarly, a Great Northern Railway caboose serves as the single unit at the **Viroqua Shortline Inn** (S6112 County Rd. J, (608) 637-3706, www.viroquashortline.com). But don't even *think* about staying in the **Presidential Caboose** downtown in Cuba City (Calhoun and Main Sts., (608) 744-2152, http://cubacity.org/visitors_center.php)—it's a visitor's center with a chief executive theme left over from the bicentennial.

Postal Route Tour

The Postal Route Tour on Lake Geneva is unique for two reasons. First, it is the only postal route in the state on which letters are delivered by boat. And secondly, it just might be the only place in the nation where you can watch postal employees actually *running* to serve their customers.

Your tour aboard the *Walworth II* takes 2.5 hours, and on the way you'll watch the "mailgirls" jump from the boat to the dock, run to each box distributing letters and junk mail (and newspapers on Sunday), and then leap back aboard. The boat stays in motion the entire time. The whole process takes about 10 seconds, and is repeated about 60 times during the tour.

Mail has been delivered like this to wealthy citizens on Lake Geneva for more than 140 years. If the carriers don't run fast enough they'll miss the boat and end up in the water. That's incentive enough to keep moving, except on blistering summer days. Then, expect a quick dip to keep them from their appointed rounds.

Geneva Lake Cruise Line Docks, Riviera Docks, 812 Wrigley Dr., PO Box 68, Lake Geneva, WI 53147

Phone: (800) 558-5911 or (262) 248-6206

Hours: June–September, 10 AM departure

Cost: Adults $30, seniors (65+) $28, teens (13–17) $22, kids (4–12) $17

Website: http://cruiselakegeneva.com/

Directions: One block south and one block west of the intersection of Rtes. 50 (Main St.) and 36 (Broad St.).

LAKE GENEVA

➡ A 30-foot serpent-like monster was spotted several times in Lake Geneva during the early 1900s. Locals dubbed the creature "Jenny."

Lake Mills
Aztalan

It's not every day you can see monuments to human sacrifice and cannibalism. The vacant lots where Jeffrey Dahmer's apartment and Ed Gein's farmhouse stood are unmarked, but Aztalan is the exception to the rule.

An early native culture settled and thrived in this part of Wisconsin from 1100 to 1300 AD, most likely descendants of those who had abandoned Cahokia in neighboring Illinois. The Pyramid of the Sun and the Pyramid of the Moon at Aztalan are the culture's most prominent surviving relics. It was atop the Pyramid of the Sun that humans were sacrificed to the gods, and it was at the nearby Pyramid of the Moon that others started to take offense—so much so they drove their cannibalistic brethren off and burned the area to purify it. Anthropologists added some of the stockade structures to give modern visitors a sense of what it might have looked like. Still, it loses some of the effect without human bones scattered all around.

Some believe there was something even more remarkable going on at Aztalan. The theories are built on the discovery of several submerged structures in Rock Lake, three miles west of the mounds. A large pyramid, 150 feet long and 12 feet wide with a rectangular base, was first spotted at the south end of the lake by local fishermen when the lake's water level dropped during a 1901 drought. Word got around town and everyone came out for a look. Kids swam around the structure. Boaters touched its peak with their oars. But then the water rose again, and nothing much was said until 1976, when a diver reported seeing several conical pyramids beneath the surface. Nobody has been able to find them again, though a dragon-shaped mound was discovered in 1998 using sonar imaging.

Author Frank Joseph believes there is a connection between Aztalan and the lost city of Atlantis, and that the cannibal culture driven out of Wisconsin became the Aztecs of Mexico. A local group, the Rock Lake Research Society, has dedicated itself to finding an answer, sponsoring ongoing dives to find the now-missing pyramids.

Aztalan State Park, c/o Glacial Drumlin State Trail, 1213 S. Main St., Lake Mills, WI 53551

Phone: Park, (920) 648-8774; museum, (920) 648-4632

Hours: Park, daily 7 AM–9 PM; museum, May–September, Thursday–Sunday noon–4 PM

Cost: Adults $2, kids (7–17) $1

Website: http://dnr.wi.gov/topic/parks/name/aztalan/

Friends of Aztalan State Park: www.aztalan.us

Directions: Take Water St. (County Rd. B) two miles east out of town.

Lodi
Home of Susie the Duck

Who is Susie the Duck? Well, she could be *any* duck, as long as she's an aggressive squatter. The first Susie nested and laid her eggs in a cement planter along Lodi's Spring Creek in 1947. Locals took a liking to her and named her Susie after the daughter of the local police chief. Maybe it's a statement on what else there is to do in Lodi when a random duck becomes a local celebrity.

Anyway, when fall came Susie and her brood moved on. The following year, another duck nested in the basket-shaped planter and she too was named Susie. A tradition was born! Today, locals hold a contest to guess the date and time when Susie's first egg will hatch. Throughout the summer the quacker is given a spot of honor in local events, and when the mallards migrate, she leaves a saddened town . . .

Goeres Park, Fair and Main Sts., PO Box 43, Lodi, WI 53555

Phone: (608) 592-4412

Hours: Always visible

Cost: Free

Website: www.lodiwisconsin.com

Directions: In the park where Main St. crosses the creek.

Lone Rock
World's Largest Highlighter

If you're the type of traveler who pulls over for every roadside marker you see, put this Lone Rock attraction on your itinerary—it's a marker of a marker. A few years back a conifer outside this bed-and-breakfast died, and rather than cut it down they carved it into a nine-foot tall yellow highlighter. They then marked the marker with a historical marker.

Merry Farm, 30999 Slow Ln., Lone Rock, WI 53556

Phone: (608) 583-3542

Hours: Daily 9 AM–5 PM

Cost: Free

Directions: North on Moss Hollow Dr. from County Rd. JJ.

Marshall
Little Amerricka

For those of you who like the atmosphere of the midway but worry about the average carnie's attention to safety, maybe Little Amerricka is more your speed. The rides are similar to those that are dragged from town to town, but are well maintained and permanently attached to the ground.

Like Disneyland, Little Amerricka has it own version of a monorail that encircles the park from a high track. Not only do you get a clear view of the rides from on high, but the adjacent cornfields and the town's cemetery. Little Amerricka has a scrambler, bumper cars, a haunted house, a Ferris wheel, kiddie rides, go-karts, miniature golf, a wooden roller coaster, and a steam train that rolls two miles over the surrounding countryside past llamas and other animals. The strangest ride of the bunch is a metal roller coaster made out of an old farm silo. You're jammed into a tiny capsule that enters the cylinder, climbs vertically through the shaft, and is jettisoned out the top. The track then spirals down around the outside of the silo before screeching to a dead stop. Ride over! You won't find thrills like that anywhere else for $1.50.

700 W. Main St., Marshall, WI 53559

Phone: (608) 655-3181

Hours: June–August, most days noon–6 PM, but check website for exact hours

Cost: Free to enter; individual rides $1.50, wristbands (access varies) $10.95–21.95

Website: www.littleamerricka.com

Directions: On Rte. 19, just east of the Rte. 73 intersection.

Round and round you'll go.

Mazomanie
Rookie's Food and Spirits

Let's face it, for all the health benefits of sports, they're also a good way to injure yourself. Why do you think baseball players wear those helmets and cups? Yet there is a way to enjoy a game without the danger of getting beaned or worse: Wiffle ball! Rookie's is your place to play.

Rookie's looks like a standard restaurant/sports bar, but out back is a "regulation" Wiffle ball field, complete with equipment, manual scoreboard, dugouts, and team pennants. The adjoining clubhouse is well stocked with beer, and burgers are a short order away. Drink all you want; there's no need for a designated hitter if you're blotto.

10267 US Hwy. 14, Mazomanie, WI 53560
Phone: (608) 767-5555
Hours: Daily 11 AM–close
Cost: Free; meals, $6–13; field, $50 per hour
Website: www.rookiesfood.com
Directions: Southeast of town, just past the Rte. 19/78 intersection.

Merrimac
The Merrimac Ferry

The Merrimac Ferry began operation in 1844, transporting people and livestock across the Wisconsin River. The privately owned craft was run by Chester Mattson, and at the time was dubbed Matt's Ferry. Mattson's business inspired other river ferries, at one time reaching a peak of 500 statewide. Early ferry operators earned their fares because they were hand-drawn. No wonder that not every kid wanted to go into the family business.

Today, the Merrimac Ferry is the only one still operating in Wisconsin. The state bought out the line in 1933 and eliminated the toll. The current motorized ferry, the *Colsac III*, can take up to 12 cars at a time. The crossing takes five minutes, and is still the quickest route between Lodi and Baraboo, unless you hit it at the height of the summer season.

Rte. 113, Merrimac, WI 53561
Phone: (608) 246-3806
Hours: Always running, weather permitting
Cost: Free
Website: www.dot.wisconsin.gov/travel/water/merrimac.htm
Directions: On Rte. 113.

Milton
Stagecoach House

Ironically, the historic Underground Railroad was neither a railroad nor underground . . . with one notable exception: Milton's hexagonal Stagecoach House. Many tales of secret tunnels have been woven around homes and businesses that were part of the effort to transport escaped slaves northward, but this is the only place where a tunnel still exists. It connects the main house through a trapdoor to an outlying log cabin.

The Stagecoach House, today called the Milton House, was the first house in the United States to be made of poured concrete. Joseph Goodrich built the home in 1844. The walls of the six-sided structure were poured a few feet at a time and allowed to harden, the forms were moved up, and another layer was added until they got to the top.

Milton House Museum, 18 S. Janesville St., Milton, WI 53563

Phone: (608) 868-7772

Hours: June–August, daily 10 AM–4 PM; September–December and February–April, Monday–
   Friday 10 AM–4 PM; January, Tuesday–Friday 10 AM–4 PM; May, Saturday–Sunday 10 AM–4 PM

Cost: Adults $6, seniors (62+) $5, kids (5–17) $3

Website: www.miltonhouse.org

Directions: At the intersection of Janesville St. (Rte. 26) and Madison St. (County Rd. M).

Mineral Point
The Ghost of William Caffee

William Caffee killed a friend in an argument in 1842, and for his actions was hanged outside of Mineral Point's Walker-Grundy House, Wisconsin's oldest inn. Instead of showing remorse or fear, Caffee banged out a tune on the lid of his coffin with two beer bottles on the way to the scaffold.

Years later people would hear the shatter of bottles on the front porch of the hotel, but no broken glass was ever found. Doors would lock and unlock when nobody was present. And the cover to a peephole into the main dining area was constantly found off. If you feel like someone or something is watching you while you're visiting, you're probably right. Caffee's ghost showed up once, without his head, on the back porch in 1981. Today the building is known as Orchard Lawn and is home to the Mineral Point Historical Society.

234 Madison St., Mineral Point, WI 53565

Phone: (608) 987-2884

Hours: May–October, Thursday–Sunday 1–5 PM
Cost: Donations encouraged
Website: www.mineralpoint.com/hist.html and www.mineralpointhistory.org/orchardlawn.html
Directions: Two blocks east of Water Tower Park and the Tourist Information Center.

The Ridgeway Phantom

Mineral Point is an old mining town with plenty of spooks, and its most notorious ghost is the Ridgeway Phantom. The general consensus seems to be that the phantom is the conglomeration of the souls of two young boys killed by rowdies at McKillip's Saloon in 1840. One boy was thrown alive into the fireplace and the other escaped into the woods, only to freeze to death. The killers may have thought it all very funny at the time, but they didn't laugh for long.

Soon a shape-changing spirit began haunting the community of Ridgeway, later renamed Mineral Point. It would show up as a variety of animals, a headless man, a ball of fire . . . you name it . . . to terrorize the living.

The Ridgeway Phantom hasn't been seen much lately, but there's no telling when it might get back into the business. If you see something strange in Mineral Point, do what everyone else does: chalk it up to the ghouls.

Ridge Rd., Mineral Point, WI 53565
No phone
Hours: After dark
Cost: Free
Directions: Along Ridge Rd. between Mineral Point and Blue Mounds.

Monroe
Monroe Means Cheese

Monroe brags that it is "Cheese City, USA," and it can make a strong case. Check out the map in the National Historic Cheesemaking Center to see the locations of all the cheesemaking operations in southern Wisconsin. Monroe is the epicenter! Only a minute fraction of these operations still exist, but cheese still runs through this town's veins. Why else would the Monroe High School's team name be the Cheesemakers? And where is Swiss Colony's headquarters still located? Monroe, that's where.

To keep its heritage alive, Monroe celebrates Cheese Days every other September, and has since 1914. A Cheese King and Queen are crowned at the Turner Hall, cows are milked for sport, children dress up in cheese-themed costumes, and Swiss folk singers yodel their tonsils out. Everywhere you turn you'll find cheese tents, cheese dances, and cheese parades.

National Historic Cheesemaking Center, 2108 Sixth Ave., PO Box 516, Monroe, WI 53566

Phone: (608) 325-4636

Hours: April–October, Monday–Saturday 9 AM–4 PM, Sunday 11 AM–4 PM

Cost: Free

Website: www.nationalhistoriccheesemakingcenter.org

Directions: At the intersection of Rte. 69 and 21st St.

If you're a brave soul, try a slice of smelly Limburger, Monroe's own. The Chalet Cheese Co-Op north of town is the only place in the United States where Limburger cheese is still made. Take a bite and you'll know why it's an acquired taste.

Chalet Cheese Co-Op, N4858 County Rd. N, Monroe, WI 53566

Phone: (608) 325-4343

Hours: Monday–Friday 7 AM–3 PM, Saturday 8–10:30 AM

Cost: Cheese sales only

Directions: Four miles north of town on County Rd. N.

CHEESY LAWS

As might be expected, Wisconsin's cheese industry is heavily regulated. Here are just a few of the stranger statutes pertaining to dairy products:

- If you purchase a meal costing more than 25¢, you are entitled to a one-ounce piece of cheese.
- Every piece of apple pie must have a slice of cheese on it to be lawfully eaten.
- You need a license to make cheese, and a Master Cheese Maker's license to make Limburger.
- Artificially-colored (that is, yellow) oleo margarine was banned from sale in the state from 1925 until 1967. It had also been classified as "the yellow stick form of Satan himself" in a proclamation signed by Governor Warren Knowles.

Mt. Horeb
The Trollway

Mt. Horeb is a small town, and though it doesn't have a tollway, it does have a Trollway. The village claims to be the "Troll Capital of the World," and to honor the little beasties, it has lined Main Street with wood carvings by local artist Mike Feeney. There's the Peddler Troll, the Old Troll, the Grumpy Troll, the Sweet Swill Troll, the Chicken Thief, the Tub Troll, the Tourist, the Accordion Player, and the Gardener. Word around town is you're not supposed to take photos of these things, either because the artist demands permission or because a snapshot would make them come alive, and Mt. Horeb could be overrun by these ugly elfs.

Main St., Mt. Horeb, WI 53572
No phone
Hours: Always visible
Cost: Free
Website: www.trollway.com
Directions: Along Business 151, the main east–west street in town.

New Glarus
Decorated Garages

Aluminum siding is a cost-effective material to protect a home or garage, but nothing is as durable as quick-set concrete. That's what Fred Zimmerman used to coat his garage in the 1920s, and it's still holding strong. Knowing that out-of-the-sack concrete has an ugly finish, even when painted, Zimmerman decided to embed objects in the still-wet surface to liven it up. Broken dishes, marbles, stones, metal toys . . . every square inch is adorned with the stuff. Fred arranged some of the colorful pieces into American and Swiss flags and a blue star, but for the most part they are randomly placed.

Adjacent to the garage is an encrusted bird house, and in the side yard is a decorated flagpole. The Zimmermans no longer live on the property, but the current residents maintain their wacky shed with loving care.

1319 Second St., New Glarus, WI 53574
Private phone
Hours: Private property; view from street
Cost: Free
Directions: At Second St. and 14th Ave.

Another garage, just down the road, is also embellished in a unique manner. The owner of this structure has mounted the back end of a Chevy Impala sticking out a fake hole in one end, making it look as if the driver entered from the wrong end.

County Rds. CC and W, New
  Glarus, WI 53574
Private phone
Hours: Private property; view
  from street
Cost: Free
Directions: Three miles east of
  town on County Rd. W.

Patriotism in porcelain.

Swiss Historical Village

In 1845 a group of 108 Swiss immigrants arrived in Wisconsin to settle 1,280 acres purchased for them (at $1.25 per acre) by the Swiss government. Economic hardships in Europe made it more cost-effective to export their citizens than to feed them. The settlers cleared the land, brought in cows, and christened the town New Glarus. A century and a half later, residents are still neutral and prone to yodeling.

On the edge of town is a historic village that recreates the life of the early settlers. You can see costumed docents farm, blacksmith, go to school, hide money in numbered accounts, and inoculate, cure, wrap, label, and sell cheese.

Twice a year the population pulls itself away from curds long enough to throw two celebrations. In June it's the Heidi Festival Pageant, and on Labor Day weekend it's the Wilhelm Tell Festival. One lucky local boy is chosen to have an apple shot off his head with an arrow, all for the glory of Switzerland.

612 Seventh Ave., New Glarus, WI 53574

Phone: (608) 527-2317; visitor information, (800) 527-6838

Hours: May–October, daily 10 AM–4 PM

Cost: Adults $9, kids (6–13) $3

Website: www.swisshistoricalvillage.org and www.swisstown.com

Directions: On the west side of town at Sixth St.

North Freedom
The *Forevertron*

Tom Every ran a salvage business for 30 years, but it depressed him; when he finished a job there was no evidence that anyone had ever been there. So he decided in 1983 to focus his energy on a constructive enterprise, the *Forevertron*, and began calling himself Dr. Evermor.

The *Forevertron*, a 320-ton sculpture, will transport the "Time-Binding" Dr. Evermor to who knows where, maybe Heaven, on a magnetic force beam when his time has come. It is constructed from, among other things, the decontamination chamber from the *Apollo 11* mission, copper

Beam me up, Doc. Photo by author, courtesy of the Evermor Foundation

kettles from a brewery, a gazebo intended for the Royal Family, a Mississippi River barge, and a mobile home, all sitting on the foundation of a former school.

And that's not the half of it. Using what he calls "historic industrial pieces," Evermor has built a giant spider and a plane-size wasp. Scattered through a field behind the *Forevertron* is a 70-piece Bird Band made from discarded musical instruments.

Dr. Evermor suffered a stroke a few years back, but he still manages to make it out to the sculpture park he created to visit with admirers, who are numerous.

S77030 Rte. 12, North Freedom, WI 53591

Phone: (608) 219-7830

Hours: April–November, Thursday–Monday 11 AM–5 PM

Cost: Free

Website: http://worldofdrevermor.com/

Directions: Seven miles north of Sauk City on Rte. 12, just south of and behind Delaney's Surplus.

THE DREAMKEEPERS

If you're in Madison, check out two of Dr. Evermor's works—*The Dreamkeepers*—outside the building at 211 South Paterson Street. The two long-necked birds stand 35 feet tall and are named Yon and Beyond.

Platteville
World's Largest "M"

Given the choice of a letter to paint on the side of a hill outside Platteville's University of Wisconsin campus, what would you choose? A "W" for Wisconsin? A "P" for Platteville? A "B" for the road it's on? Well, students chose none of these. It's an "M" for "Mines."

The University of Wisconsin, Platteville is sometimes known as the School of Mines, and they don't like to be confused with those liberal arts types in Madison, even though Madison starts with "M." The giant letter was first built in 1937 by students with a lot of time on their hands. The letter is 214 feet wide and 241 feet tall, made of whitewashed granite stones piled on a cleared hillside. Each year the school's freshmen are required to repaint it, thereby ensuring the survival of the 13th letter of the alphabet, at least in this town.

Hiawatha Pioneer Trail, Platte Mound, County Rd. B, Platteville, WI 53818

No phone

Hours: Always visible; illuminated twice a year

Cost: Free

Website: www.uwplatt.edu, http://plattevillerealestate.net/PlattevilleWI/thingstodo.html

Directions: Head west out of town on County Rd. B and look for the "M."

Poynette
Aliens and Oddities of Nature Museum

Have you ever seen a hermaphroditic pheasant? Siamese raccoons? An albino catfish? No? Then head on over the Aliens and Oddities of Nature Museum at the MacKenzie Environmental Education Center! This tiny, four-room shed is a small part of the larger nature complex, but it's the best part. The first large display case you'll see is filled with stuffed albino crit-

Like Gary Busey but hairier. Photo by author, courtesy of the MacKenzie Environmental Education Center

ters: a deer, a porcupine, a catfish, a fawn, a possum, a mink, a muskrat, and a squirrel. Another case has three examples of melatonism, the opposite of albinism, in which a creature's coloring is completely black, including a striking "red" fox.

Still another wall of oddities is devoted to hermaphrodites. Three deer skulls, one male, one female, and one somewhere in between, rest in a case. Three full, stuffed pheasants demonstrate a similar point.

In a final display are three jars of mutations. They've got conjoined raccoons, a four-legged pheasant, and a two-headed pig. This pig had the misfortune of being stolen on May 20, 1999. Two teenagers later apprehended with the jar claimed they dipped cigarettes in the formaldehyde and smoked them. The pig was returned by the authorities to the museum with fresh formaldehyde.

The "alien" portion of the museum is somewhat disappointing. No, they don't have stuffed Martians, but they do have examples of foreign species introduced into North America, such as the Chinese ring-necked pheasant. Aliens? Yes. Exciting? Not really.

MacKenzie Environmental Education Center, Wisconsin Department of Natural Resources,
  W7303 County Rds. CS and Q, Poynette, WI 53955
Phone: (608) 635-8105
Hours: May–October, daily 8 AM–4 PM; November–April, Monday–Friday 8 AM–4 PM
Cost: Free
Website: www.mackenziecenter.com
Directions: Two miles east of Rte. 51 on County Rd. Q.

Prairie du Chien
Medical Progress Museum

Were it not for Alexis St. Martin, better known as the Man with the Hole in His Stomach, nobody would have ever heard of Dr. William Beaumont. St. Martin, a man Beaumont called a "dirty, slovenly fellow, unreliable and given to drink," was shot in the stomach at Ft. Mackinac in 1822. The wound never healed, and Beaumont seized on St. Martin's misfortune to poke around in his stomach during the 1820s and '30s. Beaumont would place pieces of food on string, push them through the hole in St. Martin's side, and pull them out later for analysis. Through this work he was able to learn how quickly certain foods digested.

Beaumont published his findings in 1838 and became famous. And why did Beaumont never stitch the hole closed? He claimed the shock of surgery might kill the old trapper, and that he was only looking out for his well-being. Small wonder St. Martin was cranky.

Other medical items can be found at this unique museum, including the Transparent Twins from the 1939 World's Fair in Chicago. The women's skins are made of Lucite so that you can see all their glowing guts. Each body system lights up in succession as they tell you the story of how their organs work to keep them healthy. Nearby a mannequin, confined to an iron lung, is forced to listen to the twins repeat their message day after day after day. Poor guy.

The museum has other exhibits not related to Beaumont, St. Martin, or medicine. Fort Crawford's most famous commandant was Colonel (later US President) Zachary Taylor, whose daughter married Lieutenant (later Confederate President) Jefferson Davis, an officer at the fort. She died of malaria within three months of their vows. Sauk chief Ma-Ka-Tai-Me-She-Kia-Kiak (Black Hawk) surrendered at Fort Crawford and was imprisoned here following the Battle of Bad Axe, which ended the Black Hawk War. His cell is gone, but the bars are still on display.

Fort Crawford Medical Museum, 717 S. Beaumont Rd., PO Box 298, Prairie du Chien, WI 53821

Phone: (608) 326-6960

Hours: May–October, daily 9 AM–4 PM

Cost: Adults $5, seniors $4, kids (under 12) $3

Website: www.fortcrawfordmuseum.com

Directions: One block east of the riverfront, four blocks south of the Rte. 18 bridge.

Racine
John Dillinger's Submachine Gun

On November 20, 1933, John Dillinger's gang entered Racine's American Bank and Trust at Main and Fifth Streets and demanded all the money. When a teller ignored the hoodlums he was promptly shot in the arm. Someone tripped an alarm and the bells drew a crowd who, against all common sense, peered through the bank windows at the hold-up in progress.

Three police officers then arrived at the scene. The first ran into the bank with his machine gun drawn and was captured. The next cop ran inside, was wounded, and lay bleeding on the floor until the crime was completed. The third policeman thought better of going in and headed in the opposite direction.

To escape, the gang used two employees and the first cop as human shields. The officer was dumped at the edge of town; the other two hostages were released in Waukesha, west of Milwaukee. In all, the bank robbers got $28,000, but the local police got Dillinger's 1928 Thompson submachine gun. During the commotion, the gangster forgot it at the bank. After Dillinger was captured in Tuscon, Arizona, and returned to Indiana, he autographed the stock of the gun.

Today you can see the gun and the black shoelaces he used to tie bank president Grover Weyland and employee Ursula Patzke to a Waukesha tree in the lobby of the Racine Police Department. The American Bank and Trust was eventually torn down and a new building, the M&I Bank, stands on the site today (441 S. Main St.).

Racine Police Headquarters, 730 Center St., Racine, WI 53403

Phone: (262) 635-7700

Hours: Always visible

Cost: Free

Website: www.cityofracine.org/police.aspx

Directions: Just south of Rte. 32 as it becomes Seventh St., six blocks west of Main St. (Rte. 32).

Kewpee Restaurant

It can be rather unnerving having hundreds of naked pixie dolls staring at you while you eat, but since this is one of the cheapest meals around, I suggest you put your uneasiness aside. The Kewpee doll was created in 1909 by Rose O'Neil after she saw a vision of them dancing in her head. Those popular dolls eventually became the mascot for one of the first restaurant franchises in the United States. Once numbering in the 200s, only six Kewpee restaurants survive today, and this is the only one in the Cheese State.

The original Racine Kewpee was built in the 1920s, and the city grew up and over it—literally. The ramp from a downtown parking structure once passed right over the roof. When that lot had to be torn down in 1997, the old Kewpee went with it. But just a few months later, a new restaurant was opened on the freshly cleared site. It faithfully recreated the Art Deco design and installed a large display case for hundreds of dolls from the owner's collection.

520 Wisconsin Ave., Racine, WI 53403

Phone: (262) 634-9601

Hours: Monday–Friday 7 AM–6 PM, Saturday 7 AM–5 PM

Cost: Free; meals, $2–6

Website: www.kewpee.com

Directions: One block west of Main St. (Rte. 32) between Fifth and Sixth St.

Richland Center
Where, Oh Where, Was Little Frank Born?

Frank Lloyd Wright is to southern Wisconsin what Kurt Cobain is to Seattle: a local bad boy turned Messiah in death. So in which Richland Center manger was he born on June 8, 1867? No less then seven sites have been suggested. A definitive birth record—on which he would have been listed by his original name, Frank *Lincoln* Wright—has never been located, and Wright himself contributed to the confusion by pointing out different homes on separate occasions. Since the accuracy of his firsthand account is suspect, his input is treated with a grain of salt.

Five candidates are on or just off a five-block stretch of Church Street. The most commonly cited location is a home at **518 Church Street**. It is the only building of the seven still standing, and for that reason is a popular choice of local boosters. Or could Frank have entered the world where the house at **255 Mill Street** now stands? Perhaps the parking lot at **Park and Seminary Streets**, or under the new post office at **213 South Central Avenue**? Maybe he was born at a home that stood where Papa's Donuts now sits at **101 South Church Street**? Another possible location is at the south end of town at **810 Park Street**, today occupied by a one-car garage.

The final suggested birthplace isn't in Richland Center at all, but in neighboring Bear Valley. This location is favored by the head of the town's local historical society, but by almost nobody in Richland Center. Wright's father was a minister and had been called to preside over a funeral in Bear Valley; records show the expectant couple was staying with relatives of his late first wife, and that the funeral was the day *after* Frank's birth. That's a convincing case.

All over town, Richland Center, WI 53581
No phone
Hours: Always visible
Cost: Free
Website: www.richlandchamber.com
Directions: Ask around.

WHILE YOU'RE IN TOWN

As long as you're in Richland Center looking for something that probably no longer exists, you might as well see something that does: the **A. D. German Warehouse**. Wright designed the building in 1915, and it was constructed from 1917 to 1921. The warehouse was not used to store Germans but rather sugar, coffee, tobacco, and flour—all you needed for a 1910 breakfast. You can find it at 300 South Church Street.

The White House?

Most Ramada Inns aren't known for their architectural grandeur, but there's one in Richland Center that's a real eye-catcher. Rising above this otherwise plain chain motel is a dome reminiscent of the US Capitol building. The strictly ornamental structure was added to the roof to attract customers to the White House Supper Club. Inside was a replica of the Oval Office, which was decorated with portraits of the presidents.

Confused? So was the public—the restaurant is now out of business. However, the dome remains, and today the Ramada offers a nod to the national theme by naming its rooms after various states.

Ramada Richland Center, 1450 Veterans Dr., Richland Center, WI 53581
Phone: (608) 647-8869
Hours: Always visible
Cost: Free; Rooms, $70 per night and up
Website: http://www.ramada.com/hotels/wisconsin/richland-center/ramada-richland-center/
 hotel-overview
Directions: On the west side of Rte. 14, two blocks south of Rte. 80 (Main St.).

Sauk City

The Press Box Bar & Grill

They're creepy in the way mannequins always are—stiff and glassy-eyed, their elbows and wrists twisted at slightly unobtainable angles. But the figures over the entrance to this sports bar look even more disturbing because they are all cut off at the torso. No hips, no legs, no feet.

There are six in all, five men and one Victorian-clad woman, all staring out from a long chicken-coop case intended to resemble a press box. One guy holds a football, another a game program, and one is dressed as a referee holding a pair of binoculars, a Swingline phone nearby to call in the score.

809 Water St., Sauk City, WI 53583

Phone: (608) 643-6666

Hours: Daily 10 AM–2 PM

Cost: Free

Website: www.facebook.com/pages/Press-Box/139085672786371

Directions: One block north of Rte. 12/78 (Philips Blvd.) on the first street west of the river.

Spring Green

Acrobatic Goats

They sing! They dance! They walk the high wire! They're the Acrobatic Goats of Peck's Farm Market!

Don't jump! Life's not so bad!

OK . . . so maybe they don't sing or dance, but they *are* acrobatic. Peck's Farm Market has built three towers of increasing height in the goat pens at their petting zoo. Each tower is connected by a narrow wooden ramp, and each platform is linked to the public by a cup on a clothesline pulley. Place a quarter's worth of corn in the cup and wheel it to the top, and watch those frisky goats climb!

The heights of the towers seem more ominous and impressive because these sure-hoofed goats are pygmies. The tallest tower is at least ten times as high as a goat's length. Translated, that would be like you scrambling up the ledges of a six-story building for a chocolate bar.

Peck's Farm Market East, 6445 US Hwy. 14, Spring Green, WI 53588

Phone: (608) 588-7177

Hours: June–October 8 AM–8 PM; goats only outside in good weather

Cost: 25¢ per cup

Website: www.pecksfarmmarketeast.com

Directions: East of town on Rte. 14, just east of the County Rd. C intersection.

House on the Rock

Hell hath no fury like an architect scorned. When Frank Lloyd Wright dismissed Alex Jordan Sr. from nearby Taliesin stating, "I wouldn't hire you to design a cheese crate or a chicken coop. You aren't capable," Jordan decided to get even. *And how.* Jordan purchased the land overlooking Wright's beloved studio and started building a home to rival Mr. Bigshot's Taliesin, and the project didn't let up until the death of his son, Alex Jordan Jr., in 1989.

Most of the work was done by young Alex, known to everyone as Junior. The first structure was the actual House on the Rock, a cramped, Asian-inspired bachelor pad perched atop Deer Shelter Rock. To blast the top of the rock level, Junior hired drunks and bums in Madison whom he paid with bottles of whiskey for the hazardous duty. To demonstrate his sense of style while the work progressed, Junior would drive around Madison and out to Spring Green in a 16-cylinder, 22-foot-long, two-seater black Cadillac convertible. Seeing young Alex, Wright must have been insanely jealous or incredibly pissed off. Either emotion would have satisfied the Jordans.

House on the Rock grew out, over, and beyond Deer Shelter Rock into a 30-acre collection of everything under the sun. To see it all you must prepare yourself to run the Boston Marathon of museums. The self-guided tour snakes through 2.5 miles of displays in dozens of themed outbuildings covering 200 acres. House on the Rock won't sell you a ticket less than 2.5 hours before closing time for fear you won't get through it all and they'll have to send out a search party. Among the wonders you'll see are:

- the World's Largest Carousel—it weighs 35 tons, stands two stories high, has 182 chandeliers, and contains 269 characters (but no horses), including a cat with a fish in its mouth and a bare-breasted female with a rooster's lower body . . . and you're not allowed to ride any of them;
- the World's Largest Cannon;
- the World's Largest Fireplace—it can burn an entire tree at one time and barbecue an entire cow;
- the Infinity Room, a glass hallway dangling 156 feet over the Wyoming Valley (unsupported for its final 218 feet) with 3,264 panes of glass;
- replicas of England's Crown Jewels;
- a 200-foot fiberglass whale battling a giant squid;
- chipmunk dioramas in a men's bathroom;
- a wooden leg with a gun holster embedded in it;
- a musical Richard Nixon mannequin in the Circus Exhibit;
- the bottled head and hands of a criminal in the Sheriff's Office; and
- 6,000 Santas placed throughout the attraction at Christmastime.

How could Jordan afford such a lavish collection of knickknacks? The answer is found in what you *don't* see: placards detailing where these items came from. Back in the 1970s the Wisconsin Justice Department demanded Jordan remove all signs making unsubstantiated claims about what people were seeing. In reality, many of the "antiques" you see today were purchased at a local K-Mart and only look old because they're placed at a distance, behind glass. The music that appears to be coming from the mechanical orchestras is often piped in. Much of the ivory is fake, including the impressive Oriental Boat.

But in the end, WHO CARES!??!! There is no tour in the Badger State that inspires more wonder and awe than the Mighty, Gaudy, Fantabulous Forced March Through the World's Largest Barn of Crapola, better known as House on the Rock. Miss it and you'll die a lesser person.

5754 State Rd. 23, Spring Green, WI 53588

Phone: (800) 334-5275 or (608) 935-3639

Hours: March–April, Thursday–Monday 9 AM–5 PM; May and September–November, daily

9 AM–5 PM; June–August, daily 9 AM–6 PM

Cost: Adults $28.50, seniors (65+) $26.50, kids (4–17) $15.50

Website: www.thehouseontherock.com

Directions: Off Rte. 23 between Spring Green and Dodgeville, it's hard to miss.

ALEX JORDAN'S FIRST SCHEMES

Alex Jordan Jr. was handy with a camera in his early years, but it got him in a lot of trouble. First, he took infrared photos of a stripper in a Green Bay club, but was threatened with death when the proprietors found out. He quickly returned the negatives. Junior used the same camera in 1939 to take photos of his lifelong companion, Jennie Olson, having sex with prominent Madison businessmen in an extortion scheme. It worked on several men before the pair were caught, convicted, and sentenced, Jordan with a $500 fine and six months in jail, Olson with $300 and three months in the Big House. Alex Jordan Sr. strongly suggested his son spend more time working on the House on the Rock to keep him out of Madison, away from his former victims. For all the salacious details, check out *House of Alex* (Waubesa Press, 1990) by Marv Balousek.

Taliesin

The second-best architect in this region (after Alex Jordan Jr.) is, of course, Frank Lloyd Wright. His Wisconsin studio and home, Taliesin, are located in the Wyoming Valley where you can see them all . . . for a pretty penny. Taliesin is Welsh for "Shining Brow" and is a name more fitting for House on the Rock, but Wright took it first. If you take the tour you will no doubt be barraged with details of Wright's genius, but what you won't hear are the gory details of a mass murder at this very site.

On August 15, 1914, a Barbadian butler named Julian Carleton executed his own crazy plan to murder Mamah Cheney Borthwick, Wright's mistress, and others as they sat down to lunch. During the meal he walked in, split open Borthwick's head with an ax, struck and killed both her children. He then went to the home's other wing to attack several of the architect's employees. Those unlucky men he sealed in a dining room, poured gasoline under the bolted door, and set aflame. All exits were blocked except for the one behind which Carlton waited, ax in hand. As they tried to flee he struck them with blows to their heads. Before it was over, Borthwick and six others were dead. Though later captured, Carlton had ingested muriatic acid and died in jail two months later after a hunger strike. He never explained why he did it.

Wright was out of town and escaped the carnage. In the years to follow, Wright would ramble around in the charred shell of Taliesin while it was being rebuilt. He never quite recovered, and neither did mistress Mamah. She is believed to haunt the Tan-Y-Deri shed out back. Ask the guides about it . . . they never mention the murders in the home's promotional material, nor are they allowed to tell grisly stories during the tour. But you can ask.

Frank Lloyd Wright Visitor Center, Rte. 23 and County Rd. C, Spring Green, WI 53588

Contact: Taliesin Preservation, Inc., 5607 County Rd. C, Spring Green, WI 53588

Phone: (877) 588-7900 or (608) 588-7900

Hours: Visitor center, May–October, daily 9:00 AM–5 PM; tours, call ahead for reservations

Cost: Hillside Studio and Theater Tour $16, House Tour $47, Highlights Tour $52, Estate Tour $80

Website: www.taliesinpreservation.org

Directions: On Rte. 23, two miles south of Spring Green.

SLEEPING WITH FRANK

If you want to spend the night at a Frank Lloyd Wright house, there is only one place to do it: at the **Seth Peterson Cottage** in Mirror Lake State Park. Seth Peterson never lived in the building he commissioned; he shot himself in 1958 after being dumped by his girlfriend. For a small fee, you can take a tour of the house (every second Sunday of the month from 1 to 4 PM), or for a much larger fee you can rent the place for short vacations throughout the year. (E9982 Fern Dell Rd., Reedsburg, (877) 466-2358, www.sethpeterson.org)

And though the **Usonian Inn** was not designed by Wright, it was designed by his apprentice, J. C. Calloway and was based on Wright's "architecture for everyone" aesthetic. The current owners have also cranked the "green" emphasis to 11. (E5116 US Hwy. 14, Spring Green, (877) USONIAN, www.usonianinn .com)

Frank Lloyd Wright's Empty Grave

Just down the hill from Taliesen, Frank Lloyd Wright was laid to his not-so-final rest in 1959, beneath a monument of his own design. The stone marker was a rough-hewn hunk of native rock with a cantilever nameplate. But before the worms got a bite, folks realized they had not put Frank in the ground according to his final wishes, which was to be facing his beloved studio. So Frank was later exhumed, turned, and reburied.

Wright's third wife, Olgivanna Milanov, had no intentions of being planted in the cold Wisconsin soil beside her husband, or in the same cemetery as his murdered mistress Mamah Borthwick, so she ordered that upon *her* death Wright would be exhumed, cremated, and reburied with her in Scottsdale, Arizona, near Taliesen West.

Milanov died of a stroke in 1985 and her grave-robbing plot was carried out. Though the monument to Wright still marks a grave, nobody's home below. But if you want to see a real, dead celebrity, actress Anne Baxter, granddaughter of Wright, has been planted in this small burial ground. (Borthwick's grave is unmarked.)

Lloyd-Jones Family Cemetery, Unity Chapel, 6514 Hillside School Rd., Spring Green, WI 53588

No phone

Hours: Always not visible

Cost: Free

Website: www.unitychapel.org

Directions: Two miles south of town, just off Rte. 23 on County Rd. T (Hillside School Rd.).

Union Grove
Great Lakes Dragaway

The trouble with most racing venues is that the average Joe or Josephine isn't allowed to participate. Not so at Great Lakes Dragaway. If you've got wheels and $35 you can drag all you want on their quarter-mile track. Of course, the place is primarily frequented by serious gearheads, but you'll still see people racing everything from station wagons and minivans to dragsters and nitro-burning funny cars. Motorcycles and snowmobiles are also welcome. That's right: a modified snowmobile, its skids replaced with tiny wheels, can gobble up a quarter-mile in under 10 seconds.

The Dragaway was built by "Broadway" Bob Meltzer (who passed away just as this book was completed) and has not changed much since it opened, not even the music selection; you'll hear healthy doses of George Thorogood, Journey, and AC/DC over the loudspeakers. Sitting in the grandstands, looking out over the cornfields while blue smoke curls up from a Chevy Nova's tires to the sounds of Styx, makes for a surprisingly relaxing and entertaining evening. But maybe that's just the beer talking.

City Line Rd., Union Grove, WI 53182

Phone: (262) 878-3783

Hours: April–October, Tuesday–Sunday; check website or call for race times

Cost: Spectators $15, racers $35

Website: www.greatlakesdragaway.com

Directions: East of town on County Rd. KR (City Line Rd.).

Watertown
The Nation's First Kindergarten

Years ago Friedrich Frobel came up with the revolutionary concept that young children should be prepared for entry into the school regimen, and in 1837 he founded Europe's first *kindergarten*, "a garden for children." The experiment made an impact on one of Frobel's students, Margarethe Meyer Schurz, who later founded America's first kindergarten on August 26, 1856, in her front parlor in Watertown.

There were only six students in the first class, and two were her own children. Lessons were given in German. A friend, Elizabeth Peabody, copied Schurz and opened an English-speaking classroom for tots in Boston.

Today, few children enter the first grade without spending some time eating paste, taking naps, and finger-painting with their peers.

Schurz's home was restored in 1956 and the building was moved from downtown to its present site next to the Octagon House. There haven't been classes here for many years, so don't worry about catching the funky odor of vomit-absorbing sawdust.

Octagon House Museum, 919 Charles St., Watertown, WI 53094

Phone: (920) 261-2796

Hours: June–August, daily 10 AM–4 PM; September–October and May, daily 11 AM–3 PM

Cost: Adults $7, seniors $6, kids (6–17) $4

Website: www.watertownhistory.org

Directions: Two blocks south on Concord Ave. from Rte. 19 (Main St.), turn west on Western Ave., south on Harvey, then one block east to Charles St.

Williams Bay
World's Largest Refracting Telescope

The telescope at Williams Bay's Yerkes Observatory, with its 40-inch refractor, is the world's largest refracting telescope. It is owned and operated by the University of Chicago, and is located far north of that metropolis to avoid the smog and light pollution of the big city. Few refracting telescopes are still used today; reflecting telescopes are more common, so Yerkes may hold its record forever.

The story of how this telescope was funded is as interesting as anything it has discovered. Charles Yerkes was a public transportation tycoon who owned the streetcars on the north side of Chicago and built the elevated Loop. He was not above lining his own pockets at his investors' and riders' expenses. In fact, he spent time in prison earlier in life for misappropriating public funds in Philadelphia in 1871. And though he was rich as Midas, he didn't have the approval of the Chicago social elite, many of whom summered on the shores of Lake Geneva.

Enter U of C President William Harper and astronomer George Hale. They suggested that Yerkes fund the world's largest telescope to be placed on the same shoreline as the socialites' homes. That would certainly win over his critics! After considerable funds had been plowed into the project, the telescope was finished in 1897. And though Yerkes was praised at its dedication, he never was invited to join the upper crust.

Yerkes Observatory, 373 W. Geneva St., Williams Bay, WI 53191

Phone: (262) 245-5555

Hours: Saturday tours 10 AM, 11 AM, and noon

Cost: Free; donations accepted

Website: http://astro.uchicago.edu/yerkes/

Directions: On Rte. 67, just east of Theatre Rd.; at latitude 42 34.2, longitude –88 33.4.

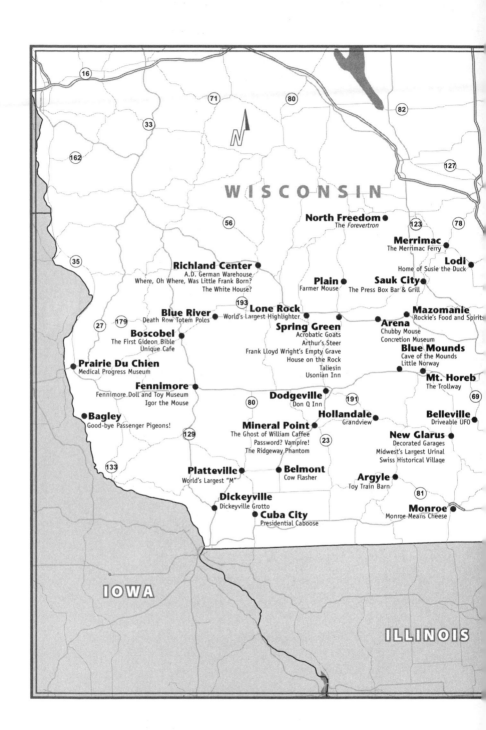

WISCONSIN

North Freedom ●
The *Forevertron*

Merrimac ●
The Merrimac Ferry

Lodi ●
Home of Susie the Duck

Richland Center ●
A.D. German Warehouse
Where, Oh Where, Was Little Frank Born?
The White House?

Plain ●
Farmer Mouse

Sauk City ●
The Press Box Bar & Grill

Blue River ●
Death Row Totem Poles

Lone Rock ●
World's Largest Highlighter

Mazomanie ●
Rockie's Food and Spirits

Spring Green
Acrobatic Goats
Arthur's Steer
Frank Lloyd Wright's Empty Grave
House on the Rock
Taliesin
Usonian Inn

Arena ●
Chubby Mouse
Concretion Museum

Blue Mounds ●
Cave of the Mounds
Little Norway

Mt. Horeb ●
The Trollway

Boscobel ●
The First Gideon Bible
Unique Cafe

Prairie Du Chien ●
Medical Progress Museum

Fennimore ●
Fennimore Doll and Toy Museum
Igor the Mouse

Dodgeville ●
Don Q Inn

Hollandale ●
Grandview

Bagley ●
Good-bye Passenger Pigeons!

Mineral Point ●
The Ghost of William Caffee
Password? Vampire!
The Ridgeway Phantom

Belleville ●
Driveable UFO

New Glarus ●
Decorated Garages
Midwest's Largest Urinal
Swiss Historical Village

Platteville ●
World's Largest "M"

Belmont ●
Cow Flasher

Argyle ●
Toy Train Barn

Dickeyville ●
Dickeyville Grotto

Cuba City ●
Presidential Caboose

Monroe ●
Monroe Means Cheese

IOWA

ILLINOIS

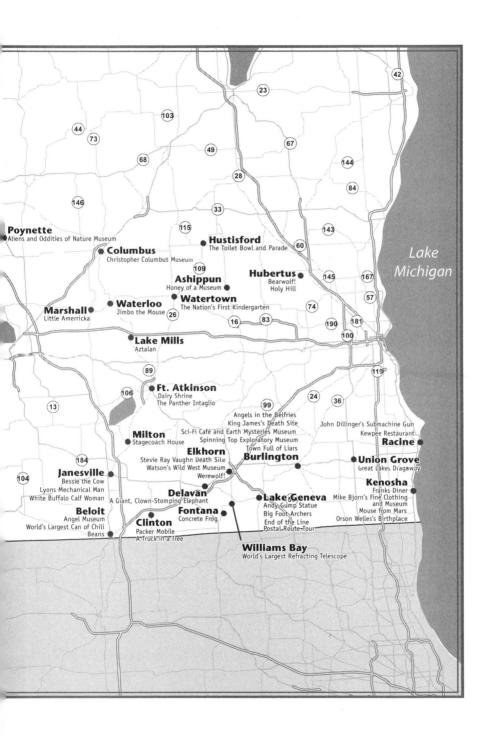

Poynette
Aliens and Oddities of Nature Museum

Columbus
Christopher Columbus Museum

Hustisford
The Toilet Bowl and Parade

Ashippun
Honey of a Museum

Hubertus
Bearwolf!
Holy Hill

Watertown
The Nation's First Kindergarten

Marshall
Little Amerricka

Waterloo
Jimbo the Mouse

Lake Mills
Aztalan

Ft. Atkinson
Dairy Shrine
The Panther Intaglio

Angels in the Belfries
King James's Death Site

Milton
Stagecoach House

Sci-Fi Café and Earth Mysteries Museum
Spinning Top Exploratory Museum
Town Full of Liars

John Dillinger's Submachine Gun
Kewpee Restaurant

Racine

Elkhorn
Stevie Ray Vaughn Death Site
Watson's Wild West Museum
Werewolf!

Burlington

Union Grove
Great Lakes Dragaway

Janesville
Bessie the Cow
Lyons Mechanical Man
White Buffalo Calf Woman

Delavan
A Giant, Clown-Stomping Elephant

Kenosha
Franks Diner
Mike Bjorn's Fine Clothing
and Museum
Mouse from Mars
Orson Welles's Birthplace

Beloit
Angel Museum
World's Largest Can of Chili
Beans

Fontana
Concrete Frog

Clinton
Packer Mobile
A Truck in a Tree

Lake Geneva
Andy Gump Statue
Big Foot Archers
End of the Line
Postal Route Tour

Williams Bay
World's Largest Refracting Telescope

Lake Michigan

MAP OF SOUTHERN WISCONSIN **191**

Mad Town

isconsin governor Lee Sherman Dreyfus once described Madison as "thirty-six square miles surrounded by reality." Whether it is due to the university or the state lawmakers, Madison had long been known as Mad Town or Mad City, home to Cheese State bureaucrats and radicals, or at least radicals by Wisconsin standards. But blaming the policy wonks and old hippies would be too easy, and not exactly fair. There's something else going on here. Something weird. Something abnormal.

Take, for example, a recent study on rhinotillexomania performed by the University of Wisconsin. Rhinotillexomania is better known by its street name: nose-picking. Researchers wanted answers to such important questions as which finger subjects used and how often they examined their boogers after extracting them. Researchers had no difficulty signing up 1,200 Madison residents as subjects.

Thinking about this study will give you peace of mind as you visit the capital city. Suddenly you won't feel so self-conscious about hopping on the merry-go-round at Ella's, paying respects to the King's karate skills, or waiting for a groundhog to predict what the weather will be like in spring. Next to these booger-digging bureaucrats, you're almost normal.

Almost.

Madison

Bombing at the Army Mathematics Research Center

On August 24, 1970, a 1967 Ford Falcon Deluxe station wagon parked outside Sterling Hall on the UW campus exploded. The car bomb killed one research scientist, Robert Fassnacht, and injured three others. Sterling Hall was targeted because it housed the Army Mathematics Research Center, and the Vietnam War was raging.

The homemade bomb was detonated by the New Year's Gang, aka the Vanguard of the Revolution, who had three basic demands: (1) release a Milwaukee Black Panther Party official being held for the attempted murder of a policeman, (2) expel the ROTC from campus, and (3) abolish "women's hours" at UW-Madison.

The New Year's Gang had named themselves after a previous, failed attempt to level the Badger Army Ammunition Plant in nearby Baraboo. On December 31, 1969, they dropped three jars of a fuel oil and nitrogen fertilizer mixture from a low-flying Cessna, hoping to set off a chain reaction at the plant. The plan didn't work.

Unfortunately for Fassnacht, their second plan *did* work in Madison, at least as far as the explosion was concerned. But the unintended consequence of the murder was a backlash against antiwar protests that had grown increasingly violent.

Eventually four men were charged in the crime. Karleton Armstrong was captured in Toronto in February 1972 after trying to get a passport to Algeria under the assumed name of David Weller. (He drew a 23-year sentence.) David Fine was nabbed in San Rafael, California, in 1975 while attending Marin Community College as William Lewes. (He got seven years.) Dwight Armstrong was apprehended in Toronto in April 1977, living as Gary Mitchell. (He also got seven years.) But the final accomplice, Leo Burt, has never been captured.

Sterling Hall was repaired and is still in service today. There is a memorial plaque on the south side of the building.

Sterling Hall, University of Wisconsin at Madison, 475 N. Charter St., Madison, WI 53706

No phone

Hours: Always visible

Cost: Free

Directions: North on Charter St. off University Ave., just east of the University/Linden Dr. intersection.

MADISON

➡ The University of Wisconsin–Madison was the first college to ever offer correspondence courses.

➡ *The Onion*, America's satirical newspaper, was founded in Madison by Christopher Johnson and Tim Keck in 1988.

GOOD THING THIS ISSUE CAME OUT LATER!

The Vanguard of the Revolution might have been able to level the Badger Army Munitions Plant had they waited a decade. A working blueprint for a hydrogen bomb was published in the *Madison Press Connection* in September 1979. Later, Madison's *Progressive Magazine* attempted to do the same but was blocked by the Pentagon.

Car-Washing Octopi

To give your car a thorough scrubbing you almost have to be an octopus. As luck would have it, three businesses in Madison do just that: the Octopus Car Washes! Their signs are difficult to miss; a smiling, pistachio-colored octopus (named Ozzie) grips a pail, sponge, vacuum, and brush in his writhing tentacles. Whether your car is spattered with bugs or bird doo-doo, this cephalopod looks up to the job. Yet Ozzie stays atop his pole

Eight hands are better than two.

and humans do most of the work on your vehicle. What gives? Their slogan says it all: "Many *Hands* to Serve You"—not *tentacles*.

Octopus Car Wash, 907 S. Park St., Madison, WI 53715

Phone: (608) 257-3991

Octopus Car Wash, 1039 E. Washington Ave., Madison, WI 53703

Phone: (608) 257-2929

Octopus Car Wash, 2202 University Ave., Madison, WI 53729

Phone: (608) 238-1111

Hours: Always visible; car washes, Monday–Saturday 8 AM–5:30 PM, Sunday 9 AM–4:30 PM

Cost: Free; washes, $9.48–$19

Website: www.octopuscarwashes.com/wi/

Directions: Location 1, on Park St. (Rte. 151) just north of the Fish Hatchery Rd. (Rte. D) intersection; Location 2, on Washington Ave. (Rte. 151) at Haywood Dr., nine blocks northeast of the Capitol building; Location 3, on University Ave., one block south of Campus Dr., three blocks east of Highland Ave.

 FAR-REACHING TENTACLES

In addition to the three locations in Madison, there is an **Octopus Car Wash** in Milwaukee (4519 N. Green Bay Ave., (414) 265-2233), as well as two locations in nearby Rockford, Illinois.

Chris Farley's Tomb

Contrary to what you might have heard, Chris Farley was not buried in a van down by the river. After the comedian died in the foyer of his Chicago condo on December 18, 1997, his body was returned to Madison, his hometown.

Chris Farley's family lived in the Maple Bluff neighborhood when he was born on February 15, 1964. Farley was the class clown and his idol was John Belushi. Clearly he took the idol worship too far, copying Belushi's excesses in food, alcohol, and drugs. Farley died at the age of 33 of a heart attack brought on by a long night of partying with a hired stripper.

The location of Farley's tomb in the mausoleum would suggest he was a bishop. Perhaps in Madison he was. He's interred just past the altar, on the left, as you enter the interior mausoleum. A long kneeler in front can accommodate several fans at once.

Resurrection Chapel Mausoleum, 2705 Regent St., Madison, WI 53705

Phone: (608) 238-5561

Hours: Monday–Friday 8:30 AM–4:30 PM, Saturday 9 AM–noon

Cost: Free

Website: www.madisondiocese.org/diocesancemeteries/Locations/ResurrectionCemetery-
   Madison.aspx

Directions: At the corner of Franklin Ave. and Regent St.

Ella's Kosher Deli & Ice Cream Parlor

The name of this establishment suggests you might find a traditional eatery, but there is nothing traditional about Ella's. The food and desserts are average, but the decor is a Mel Blanc acid trip. Animatronic cartoon characters fly overhead on wires, turn, and return for another pass. Mickey Mouse, Bart Simpson, Superman, Batman, Spongebob Squarepants, and a genie on a flying carpet are some of the tamer robots. Popeye rises into the air

Look out above! Photo by author, courtesy of Ella's

on a rocket ship, workshop tools come alive and dance, and three brightly-dressed clowns stretch like rubber, changing height before your very eyes. Guitar-plucking cowboys, the Beatles, and Mozart add music to the mix.

If you can take your eyes off the ceiling long enough, check out your table. Each glass-topped booth is filled with a collection of toys or interactive games. Those seated at certain tables are given magnetic wands to pull iron-filing beards and hair on the bald heads beneath the glass. Others are filled with marble games, or optical illusions. You can also find collections of Pez dispensers, model trains, and yo-yos.

Outside, in the summer, is a fully operational wooden carousel. It was built in 1927 by C. W. Parker of Leavenworth, Kansas. The carousel is in mint condition, and can even support full-size adult riders who have just gorged themselves inside.

2902 E. Washington Ave., Madison, WI 53704
Phone: (608) 241-5291
Hours: Sunday–Thursday 10 AM–10 PM, Friday–Saturday 10 AM–11 PM
Cost: Free; meals, $7–12
Website: www.ellasdeli.com
Directions: Three blocks south of Rte. 30 on Rte. 151 (Washington Ave.).

MADISON MUSEUMS R.I.P.

Madison was once home to several oddball collections that are now off-limits. What a shame these museums have been moth-balled, or are only open on special occasions.

International Credit Union Museum

The Credit Union National Association once maintained a credit union collection at their national headquarters. Your visit started by viewing "The Credit Union Legacy," a 24-projector, multimedia extravaganza in the association's 175-seat auditorium—no need to push, there's room for everyone! After the show you could view dioramas and maps outlining collective debt's checkered history. No longer. CUNA hopes to open the museum again someday.

Madison Museum of Bathroom Tissue

Currently "in transit," this privately-held collection has rolls "liberated" from the Alamo, the Statue of Liberty, Graceland, Caesar's Palace, and Churchill Downs . . . along with 3,000 other rolls from less ostentatious locales. Admittance was reasonable—just 25¢ and a roll of TP. But until they find a new home, they're closed to the public.

Sam Sanfillippo's Taxidermy

Located in the basement of a local funeral home, this strange collection of stuffed critters had chipmunks riding saddled plastic deer and horses and other rodents dancing in a "Topless Girlie Show," riding a Ferris wheel, or playing cards in a local saloon. Also, a dozen albino squirrels posed in pink Barbie convertibles and monster Tonka trucks. But now it's closed to the public, and the world is a lesser place.

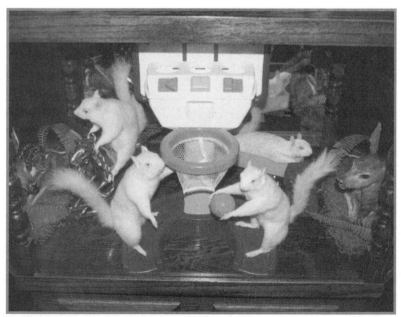

Albino squirrels just want to have fun.

Elvis to the Rescue

The King got into a lot of scraps in his day, but here is Madison is one of the few places where he *stopped* a fight. Today the historic spot is marked with a historic plaque . . . in granite!

It happened on June 24, 1977, at about 1 AM. Presley's limousine was stopped at a red light when he witnessed two teenagers beating up another in the parking lot of the Skyland Standard Service Station. Elvis hopped out (still in a blue jumpsuit from an earlier concert in Des Moines), ran up to the fracas, struck a karate pose, and announced, "If you want to fight, let's fight. . . . I'll take you on." Stunned, the hoodlums stopped their beatdown, everyone shook hands, and it was over.

Elvis did a concert at the Dane County Coliseum (today the Alliant Energy Center, 1919 Alliant Energy Center Way) the next evening. And

Where the business was taken care of.

while sitting on a toilet in Graceland 52 days later, the King went to that last final concert in the sky.

In 2007 one of Presley's admirers erected a marker at the site of the confrontation. Apparently the Wisconsin Historical Society didn't accept the momentous significance of the event, and had no part in the memorial. The gas station closed years ago, but today is a used-car lot.

Schoepp Motors Northeast, 3602 E. Washington Ave., Madison, WI 53714

No phone

Hours: Always visible

Cost: Free

Directions: At the intersection of Rte. 151 (Washington Ave.) and Rte. 51 (Stoughton Rd.).

The Rebel Dead

When Confederate soldiers were captured at Island Number 10 on the Mississippi River in 1862, they were transferred to Camp Randall's POW stockade in Madison. Conditions there were similar to prisons on both sides during the conflict: horrific. Many of the Rebs died of disease and were buried in Forest Hill Cemetery. And though these soldiers may have been hundreds of miles from home in the cold, Wisconsin soil, thanks to Abraham Lincoln they're still buried in the United States. Today, Confederate Rest at Forest Hill is the nation's northernmost Confederate burial plot.

Forest Hill Cemetery is also notable for another reason: it is one of the few urban graveyards in the United States where Native American effigy mounds are part of the land. At the southern corner of the cemetery are two panther-shaped mounds, a goose-shaped mound, and a linear mound, estimated to have been built around 900–1200 AD. The goose was accidentally "beheaded" by the Illinois Central Railroad in the 1880s, and three other linear mounds were leveled before anyone realized what they were destroying.

Forest Hill Cemetery, 1 Speedway Rd., Madison, WI 53705

Phone: (608) 266-4720

Hours: Daily 9 AM–5 PM

Cost: Free

Website: www.cityofmadison.com/parks/parks/cemetery/

Directions: South of the intersection of Regent St. and Speedway Rd.

ALSO BURIED AT FOREST HILL CEMTERY

A man who claimed to be Thomas Jefferson's son by Sally Hemings, **Eston Hemings**, is also buried at Forest Hill Cemetery. Hemings brought his family to Madison in 1852, having fled Ohio where free African Americans were being captured under the Fugitive Slave Act. His lineage was not revealed until after he died in 1856, but it wasn't until recent years that DNA tests confirmed his claim.

Sid's Sculpture Yard

Sid Boyum has never gotten his due. For years he was Alex Jordan Jr.'s right-hand man at House on the Rock (page 182). Boyum and Jordan's friendship went back to the days when they peddled a product called No Run to university women. When mixed with water it was supposed to keep snagged nylons from running. The claim was technically true, but No Run turned out to be nothing more than cement.

Though he worked in Spring Green, Boyum lived in Madison for most of his life. Over the years he built 70 sculptures in his backyard and home, many from Eastern mythology and several of them sexually explicit. In the front yard he had a chair shaped like a polar bear, and in the back was a big-breasted sphinx and the Mouth of Hell. In the years leading up to his 1991 death, his home was also filled with more than 80 cats. The living kind, not statues.

Boyum's son Steve inherited the home, the sculptures, and the cats. Rather than hide his father's artwork from the public, 13 pieces were restored and moved to locations around the Atwood neighborhood in the summer of 2000. You can find them in parks (such as at Center Ave. and Elmside Blvd.) and along parkways (St. Paul Ave.). A few are visible over the fence at his old home.

Home, 237 Waubesa St., Madison, WI 53704
No phone
Hours: Always visible
Cost: Free
Directions: Two blocks east of the intersection of Fair Oak and Atwood Aves., then north on Waubesa St.

Thornton Wilder's Birthplace

Pulitzer Prize–winning novelist and playwright Thornton Wilder was born in Madison on April 17, 1897. He was the only surviving child of a pair of twins, and spent much of his first year in a sickly state, carried around on a pillow by his mother, like a golden egg.

At the time, his father was editor of the *Wisconsin State Journal*. The Wilder family moved two blocks away, to 211 West Gilman Street, when Thornton was an infant, and through their time in Madison attended the First Congregationalist Church (1609 University Ave., (608) 233-9751, www.firstcongmadison.org).

Young Thornton inherited his father's interest in writing, and would hang out at the newspaper office or the local library. The family left town for Hong Kong when Thornton was nine, after his father was appointed American Consul General.

14 W. Gilman St., Madison, WI 53702

Private phone

Hours: Private residence; view from street

Cost: Free

Directions: Head northwest on Wisconsin Ave. from the State Capitol building, turn left on Gilman, one block short of the lake.

MORE MADISON BABIES

Tyne Daly: February 21, 1946
Chris Noth: November 13, 1954
Gena Rowlands: June 19, 1930

Vitense Miniature Golf

What brainiac came up with the idea that a miniature golf course had to have a theme, that it had to make *sense*? Wasn't half the fun knowing that each hole made no sense whatsoever? Well, that seems to be the thinking at Vitense Miniature Golf. Hippos are side-by-side with dinosaurs, chickens with Ferris wheels, talking trees with giraffes.

And that's just outside; wait until you see the indoor course! Here you'll find a US Capitol building, a miniature Wienermobile, a hot dog slide, and

It's a golf hole, it's a slide, it's a hot dog. Photo by author, courtesy of Vitense Golfland

a trippy black-light hole where the obstacles glow and the walls explode with neon fireworks while a Moody Blues moon rises in the distance. Even your balls glow.

Vitense Golfland, 5501 Schroeder Rd., Madison, WI 53711

Phone: (608) 271-1411

Hours: Outdoor, June–August, Sunday–Thursday 7:30 AM–11 PM, Friday–Saturday 7:30 AM–11:30 PM; indoor, September–May, daily 10 AM–7 PM

Cost: 18 holes, adults $7.75, seniors $6.50, kids (4–12) $6.50, peewee (3 and under) $3; 36 holes, adults $12, seniors $10, kids $10, peewee $4.50; 54 holes, adults $16, seniors $13, kids $13, peewee $6

Website: www.vitense.com/Miniaturegolf.aspx#

Directions: South of W. Beltline Hwy. at Whitney Way.

Washin' Up by the Dock of the Lake

Otis Redding recorded "Sittin' on the Dock of the Bay" on December 7, 1967, and three days later made an unanticipated career move: he died when his Beechcraft plane crashed into Madison's Lake Monona. The song would likely have been a hit had the 26-year-old singer not met an early, tragic death, but as Jim Croce could tell you if he were alive, the publicity doesn't hurt.

Redding was on his way to Madison from Cleveland to play at the Factory Nightclub and went down three miles short of the runway in the middle of the icy lake. Four band members (the Bar-Kays) were also killed, but one, trumpet player Ben Cauley, miraculously survived. Contrary to local legend, all the victims' bodies were found.

For years there was a three-bench memorial to Redding in Law Park. The benches faced east, in the direction of the crash site. When the Monona Terrace Convention Center was built, they were moved to the Rooftop Garden.

William T. Evjue Rooftop Garden, Monona Terrace Convention Center, 1 John Nolan Dr., Madison, WI 53702

No phone

Hours: Always visible

Cost: Free

Directions: Just southeast of the State Capitol, on Lake Monona.

Wisconsin State Capitol Building

As state capitol buildings go, the Wisconsin structure is unique in many weird ways. It is the only granite dome in the United States, and is topped with a gilded statue entitled *Wisconsin*. Though it is difficult to distinguish from the ground, this golden statue wears a badger on her head and has a corncob dangling beside each ear. She was sculpted in 1914 by Daniel Chester French who later went on to design the Lincoln Memorial, though Abe didn't end up with such silly accessories.

The highest flagpole to rise from the capitol roof was the scene of a fool-hearted gesture on Memorial Day 1911. On that day, patriotic citizen Frank E. Smith shimmied up the pole to unwind a flag that had gotten tangled 230 feet in the air. An approving crowd watched from below as Smith unfurled the banner, lost his grip, and plunged to his death.

Inside the capitol are two special features, both near the governor's office. First, the 1,000-pound bronze badger just outside once adorned the deck of the USS *Wisconsin*, but the navy removed it from the ship because they worried about shrapnel if the metalic rodent were hit by a shell. The second oddity is a doorknob in the office—it has traveled to outer space! The knob took a trip aboard the Space Shuttle *Discovery* with astronaut Daniel Brandenstein in 1985.

But as remarkable as this all is, not everyone has been impressed with the capitol or its knickknacks. Architect Frank Lloyd Wright once said, "You can't put that much stone in one pile without creating some dignity and majesty. Anyway, there it is, and we should make the best of it." Coming from Wright, it was a stellar endorsement.

State Capitol Building, Washington and Wisconsin Aves., Madison, WI 53702
Phone: (608) 266-0382
Hours: Tours, Monday–Saturday 9 AM, 10 AM, 11 AM, 1 PM, 2 PM, 3 PM; Sunday 1 PM, 2 PM, 3 PM, and 4 PM
Cost: Free
Website: www.wisconsin.gov/state/core/wisconsin_state_capitol_tour.html
Directions: On the isthmus between Lake Monona and Lake Mendota.

SUBURBS

DeForest

The Partying Pink Elephant

The partying pink elephant stares through a pair of black, horn-rimmed glasses as you pass by on Interstate 90/94. It obviously had too much of a good time the night before, because its head hangs down and its bloodshot eyes are almost closed. This pink pachyderm has stood guard over Andy's gas station for years, and you have to wonder whether it just might be time to retire from life in the shadow of a college town. It's not as easy to bounce back from a kegger these days.

Andy's Pink Elephant, 4995 County Rd. V, DeForest, WI 53532

Phone: (608) 846-2595

Hours: Always visible

Cost: Free

Directions: Off I-90/94 at Exit 126 north, head west.

Ooooooh, my aching head!

Maple Bluff
Fighting Bob's Place

Wisconsin senator Robert "Fighting Bob" La Follette certainly earned his pugilistic nickname—if there was a moneyed interest or a corrupt politician, he took them on, often to the consternation of his Republican Party.

La Follette was born three miles north of Stoughton on June 14, 1885. He was elected to three terms in the US House of Representatives, starting in 1884, served as Wisconsin governor from 1901 to 1906, and then senator from 1905 to 1925 (serving simultaneously as senator and governor in 1905). La Follette was part of the "insurgent" wing of the GOP, foes of railroads and other trusts that backed the party's powerful machine. He even exposed the state's sitting Republican senator, Philetus Sawyer, for trying to bribe him to fix a legal case. As governor he launched the "Wisconsin Idea" wherein University of Wisconsin faculty developed progressive reforms that the state legislature implemented. These included open primaries, workmen's compensation, transparent government, the minimum wage, women's suffrage, and more.

While senator, Fighting Bob began publishing *La Follette's Weekly* (today known as *The Progressive*), a forum for progressives and home to muckraking journalists. He opposed the United States' entry into World War I, the draft, and the 1917 Espionage Act, and after the war was over, the League of Nations. He helped launch the Teapot Dome investigation and in 1924 formed the Progressive Party to challenge Calvin Coolidge and the Republicans in the general election. The Progressives' platform included union protection, an end to child labor, government control of utilities and railroads, and cheap farm credit. La Follette also called for a restoration of civil liberties lost in the war, the end of American military intervention in Central and South America, and a national plebiscite any time the United States wanted to declare war. He won 17 percent of the popular vote, and carried Wisconsin.

La Follette died on June 18, 1925, and was succeeded by his son, Robert M. La Follette Jr., who would represent the state until being defeated in the 1946 Republican primary by Joseph McCarthy. Fighting Bob's Maple Bluff home is today a National Historic Landmark, though it is not open to the public. Each year Madison hosts Fighting Bob Fest (www.fightingbobfest.org) for progressives across the nation.

La Follette House, 733 Lakewood Blvd., Maple Bluff, WI 53704
Private phone
Hours: Always visible; view from street
Cost: Free
Website: www.wisconsinhistory.org/hp/register/viewSummary.asp?refnum=66000020
Directions: Take Lakewood Blvd. west/north from Sherman Ave., five blocks ahead.

Middleton
National Mustard Museum

If you thought mustard was divided into two types, yellow for sports fans and brown for people who ride in limousines, you're sadly underinformed. In actuality, there are more than 5,400 different types of mustard (and more each day!), and many of them are at the National Mustard Museum, collected by proprietor Barry Levenson and his wife Patti.

Start your visit by screening the movie *Mustardpiece Theatre*, narrated by James Earl Jones. Mustards from all 50 United States and 70 countries fill the shelves around you. After a quick survey you'll realize *anything* can be made into mustard; they've got mustards made of cranberries and apples, beer and BBQ sauce, prickly pears and chocolate fudge. Try spreading that on corned beef. The Levensons also sell products that appeal to customers' goofier sensibilities, like diplomas and T-shirts from Poupon U, or the Naughty, Bawdy, Raunchy, X-Rated, Titillating, Should-Be-Wrapped-in-Brown-Paper, Oughta-Be-Banned, We-Should-Be-Ashamed-But-We're-Not Gift Box which includes such prurient delights as Smack My Ass and Call Me Sally habañero hot sauce, Sweet Mama Jannisse's Sticky Love Sauce, Blow Hard Hot Mustard, and Dave's Burning Nuts.

Levenson, a former Wisconsin assistant attorney general, opened his establishment two decades ago in nearby Mt. Horeb, but recently moved to new digs in Middleton. The museum publishes a newsletter, *The Proper Mustard*, hosts an annual haiku contest and family reunion for people named Mustard, and is an archival repository for all things mustardy, from cartoon strips that mention the condiment to the history of Colonel Mustard of the board game Clue.

7477 Hubbard Ave., Middleton, WI 53562

Phone: (800) 438-6878 or (608) 831-2222

Hours: Daily 10 AM–5 PM

Cost: Free

Website: www.mustardmuseum.com

Directions: Two blocks south of University Ave., two blocks east of Rte. 12.

MADISON

➡ Both Vitamin A and Vitamin B were discovered in Madison.

Sun Prairie
Birthplace of Georgia O'Keeffe

It's only natural that people associate Georgia O'Keeffe with where she spent the bulk of her creative life, in the Southwest, but it is not her homeland. She was born in Wisconsin near Sun Prairie on November 15, 1887, the first daughter of Irish immigrants.

Georgia Totto O'Keeffe was the second child of seven, and by all accounts her mother's least favorite child. She was a tomboy, and to get back at her sisters for their favorable standing would bring the girls to the barn and dare them to stick their hands into the cows' mouths in order to feel their tongues. They did, and Georgia got in trouble. She was also punished by her grandmother for getting dirty while acting on her taste for fresh-tilled soil.

Georgia attended the nearby Town Hall School, and was a loner. It took a local art teacher, Sarah Mann, to draw out her creative side. Mann privately instructed the O'Keeffe girls at her home at 173 North Street in Sun Prairie. It must have worked; in addition to Georgia, two of her sisters also became artists.

The O'Keeffe family moved to Virginia in 1904, but left Georgia with an aunt in Madison who lived on Spaight Street. O'Keeffe attended Sacred Heart Academy (219 Columbus St., (608) 837-8508, www.sacredhearts. k12.wi.us) where she received her most valuable lesson at the hands of her art teacher, Sister Angelique. Georgia had drawn a baby's hand from a plaster cast given to her by the instructor. Though the rendering was accurate, the nun barked at her for drawing it too small. From that point on, O'Keeffe would think and paint large. Very large.

Birthplace, Town Hall Rd. and County Rd. T, Sun Prairie, WI 53590
No phone
Hours: Always visible
Cost: Free
Website: www.sun-prairie-wisconsin.com/georgia-okeeffe-sun-prairie.html
Directions: County Rd. N south from Sun Prairie, then east on County Rd. T to Town Hall Rd.

Jimmy the Groundhog

Pennsylvania's Punxsutawney Phil gets most of the national media attention on Groundhog Day, but for the record, Jimmy the Groundhog is more accurate on the coming of spring. So adamant are the citizens of Sun Prairie they asked the US Congress to decide which was the nation's official weathercasting rodent. Congress passed a nonbinding resolution giving equal credence to both towns' claims. Some "resolution"—thanks for nothing, gang!

In fairness to Punxsutawney, that community has been celebrating Groundhog Day since 1887. Sun Prairie has only been at it since 1949. That was the year local boosters decided that, because the holiday celebrates the *sun* coming out on the *prairie*, they were the "Groundhog Capital of the World." And Jimmy hasn't let them down. Statistically speaking, he's 79 percent accurate, while Phil has a lousy 17 percent record. For many years, Jimmy was a stuffed groundhog, which made his prognostication even more amazing.

Sun Prairie celebrates February 2 each year with a Community Breakfast at the Round Table Restaurant (1611 N. Bristol St., (608) 825-9195, www.kofcroundtable.com). If you can't make it in February, there's a statue of Jimmy in Cannery Square (Main and Church Sts.). The town also has a Groundhog Club, but you can only become a member if you were born on February 2. Those born on other February days are designated mere Woodchucks. Write the Chamber of Commerce and they'll send you a Groundhog Birth Certificate. It is not valid at US border crossings unless you look like a rodent.

Sun Prairie Chamber of Commerce, 109 E. Main St., Sun Prairie, WI 53590
Phone: (608) 837-4547
Sun Prairie Historical Society, 115 E. Main St., Sun Prairie, WI 53590
Phone: (608) 837-2915
Hours: February 2 every year
Cost: Free
Website: www.groundhogcentral.com
Directions: Start Groundhog Day at the Round Table Restaurant.

Waunakee
Bavarian Goat Tower

Who doesn't love goats? Except, of course, trolls.

Well, Larry Endres was no troll. In 1982 the then-president of Endres Manufacturing erected a small village for a family of goats—more accurately called a tribe, a trip, a drove, or a flock—adjacent to his company's new operations at the south end of Waunakee. There's a chapel and a clock and a whirligig with a guy in lederhosen, but the real eye-catcher is a screw-shaped tower that the goats just love to climb. Up the goats go, and then back down, over and over again. Who wouldn't enjoy such an idyllic life? Except, of course, a troll.

Endres Manufacturing, Kappel Park, 802 S. Century Ave., Waunakee, WI 53597

Phone: (608) 849-4143

Hours: June–August, daylight hours

Cost: Free

Website: www.endresmfg.com/goats.htm

Directions: Eight blocks south of Main St. (Rte. 19/113) on County Rd. Q (Century Ave.).

What goes up must come down.

Eastern Wisconsin

*T*hink of the East Coast of the United States and images of light-houses, overpriced restaurants, and lots of folks reminding one another they're the upper crust come to mind. Wisconsin's East Coast of is no different. The Badger blue bloods at Kohler's American Club would like you to think they're a better cut of meat, but Kohler is still just a suburb of the Sheboygan bratwurst metroplex. And after a long weekend of antiquing in oh-so-quaint Door County, you still have the shock of driving through gritty Green Bay to get back home.

Don't misunderstand: Wisconsin's East Coast is a wonderful place, not because of its myriad bed-and-breakfasts or picturesque beaches, but *in spite of* them. This region gave the world the ham-burger and the ice cream sundae. And don't forget toilet paper. Green Bay is the Toilet Paper Capital of the World! For that reason alone, this corner of the state deserves our undying gratitude and respect.

There is no Toilet Paper Monument in Green Bay, yet, but there is a Hamburger Monument in Seymour and the World's First Sundae Counter in Two Rivers. So cheer up and gas up. Eastern Wisconsin is calling to you.

Baileys Harbor
Bird Park House

For years Albert Zahn was a no-nonsense farmer, an immigrant from Ger-many and devout Lutheran. But once he retired, he decided to let loose. In 1924, he built a home for his twilight years on the north side of Baileys Harbor, a two-story structure made from tiers of poured concrete. Around it he created raised cement fishponds, and on top of them he mounted wooden carvings of birds, running dogs, angels, and more birds—so many that people started calling him the Birdman of Door County.

Zahn kept it up for more than two decades before he died in 1953. In the 1960s, the home began to deteriorate and burglars walked off with some of his smaller carvings. The rest were sold or ended up in museums. But then the new owners embarked on a detailed restoration. Though you can't enter, the outside is still impressive, and you can see the outlines of four soaring birds atop the second story.

8223 State Hwy. 57, Bailey Harbor, WI 54202

Private phone

Hours: Daylight hours

Cost: Free

Directions: Just north of town on Rte. 57.

Service by Train

How great for the servers at P. C. Junction! Unlike at most restaurants, they don't have to learn how to balance six loaded plates on their arms because a miniature train delivers all the food. All they have to do is take the orders and the choo-choo does the rest. If the central counter is full during your visit, the kitchen looks like Grand Central Station with hot dogs and BBQ sandwiches departing every minute.

Hotdog on a flatbed. Photo by author, courtesy of P. C. Junction

The restaurant continues its train theme both indoors and out. If you want to work off that pizza or A-Train Cheeseburger, the restaurant also has a number of adult-size pedal cars out back that you can use to cruise around through the trees, even after you've had a beer or two.

P. C. Junction, 7898 County Rd. A, Bailey Harbor, WI 54202

Phone: (920) 839-2048

Hours: Spring–summer, 10 AM–dark

Cost: Meals, $7–12

Website: www.pcjunctiondoorcounty.com

Directions: Southwest of town, at the intersection of County Rds. A and E.

Champion
Mary the Fire Extinguisher

On August 15, 1858, the Virgin Mary appeared to a 28-year-old immigrant from Belgium, Adele Brice, and proclaimed, "I am the Queen of Heaven who prays for the conversion of sinners." Impressed by his daughter's connections, Brice's father built a shrine on the site in Robinsonville (later renamed Champion), where Mary appeared. But that apparently wasn't enough to please the Madonna, because the building was soon threatened with destruction.

In 1871 a massive forest fire raced toward the chapel. Quick-thinking parishioners dropped their buckets, grabbed a statue of the Virgin, and began parading her around and around the shrine. Suddenly, the skies opened and a freak rainstorm doused the blaze, saving the shrine from certain immolation. Or so the story goes.

Brice felt her vision had been vindicated and further devoted herself to Mary . . . but not entirely. Sister Adele was a nun in appearance only, for though she wore a nun's habit in her later years, she never took religious vows. Brice died July 5, 1896, at the age of 66, but the shrine survives.

Shrine of Our Lady of Good Help, 4047 Chapel Dr., Champion, WI 54229

Phone: (920) 866-2571

Hours: Daily 6:30 AM–7 PM

Cost: Free

Website: www.shrineofourladyofgoodhelp.com

Directions: On County Rd. K, just east of the intersection with County Rd. P.

Dundee
Benson's Hide-A-Way

Strange things have been happening over Long Lake—just ask the patrons wearing the aluminum foil hats at Benson's Hide-A-Way. They don't wear the foil hats every day, just during the annual UFO Daze celebration thrown by owner Bill Benson. During the bar's 2002 festivities, lights were spotted over the lake by the inebriated revelers. Proof! Or at least 80 proof . . .

Bill Benson, owner of the Hide-A-Way, has been a true believer for some time, and even does some UFO research on the side. Since the late 1940s, saucers and lights have been spotted over the lake, and in recent years crop circles have appeared in the area. When Benson opened this establishment, he thought it made sense to decorate with an alien theme. The place is always fun, but come in the summer for the big green gathering.

N4241 Boy Scout Rd., Dundee, WI 53010
Phone: (920) 533-8219
Hours: Tuesday–Friday 11 AM–11 PM, Saturday–Sunday 10 AM–midnight
Cost: Free
Website: www.ufowisconsin.com/bensons/index.html
Directions: Three miles north of Dundee on Rte. 67, on the north shore of Long Lake.

Green Bay
Bay Beach Amusement Park

Sure, you can go to some Six Flags–style theme park where they start shaking you down for cash just to use their parking lot, or you can come to Bay Beach—free to park and enter, and no ride is more than a dollar. Most of the rides are for kiddies: miniature helicopters and race cars and airplanes with machine guns, a steal at 25¢. But they also have a few adult attractions, like bumper cars, a Scrambler, and a Tilt-a-Whirl. However, no visit to Bay Beach would be complete without a ride on the Zippin Pippin.

In roller-coaster lingo, a Zippin Pippin is a coaster built by John A. Miller of National Amusement Devices. He designed rides in Chicago, Pittsburgh, and Salt Lake City, but his 1912 Libertyland coaster in Memphis was the most famous. Elvis claimed that the Zippin Pippin was his favorite, and even rented out the park for himself and 10 friends on August 8, 1977. And a week later, he was dead. What a way to go.

Libertyland went bankrupt in 2005, but the visionary folks of Green Bay purchased the rights to the Zippin Pippin's design and historic items and brought them to the shores of Lake Michigan. The Bay Beach coaster tracks are brand new, though have been laid out in the same configuration as Libertyland. The renovated cars are original, so you could be sitting in the same seat the King sat in.

1313 Bay Beach Rd., Green Bay, WI 54302

Phone: (920) 448-3365

Hours: June–August, daily 10 AM–9 PM; May and September, Saturday–Sunday 10 AM–6 PM

Cost: Zippin Pippin $1; rides, 25¢–50¢

Website: www.ci.green-bay.wi.us/BayBeach/index.html and www.zippinpippin.org

Directions: Take the Webster Ave./Shore Dr. Exit from I-43, then north one block.

The Day Before the Day the Music Died

Every Buddy Holly, Ritchie Valens, and Big Bopper fan knows that they performed their last concert at the Surf Ballroom in Clear Lake, Iowa, before crashing into a cornfield shortly after midnight on February 3, 1959. But why were they in that Beechcraft Bonanza in the first place? Wisconsin is the answer.

Several days earlier, Holly and the other Winter Dance Party performers were on their way from Duluth, Minnesota, to Appleton, Wisconsin, when their bus broke down on Route 51 one mile north of Pine Lake. Before being rescued, they had to burn newspapers in the aisle to keep from freezing to death. The Iron County sheriff found them just in time and then brought them back to Hurley. The group was forced to cancel the Appleton gig and take a train directly to Green Bay.

On February 1, they played the Riverside Ballroom. Tickets were $1.25, or 90¢ if you bought them in advance. About 2,200 people attended. After the show the performers were put on another bus, this one headed for Clear Lake, Iowa. The heater conked out along the 357-mile trip, and Holly decided he'd rather fly than take another bus ride. And you know how that turned out.

Three metal silhouettes have been erected outside the Riverside Ballroom to commemorate Holly's, Valens's, and the Bopper's second-to-last concert.

Riverside Ballroom, 1560 Main St., Green Bay, WI 54302

Phone: (920) 432-5518

Hours: Always visible; check website for shows

Cost: Free

Website: www.riversideballroom.com

Directions: On Rte. 151 (Main St.) at Newhall St., one block west of Elizabeth St.

Green Bay Packers Hall of Fame

The Green Bay Packers are America's most lovable professional football team, if for no other reason than their blue-collar backing. They are the nation's only publicly-owned professional team; Curly Lambeau bought the franchise in 1919 for $50, but it went public in 1923. Eighty years later the Packers are still in Green Bay, the smallest US city with an NFL team.

Packers fans are nothing if not rabidly irrational about their team. Just read the brochure for this place: "Buckingham Palace has nothing on the Green Bay Packers Hall of Fame!" Good point. And would you ever catch Queen Elizabeth II, who's a fan of hats, sporting a foam cheesehead wedge? Not likely!

The Green Bay Packers Hall of Fame has everything a Packers fan could want to see—even the ghost of Vince Lombardi, who some believe haunts the place. Lockers from the 17 greatest Packers line the walls, each crammed with personal artifacts, like Paul Hornung's of copy of a Marlboro cigarette ad. Next, touch a section of the Louisiana Superdome goalpost given to Damon's Clubhouse in 1997. "Test Your Skills" in the amusement arcade where you can hone your football moves with pinball and pachinko, or stick the kiddies in a giant motorized Green Bay helmet. Visit the Titletown's Finest Room, bursting with fan-contributed green-and-gold doodads. Finally, see replicas of all the Vince Lombardi Trophies the team has won.

855 Lombardi Ave., PO Box 28287, Green Bay, WI 54324-0287

Phone: (888) 4GB-PACK or (920) 569-7512

Hours: Monday–Saturday 9 AM–6 PM, Sunday 10 AM–5 PM; game days, 8 AM–7 PM

Cost: Adults $10, seniors (62+) $8, teens (12–17) $8, kids (6–11) $5

Website: http://packershalloffame.com/

Directions: At the intersection of Lombardi and Oneida Sts.

MORE FOR PACKERS FANS

What's a Packers fanatic to do in the off season? Surely there must be places to visit and things to see to get through those difficult months.

Vince Lombardi's Steakhouse

333 W. College Ave., Appleton, (920) 380-9390, www.vincelombardisteakhouse.com

Though not in Titletown, this restaurant/museum is worth the drive for any true Packers fan. The place is filled with more than 400 "artifacts," including Lombardi's sunglasses, several hand-drawn football plays, and his draft card. And the menu? Mostly steak.

Green Bay Packers Receiver

Titletown Brewing Company, 200 Dousman St., Green Bay, (920) 437-BEER, www.titletownbrewing.com

Outside this brewery stands a 22-foot-tall receiver (no. 88) making an *awesome* catch. It once stood in front of the Packers Hall of Fame, but was later moved here. The brewery itself is housed in Green Bay's historic Chicago & North Western Railroad station.

Jumbo Lombardi Trophy

Stadium View Bar & Grille, 1963 Holmgren Way, Green Bay, (920) 884-3159, www.thestadiumview.com

The Lombardi Trophy—called the Super Bowl trophy by Vikings fans, not that they've ever seen one—is big, but not as big as the glimmering replica in front of the Stadium View Bar & Grille. It's as tall as the building!

Jumbo Football

Resch Center, 1901 S. Oneida St., Green Bay, (920) 405-1177, www.reschcenter.com

A giant football holds up a portico at this arena, located just across the street from Lambeau Field.

Green Bay Packers House

224 Sutliff Ave., Rhinelander

If you have to paint your house anyway, why not use the colors of your favorite football team? With bright yellow siding and green trim, not to mention Packers logos and player cutouts, this Rhinelander abode demonstrates the true commitment of a super fan.

Unique Cafe

1100 Wisconsin Ave., Boscobel, (608) 375-4465

The main floor of this unique café, the Unique Cafe, is filled with all manner of tchotchkes, but the basement dining room is reserved for *all things* Packers, and we do mean all things, from autographed items to the tackiest souvenir.

Big Packers Helmet

The Linebacker, 527 N. Tenth St., Manitowoc, (920) 682-6510

The green-and-gold awning at this neighborhood sports bar is the first clue about where its loyalties lie. The giant Packers helmet hanging above it is the other.

Home of the Cheesehead

Foamation Outlet Store, 3775 S. Packard Ave., St. Francis, (800) FOAM-FUN, www.cheesehead.com

Yes, other companies have jumped on the Cheesehead bandwagon, but Foamation gets credit for the Cheesehead hat, first injected to a wedge-shaped mold in 1987. Now they have cheese-colored top hats, crowns, baseball caps, fezzes, fedoras, sombreros, and dunce caps, all for sale at their outlet store and, basically, every cheese and gift emporium throughout the state.

Packer Mobile

8729 E. Little Ln., Clinton, (608) 676-5166, http://packermobile.com/

Though it's not for sale and only taken out on special occasions, like a 1,300-mile road trip through the snow to Superbowl XLV, this 1978 Cadillac Eldorado has been painted green and gold and its roof has been removed to make room for a large surfboard. The steer horns on the hood might confuse Cowboys fans, but then they're not a bright bunch.

The Toilet Bowl and Parade

All over town, Hustisford, (920) 349-3814, www.hustisfordfire.com

Unfortunately, not every Packers season leads to a playoff berth. If your beloved team ends up in the division toilet, you can use the time you would have spent watching the playoffs watching the Toilet Bowl and Parade, perhaps releasing some of that postseason anger. Since 1967, the Hustisford volunteer fire department has organized a January 1 fundraiser called the Toilet Bowl. After a king and queen are crowned, they're made to ride in a toilet-shaped float through town at noon. Bystanders are encouraged to chuck rolls of Charmin at them, though beware, the king and queen can return the fire. After the parade, dozens of crazy idiots play a game of no-pads, no-helmets tackle football in the Village Ballpark, snow or shine.

I Like Ike's Railroad Car

One would assume the Eisenhower staff train housed at the National Railroad Museum has been modified since its days as Ike's rolling war office in England. After all, chugging around in a train emblazoned "Dwight D. Eisenhower" is no way to elude the enemy . . . unless you're on another train. But these are the original, armor-plated London & North Eastern Railroad cars and engine used from 1944 to 1945 by the Supreme Allied Commander. Plaques point to Ike's quarters and his personal shower, but fail to detail which toilet he used, though there seem to be plenty to choose from.

Ike's train is one of 75 different railroad cars and engines housed at this museum. You'll see Union Pacific's impressive Big Boy, the largest steam locomotive in the world at 600 tons and 133 feet long. Check out General Motor's futuristic Aerotrain, a prototype built with Greyhound bus parts. Meet Lydia, Josephine, Winona, and Miss Bud, not staff members but passenger cars. The museum also houses a 72-by-33-feet, HO-scale model railroad being built by local hobbyists. Stop by on Thursday night and you'll see the builders in action.

Included in the price of admission is a ride around a 1.5-mile loop pulled by a diesel engine. The tracks pass over creaking trestles, through repair and restoration areas, and stop briefly at a Hobo Camp. There you'll see "signatures" for Boxcar Betty and Bozo the Clown chalked on boxcars, and learn the difference between a hobo, a tramp, and a bum. (Hint: Be most offended when somebody calls you a bum.)

National Railroad Museum, 2285 S. Broadway, Green Bay, WI 54304

Phone: (920) 437-7623

Hours: January–March, Tuesday–Saturday 9 AM–5 PM, Sunday 11 AM–5 PM; April–December, Monday–Saturday 9 AM–5 PM, Sunday 11 AM–5 PM; train rides, May–September 10 AM, 11:30 AM, 1 PM, 2:30 PM, and 4 PM

Cost: Museum, adults $9, seniors (62+) $8, kids (3–12) $6.50; museum and train ride, adults $11, seniors (62+) $10, kids (3–12) $8.50

Website: www.nationalrrmuseum.org

Directions: Ashland Ave. Exit from Rte. 172, north to Cormier Rd., east to Broadway to the Fox River.

McDonald's Arch

Gather 'round, children, and I'll tell you a story of a long, long time ago, a time when phones were attached to buildings with wires, when TV had only four channels, and when McDonald's had *only one arch*.

Don't believe me? Stop on by this west-side McDonald's and see for yourself. Built in 1959, its sign sports a single yellow arch topped by Speedee, the burger-headed mascot that was bumped off by Ronald McDonald in 1963. This Green Bay store was franchise number 91, but its signage is the nation's second oldest, bested only by the first franchise erected in Downey, California. It is not only listed as a Green Bay Historic Site, but can be found on the National Register of Historic Places.

1587 Shawano Ave., Green Bay, WI 54303

Phone: (920) 494-4472

Hours: Always visible

Cost: Free

Directions: Just west of Military Ave. on Rte. 29 (Shawano Ave.).

Kewaunee
Custer's Last Stand

George Armstrong Custer may have made his last stand many years ago, but it lives on forever in this small Wisconsin museum. Two local clock makers spent more than six years carving an intricate depiction of the general's final moments in bas relief. Why did it take so long? The sculpture measures 30 square feet!

That's not all you'll find in this converted town jail. They've also got a letter written by George Washington, life-size statues of Father Marquette arriving in Kewaunee in 1674, and an exhibit on the USS *Pueblo*, built and launched in Kewaunee in 1944, today in the service of the North Korean Navy (not by choice).

Kewaunee Historical Jail Museum, 613 Dodge St., Kewaunee, WI 54216

Phone: (920) 388-3858

Hours: June–August, daily noon–4 PM; September–May, by appointment

Cost: Adults $2, kids free

Website: www.cityofkewaunee.org/jail%20museum.htm

Directions: On the courthouse square at Vliet St.

World's Largest Grandfather Clock

In general it is not a good idea to leave a fine piece of furniture outside in the rain and snow. But the 35-foot grandfather clock that towers over the now-closed Top of the Hill Shop is an exception. Unlike the other handcrafted timepieces made at Svoboda Industries, this one was built to withstand the harsh Wisconsin elements.

The World's Largest Grandfather Clock was constructed in 1976 for the nation's Bicentennial, yet it was not painted red, white, or blue. It's a respectable brown. The clock kept accurate time for many years, but eventually broke down. Now the gift shop has gone out of business, there's little chance that the timepiece will be repaired. Svoboda is a woodworking operation, not a clock shop.

If you think that's big, you should see Grandpa.

624 N. Main St., Kewaunee, WI 54216
Phone: (800) 678-9996 or (920) 388-2691
Hours: Always visible
Cost: Free
Website: www.mastersofwood.com
Directions: At the north end of town, north of Rte. 29.

Kohler
The Great Wall of China

Why travel all the way to one of the last surviving Communist countries on earth to see the Great Wall when you can see it here, just down the road from Joseph McCarthy's hometown? True, this wall isn't quite the size of the original—you can't see it from outer space—but then the original isn't made of sinks, tubs, urinals, and toilets. No, *this* Great Wall is built using the latest designs from Kohler, first in bathroom fixtures.

The Kohler Design Center is a fixer-upper's fantasyland, and you can pick up more than a few decorating ideas that won't take 300,000 laborers and 150 years to finish. If you're a true bathophile, come at 8:30 AM on a weekday and take the three-hour plant tour. Then visit the Design Center's basement museum dedicated to discontinued models, many of which you can still see in economy hotels across the nation.

Kohler Design Center, 101 Upper Rd., Kohler, WI 53044
Phone: (920) 457-3699
Hours: Monday–Friday 8 AM–5 PM, Saturday–Sunday 10 AM–4 PM
Cost: Free
Website: www.us.kohler.com/designkb/designcenter/designcenter.jsp
Directions: On County Rd. Y, just south of the Rte. 23 intersection.

Malone
Big Al Capone's of Pipe

Lots of old roadhouses in Wisconsin claim to have been stopovers for gangster Al Capone. He would head north whenever things got hot in Chicago. But this establishment goes one step further with its name and decorating scheme. Inside you'll find a bullet-ridden 1948 Chevy on the dance floor, machine guns and violin cases on the walls, and a statue of Big Al chomping on a cigar up in one corner. It then goes one step too far in naming items on its menu after famous mobsters: Bugs Moran Chicken Parmesan, the Frankie Frotto Haystack Salad, the Alcatraz BBQ Pulled Pork Sandwich, the Enforcer Patty Melt, the Prohibition Meatball Sandwich, and, for the little ones, a cheeseburger called the Hitman Jr.

N10302 Hwy. 151, Malone, WI 53074

Phone: (920) 795-4140

Hours: Sunday–Thursday 11 AM–9 PM, Friday–Saturday 11 AM–10 PM

Cost: Free; meals, $4–10

Website: www.caponesofpipe.com

Directions: At the intersection of Rte. 151 and County Rd. W.

Manitowoc
Sputnik IV Crash Site

Contrary to the popular song, what goes up does not always come down. But *Sputnik IV* did, on Manitowoc. It was launched on May 14, 1960, and stayed in orbit for five days. But when Soviet controllers fired its reentry rockets, the fuel tank exploded and the spacecraft spun out of control. Remarkably, what was left of the orbiter stayed aloft for two more years. Then, sometime during the night of September 4–5, 1962, the satellite reentered the Earth's atmosphere, broke into pieces, and burned up. Mostly.

A 20-pound chunk that didn't was found in the middle of a city street by police officers Marvin Bauch and Ronald Rusboldt. They ignored it at first, but returned when they heard reports that a satellite had crashed. At first the bowl-shaped hunk of metal was too hot to touch, but after it cooled they brought it into the station. (A few other small pieces were found on a nearby church roof.)

The fragment was later turned over to NASA, which made two replicas for the town. One can be seen at the Visitors Information Center (I-43, exit 149), the other at the Rahr-West Art Museum, which coincidentally stands just only feet from where the piece was found. That historic spot is marked with a brass ring in the middle of the street; watch for traffic before you go out to take a picture. If that isn't enough, come to Manitowoc in September for its annual Sputnikfest.

Rahr-West Art Museum, 610 N. Eighth St., Manitowoc, WI 54220

Phone: (920) 686-3090

Hours: Plaque, always visible; museum, Monday–Friday 10 AM–4 PM, Saturday–Sunday 11 AM–4 PM

Cost: Free; museum, adults $4, kids $2

Website: www.rahrwestartmuseum.org, www.sputnikfest.com

Directions: On Rte. 10 (Eighth St.) at Park St.

Chicken Little was right.

USS *Cobia*

The Manitowoc Shipbuilding Company played an important role in World War II submarine production, so it seems appropriate that a maritime museum be located in town. Unfortunately the museum's crown jewel, the USS *Cobia* was not built in Manitowoc but in Groton, Connecticut, by the Electric Boat Company. None of the 28 subs constructed here between 1942 and 1945 were afloat or available when this museum was established.

The USS *Cobia* has been restored to its WWII appearance since its decommissioning. The sub is 311 feet long and needed 80 crew to operate it. It was credited with sinking 13 Japanese ships between 1944 and 1945, mostly merchant marine vessels.

It is hard to appreciate just how cramped submarine service must have been until you stand belowdecks with a 20-person tour and imagine four times the number of crew aboard. Also consider that the men showered once a week (unless they were mess workers), and it makes for a tight, stinky stew. Two stairways have been installed to get tours in and out, but that's all the help you'll get maneuvering from stem to stern. A good portion of the 45-minute tour is watching and helping the senior guests bend their way through the bulkheads.

In addition to the USS *Cobia*, the museum contains an impressive collection of maritime artifacts that will impress gobs and landlubbers alike. Diving suits and miniature ship models, stuffed seagulls and a re-created fishing dock. All that's missing are the Village People.

Manitowoc Maritime Museum, 75 Maritime Dr., Manitowoc, WI 54220

Phone: (866) 724-2356 or (920) 684-0218

Hours: July–August, daily 9 AM–6 PM; March–June and September–October, daily 9 AM–5 PM; November–March, Monday–Friday 10 AM–4 PM, Saturday–Sunday 9 AM–4 PM

Cost: Adults $12, kids (6–15) $10

Website: www.wisconsinmaritime.org

Directions: Downtown, east of the Eighth St. bridge, north of the river.

Peshtigo
Fire Museum and Mass Graves

On the same day as the Great Chicago Fire, October 8, 1871, a much more deadly fire raged through the town of Peshtigo, Wisconsin. Some would say they were inviting it. The town and its mills were cutting 5.7 million board feet of lumber each year and loggers left a quarter again more on the forest floor as waste slash, the perfect fuel for fires. And worse, Peshtigo's town streets were "paved" with sawdust to suppress the flying dust.

The inferno began as a forest fire and engulfed the town before anyone had a chance to escape. Reports say the "fire cyclone" consumed the town in 10 minutes and burned out within an hour. Residents dashed for the Peshtigo River but many didn't make it. Some people hid in brick buildings, others in ditches and open fields. All who tried died. Those lucky enough to make it to the river suffered hypothermia or were drowned by livestock swimming to safety.

The heat of the fire was so intense that not even the bones of many of the 800-plus victims (some say as many as 1,200 or even 2,400) remained. For those who weren't already cremated, coffins were built at the Peshtigo Harbor sawmill several miles away. It had miraculously escaped the fire. In all, 2,400 square miles of northern Wisconsin were incinerated on both sides of Green Bay.

In some of the more bizarre tales to come out of the event, a man hanged himself on a well's chain rather than be burned alive. The tabernacle from the Catholic Church was found free of charring by the side of the river, where the priest had abandoned it during the hellish inferno. And a looter found in the village after the fire was sentenced to death in a quickly convened court but escaped execution because neither a rope nor a tall tree could be found.

About 350 victims were buried in a mass grave on the edge of town. A church built next to the cemetery just after the firehouses a museum dedicated to the disaster. In it you'll see a few of the relics that survived the tragedy, all charred or melted, and a map showing the fire's deadly path. The cemetery contains a monument to the victims.

Peshtigo Fire Museum, 400 Oconto Ave., Peshtigo, WI 54157

Phone: (715) 582-3244

Hours: May–October 8, daily 10 AM–4 PM

Cost: Free

Website: www.peshtigofire.info

Directions: One block north of Rte. 41, two blocks west of the river.

Poland
UFO Landing Port

Bob Tohak is a welder by trade and a sky-watcher by choice. He builds picnic tables and custom trailers, bridges and park benches, but his greatest achievement to date is a 40-foot tall UFO Landing Port just off his driveway.

Bob has big plans for the port. This former grain silo opens at the top like a flower, making a flat docking surface for a flying saucer. Aliens are protected from falling off with old metal headboards. A large fluorescent sign invites Martians and reminds Earthly visitors "We are not alone." It also asks, "If the Government has no knowledge of Aliens, why do they

Ready for a close encounter.

make it illegal for U.S. Citizens to have any contact with Extraterrestrials or their vehicles, per Title 14, Sec. 1211, implemented on July 16, 1969?"

Well, Bob doesn't give a damn about Title 14, Sec. 1211—he's even installed blue landing lights to guide the spacecraft to his backyard and an interior spiral staircase to help them reach the ground. You're welcome to view his future historic site from the road, and if he's around he just might show you his submarine (a work in progress) or two pet miniature horses. The animals have their own TV in the barn and love soap operas.

Tohak & Son Welding, 4885 Rte. 29 E, Green Bay, WI 54311

Phone: (920) 863-2541

Hours: Always visible; view from road

Cost: Free

Directions: One block west of County Rd. T on Rte. 29, in unincorporated Poland.

THEY LANDED OFF COURSE . . .

Some people build UFO landing pads, others build UFOs. Enterprising welders have created a **flying saucer and rocket** that can be seen at the intersection of Route 10 and County Road OOO west of Osseo, a **driveable UFO** that is usually parked three miles north of Belleville on County Road D (www.belleville-wi .com/ufoday/), and several **alien spacecraft** in the parking lot of Sailer's Meat Market in Elmwood (600 W. Winter Ave., (715) 639-2191, www.sailersmeats.com). The **large rocket** at Route 29 and County Road CC in Spring Valley does not honor Martians, but the US Apollo program. It's 16 feet tall and weighs almost two tons.

Port Washington
Pebble House

No, this isn't the prehistoric home of the Flintstones . . . that's in Bedrock. This place is younger, built in 1848 by Elizabeth and Henry Dodge with pebbles they collected along the Lake Michigan shoreline. Its walls are 20 inches thick and covered with stones battered smooth and round by waves over thousands of years.

The Pebble House was moved to its downtown location in 1985 where it reopened as the city's Chamber of Commerce and Tourist Information Center. You can gather information on local attractions and events during regular business hours.

Port Washington Chamber of Commerce and Tourist Information Center, 126 Grand Ave., Port
 Washington, WI 53074
Phone: (262) 284-0900
Hours: Always visible
Cost: Free
Website: www.visitportwashington.com/chamber/
Directions: On Rte. 33, just before it turns north and becomes Rte. 32.

Scott
Jean Nicolet Reaches "China"

Sometimes you have to put the best face on a botched job. Jean Nicolet had been sent in 1634 by the governor of New France, Samuel de Champlain, to discover a Northwest Passage to China. Rumors that an Asiatic tribe (actually, the Winnebagos) lived across a large body of water (Lake Michigan) got Nicolet packing . . . an embroidered Oriental robe.

When Nicolet, assisted by a group of Hurons, waded ashore near Scott he was wearing an elaborate damask costume festooned with birds and flowers. If that didn't impress the locals, the two pistols he fired into the air sure did. He then brought out gifts and that whole gown-and-gun show was forgiven.

Though Nicolet came up a bit short of China, whatever he did must have made a positive impression because the Winnebagos were loyal to the French for another 150 years. A statue of Nicolet wearing his full-length robe stands near the point where it all happened. The statue was crafted in 1939 by Sidney Bedore. It was recently moved from Red Banks to this new location.

Wequiock Falls County Park, 3426 Bay Settlement Rd., Scott, WI 54311
No phone
Hours: Always visible
Cost: Free
Directions: At Van Lanen Rd. and Rte. 57.

Seymour

Birthplace of the Hamburger

Just ask anyone in Seymour: the hamburger was invented here by "Hamburger Charlie" Nagreen. Charlie first flattened his poor-selling, hard-to-eat fried meatballs into patties and placed them on bread for customers at

Charlie Nagreen, visionary.

the 1885 Seymour-Outagamie County Fair. They were a big hit, and Charlie sold them every year until he died in 1951.

The town has never forgotten Charlie's contribution to gastronomy. Every first Saturday in August, Seymour celebrates Burger Fest with a Bun Run, pickle- and burger-tossing contests, a catsup slide, stale-bun stacking for the kids, and a Hamburger Parade, among other events. In 1989 they capped off the celebration by frying the World's Largest Hamburger. It had a 5,445-pound patty and fed 13,000 hungry celebrants. Unfortunately, Seymour was bested by a Montana town a decade later, but then it reclaimed the *Guinness World Records* title in 2001 with an 8,266-pound patty. The grill used to cook the patty still stands on Depot Street.

Seymour once had a small Hamburger Hall of Fame in a storefront on Main Street, crammed with hamburger-themed items, but it has closed its doors. Also dead are plans for an even larger museum, an $8 million hamburger-shaped structure that was to attract burger lovers from around the world. The main building was to be a four-story cheeseburger with a pile of fries as an entryway and a green, dill-pickle-shaped outdoor pavilion. So sad.

But all is not lost. In 2005, the town did erect a 12-foot tall statue of Charlie, burger in hand.

Depot and Main Sts., Seymour, WI 54165
Phone: (920) 833-6053
Hours: Always visible
Cost: Free
Website: www.homeofthehamburger.org
Directions: Just east of Rte. 55 (Main St.) on Depot St.

WOULD YOU LIKE JUMBO FRIES WITH THAT?

When a 6.75-inch french fry was discovered in June 2003 by workers at the Culver's in Wisconsin Rapids (2711 Eighth St. S., (715) 421-1112), they knew they had something special. Declared the **World's Largest French Fry**, it was put up for auction on eBay and sold for $202.50.

Sheboygan
Art in the Bathrooms

It's not often a museum asks you to pee on a work of art, at least outside of New York, but the Kohler Arts Center is not a typical art museum. You're not allowed to relieve yourself on any work you choose, just those commissioned for the bathrooms. Originally two artists, Ann Agee and Matt Nolan, designed the tile and fixtures in two men's rooms, including the urinals, inside and out. Four other artists have since added to the museum's privy collection, both men's and women's.

The remainder of the museum has expanded greatly in recent years. You can see art on loan from the Kohler Foundation's restorations around the state, most of which are included in this travel guide—Grandview, the Painted Forest, Fred Smith's Wisconsin Concrete Park, the Paul and Matilda Wegner Grotto, and the Prairie Moon Sculpture Gardens. They also have the jewel-encrusted living room of Loy Allen Bowlin, the original Rhinestone Cowboy, as well as his suits, clothes that would put Elvis to shame.

John Michael Kohler Arts Center, 608 New York Ave., Sheboygan, WI 53081

Phone: (920) 458-6144

Hours: Monday, Wednesday, Friday 10 AM–5 PM; Tuesday, Thursday 10 AM–8 PM;
Saturday–Sunday 10 AM–4 PM

Cost: Free, donations encouraged

Website: www.jmkac.org

Directions: Two blocks north of Pennsylvania Ave., four blocks east of the river, between Sixth and Seventh Sts.

SHEBOYGAN

➡ Sheboygan claims to be the "Wurst Capital of the World," as in bratwurst. Each August they celebrate Bratwurst Days (http://brat-days.com/).

➡ Jackie Mason was born in Sheboygan on June 9, 1936.

➡ Sheboygan began flouridating its drinking water in 1946, the first Wisconsin town to do so.

➡ "Sheboygan" is Potawatomi for "rumbling waters."

James A. Tellen Jr.'s Woodland Sculpture Garden

There are certain weekend warriors that put us all to shame. Thinking his lakeside cabin needed a little sprucing up, in 1942 James Tellen began creating statues to keep him company. Over the next decade and a half he built 14 sculptural tableaus that he placed around his property. Most are strangely realistic and in an evening light look almost human, or elfin.

The entrance to the property is guarded by a Native American chief with a large headdress and a woman with a baby on her back. The chief is straddling a concrete log fence on which the woman is leaning. Around the grounds are more full-size statues with varying subjects: Abraham Lincoln splitting rails, elves playing musical instruments, a man on horseback greeting a woman at a well, the Virgin of Fatima, a goat retreating from a skunk, and more.

Frozen forever. Photo by author, courtesy of the Kohler Foundation

The site fell into disrepair after Tellen's death but was restored a decade ago by the Kohler Foundation.

5634 Evergreen Dr., Sheboygan, WI 53081

Phone: (920) 458-6144

Hours: Always visible; view from road or by appointment

Cost: Free

Website: www.kohlerfoundation.org/tellen.html

Directions: One block south of the intersection of Evergreen Dr. and Indian Mound Rd. on the south side of Sheboygan.

Stories on the Wall

Viking raiders! Marauding Cossacks! Keystone Cops! They're all here . . . in cement . . . in Sheboygan. No, none of these individuals have had anything to do with the history of the Bratwurst Capital of the World, but they were still interesting to Dan Erbstoesser, the retired policeman who created them on a wall adjoining his house. He also rendered his own version of *American Gothic*, a log cabin in the woods, and a metal worker pouring molten steel from a cauldron.

Erbstoesser began the bas-relief panels in the 1950s and finished his final piece in 1976. Working slowly over two decades, he completed only four panels along the exterior sidewalk. Each piece was carefully painted and are all still in relatively good condition. Erbstoesser has since passed away, but his creation remains, though it has started to crumble a bit. See it while you still can.

548 Whitcomb Ave., Sheboygan, WI 53081

Private phone

Hours: Private residence; view from sidewalk

Cost: Free

Directions: One block north of Wilson Ave. at the corner of Lake Shore Dr. and Whitcomb Ave.

SHIOCTON

→ Each September Shiocton hosts the **World Championship Cabbage Chuck and Sauerkraut Wrestling Festival** (www.cabbagechuck.com).

John Schnieder? Shelley Fabares?! Gilbert Gottfreid?!!? Photo by author, courtesy of Back Door Bakery

Sister Bay
Coffee Cup Museum

For years, Spike O'Dell interviewed celebrities and politicians, authors and sports figures, has-beens and gonna-bes, on WGN radio in Chicago. Most of these guests were offered coffee or water, and when they were done they were asked to autograph their paper cups. Thousands of shows later, O'Dell had a pretty impressive collection, and today it's on display at this Door County bakery/art gallery.

Who's here? Rod Blagojevich, Tommy Chong, Marie Osmond, Tony Randall, Michael Flatley, Vince Van Patten, Jane Fonda, Henry Kissinger, George Wendt, astronaut Jim Lovell, Jimmie "J. J." Walker, Dusty Baker,

John McCain, Gunther Williams, and Jean Vander Pyl, voice of Wilma Flintstone. And that's just for beginners—there are *hundreds*.

Back Door Studio, Door County Bakery, 10048 Hwy. 57, Sister Bay, WI 54234

Phone: (888) 39-BREAD or (920) 854-1137

Hours: Tuesday–Saturday 8 AM–5 PM; Sunday 8 AM–4 PM; Monday 8 AM–3 PM;

Cost: Free

Website: www.doorcountybakery.com

Directions: Just north of County Rd. Q.

Al Johnson puts his goat on a pedestal. Photo by Annice Tatken

Goats on the Roof

The thought of eating a meal while a goat struts around above your head might sound unappetizing, but only if you've never been to Sister Bay. At Al Johnson's the food may be Swedish, but the building is all Norwegian.

Apparently in Norway a good place to raise goats is on your sod-covered roof. The roof is peaked and steeper than you'd expect, but these goats are mountain lovers. Currently three different breeds live up there, and have since 1973. Don't worry that they might fall off; they're taken down at night, in the winter, and during storms or high winds.

Al Johnson's specializes in breakfasts and meatballs. They open at 7 AM, which makes it a good first stop on a road trip. Still, it's a popular eatery, and people often line up for lingonberries before the doors even open.

Al Johnson's Swedish Restaurant & Butik, 10698 Bay Shore Dr., PO Box 257, Sister Bay, WI 54234

Phone: (920) 854-2626

Hours: Daily 7 AM–8 PM

Cost: Breakfast, $7–10; lunch, $7–12; dinner, $9–15

Website: www.aljohnsons.com

Directions: Two blocks north of County Rd. ZZ (Maple Dr.) on Rte. 24 (Bay Shore Dr.).

Two Rivers
Birthplace of the Sundae

Two Rivers claims to be the "Coolest Spot in Wisconsin," not because it is particularly frigid or hip, but because the ice cream sundae was invented here. A local man named George Hallauer requested the as-yet-unknown treat on July 8, 1881, at an ice cream parlor run by Edward Berner. Hallauer wanted chocolate sauce poured over his ice cream; until that moment, chocolate sauce was only used in ice cream sodas. The new 5¢-dish was a hit, but for a while it was only sold on Sundays. Soon people, led by a vocal 10-year-old girl visiting George Giffy's parlor in nearby Manitowoc, were demanding it every day of the week. The name sundae was born. (Some say that they got their name after an order for glass ice cream boats was misspelled.)

Ed Berner's original parlor stood at 1404 Fifteenth Street, but since 1979 the site has been a parking lot. You can visit another parlor named in his honor a few blocks away on the ground floor of historic Washington House, home of the Two Rivers Historical Society. Their specialty is a "Washington House Sundae." It's red, white, and (ugh!) blue.

After you've enjoyed your treat, head upstairs to Washington House's second-floor ballroom, sometimes called the Sistine Chapel of the Midwest.

There you'll find murals painted in 1906 by a traveling artist in exchange for room and board. The murals depict bucolic scenes of Wisconsin life and Lake Michigan. Like the Sistine Chapel, these masterpieces were also recently restored.

Ed Berner's Ice Cream Parlor, 1622 Jefferson St., Two Rivers, WI 54241

Phone: (888) 857-3529 or (920) 793-2490

Hours: November–April, daily 9 AM–5 PM; May–October, daily 9 AM–9 PM

Cost: Single scoop $1, sundae $2.50

Website: www.tworiverseconomicdevelopment.org/tourism/visitor.htm

Directions: At the corner of Jefferson and 17th Sts.

IF YOU SCREAM FOR ICE CREAM

Maybe sundaes aren't your thing. Maybe you prefer your ice cream straight up, on top of a cone. Well, the roadside gods have some fiberglass shrines for you, too.

Big Pink Cone

Hawkeye Dairy, 118 S. Fourth St., Abbotsford, (715) 223-6358, www.hawkeyedairy.com

The giant strawberry ice cream cone outside the Hawkeye Dairy not only has its own stone pedestal, but it is propped up on two enormous fiberglass cheese wedges.

Medium Pink Cone

Roseville Mini-Golf & Shops, 1151 Main St., Wild Rose, (920) 622-5090

A less-giant strawberry ice cream cone outside the putt-putt golf course southwest of Wild Rose doesn't need cheese to hold it up—it's a flat-based sugar cone.

DQ Soft-Serve (with Swirl)

Dairy Queen, 290 S. Main St., Clintonville, (715) 823-3644,
www.dairyqueen.com

The eight-foot-tall vanilla cone at the Clintonville DQ was obviously made by one of its employees—it has the telltale swirl on its tip.

Ice Cream Slide

Schopf's Dairy View, 5169 County Rd. I, Sturgeon Bay, (920) 743-9779,
www.dairyview.com

This two-scoop cone is tall and big enough for children to crawl through the top scoop onto a slide stretching down to the ground.

Hamilton Wood Type and Printing Museum

The Hamilton Wood Type and Printing Museum is the first and only wood type museum in the world. Imagine being transported to your high school shop class, without the bitter shop teacher barking at you as you struggled to build a crummy spice rack, and you'll get a feel for this place.

In the days before modern printing, every newspaper, book, and poster was printed using movable type. While metal type was fine for small print, it was hardly cost effective for large jobs. Posters and headlines needed something lighter and cheaper. That's where wood type was used.

At the museum, you'll follow the entire process by which a simple log is transformed into a banner headline that might read, TITANIC SINKS! Cross-sections were cut and dried, trimmed and planed, sanded and polished, and eventually checked for minute deviations and blemishes. Only a small fraction of the slabs ever made it to the point where they were etched into a giant *Z* or *G* using reproduction machines perfected by James E. Hamilton, the man for whom this museum is named.

At the turn of the century, Hamilton's company manufactured more wood type than any other company in the United States. A half million original "masters" cover the walls and fill the cabinets here in all sizes and fonts. Today, at the museum, printing artists-in-residence use these masters to make elaborate compositions.

And if none of this sounds thrilling to you, might they interest you in the world's first residential gas-powered clothes dryer, circa 1938? It's also on display here. Now we're talking excitement!

1315 17th St., Two Rivers, WI 54241

Phone: (920) 794-6272

Hours: May–October, Tuesday–Saturday 9 AM–5 PM, Sunday 1–5 PM; November–April, Monday–Friday 9 AM–5 PM

Cost: Free; donations encouraged

Website: http://woodtype.org/

Directions: Across the street from the Historical Society at 17th and Jefferson Sts., one block east of Rte. 42.

Point Beach Energy Center

Who ever thought a nuclear power plant could be so much fun? Three Mile Island? Fukushima? Oh, don't be a wet blanket! Drive on up to the reactor and hang a right and you'll find a nifty science museum. Larry the Lightbulb is your tour guide through the Point Beach Energy Center, or will be until he burns out on the job.

At Point Beach you'll see dozens of interactive exhibits, like a sparking eight-foot Jacob's Ladder. It discharges a bolt when you trip an electric eye. View a cutaway model of the main building, which looks as if its top was blown off on in a Chernobyl-style mishap. Take a trip "inside containment" to see nuclear fuel rods being pulled out of the core. Yellow danger lights flash in this mock containment chamber that is so realistic you'll wish you'd pulled on your lead-lined undies.

Best of all is the Energy Detectives' Clubhouse. Four rooms appear to have been modeled on Pee Wee's Playhouse, only in this clubhouse somebody's wasting energy . . . LOTS of it! Who left the water running in the sink? Who installed a 100-watt bulb in the table lamp when a 60-watt would have worked just fine? The goal is to get little visitors to spot the culprits and, one would assume, turn them in to the Energy Police.

6400 Nuclear Rd., Two Rivers, WI 54241

Phone: (800) 880-8463 or (920) 755-6400

Hours: Tuesday–Saturday, daily 9:30 AM–4 PM

Cost: Free

Directions: Ten miles north of town on Rte. 42, turn east on Nuclear Rd.

Washington Island
Colossal Coffee Pot

Before there was tall, grande, and venti, there was *gifurlegur*, Icelandic for enormous, the size of the coffee pot that greets you as you step off the Washington Island ferry. The toll ware pot was built in 1941 and for years served as a tourist information center called the Velkommen Coffee Pot. (Though this island is the nation's largest Icelandic settlement, the builders went with the Norwegian spelling.)

Oddly enough, though Americans have gone cuckoo over coffee, this percolator has gone idle—no information for *you*. And though Starbucks has outlets on every other block in America, for some reason they're not on Washington Island. Yet.

County Rd. W, Washington Island, WI 54246

No phone

Hours: Always visible

Cost: Free

Website: www.washingtonisland.com

Directions: Just past the ferry dock in Detroit Harbor.

Waubeka
First Flag Day

Bernard J. Cigrand helped write the Pledge of Allegiance, but that wasn't enough for this zealous patriot. The young Waubeka schoolteacher, just 19 years old, wanted a day set aside each year to celebrate Old Glory, so on June 14, 1885, he propped up a 38-star US flag on the desk of his Stony Hill School and declared the event Flag Day.

Why June 14? In 1777, the Second Continental Congress adopted the Stars and Stripes as the nation's official flag. The US Congress had previously declared a Flag Day on the banner's 100th anniversary, but one day

First in flag fests.

a century wasn't enough for Cigrand. His solitary schoolhouse gesture was a start to a tireless campaign to enact a national holiday. Thirty-one years later, on June 14, 1916, president Woodrow Wilson signed the law that made the holiday official.

N5595 County Rd. I, PO Box 55, Waubeka, WI 53021

Phone: (262) 692-9111

Hours: Always visible

Cost: Free

Website: www.nationalflagday.com

Directions: On County Rd. I, just south of the Rte. 84 (Kohler–Fredonia Rd.) intersection.

West Bend
Lizard Mounds

What's a zoomorph? Glad you asked: it's a physical representation, in this case a dirt effigy mound, of an animal used by Native American cultures during spirit-calling ceremonies. Ninety percent of all North American effigy mounds are found in Wisconsin and can take the shape of birds, buffalo, mythical creatures, panthers, bears, and more. Often times a body is found ceremoniously interred within a mound.

Most of the 31 zoomorphs at Lizard Mounds State Park take the shape of (surprise!) a lizard. Others are conical. The mounds are no more than 3 or 4 feet high, but they can be as long as 300 feet and would be hard to identify from ground level were it not for the interpretive signs.

Because they are so large and best viewed from above, some have suggested a connection between effigy mounds and prehistoric visits from UFOs. Maybe they're landing markers for flying saucers! But think about it: if early humans were descendants of aliens, why did they build their effigies out of common, everyday dirt? Why not something flashier, like fiberglass? That would really impress their Martian relatives!

Lizard Mounds State Park, 2121 County Rd. A, PO Box 1986, West Bend, WI 53095

Phone: (262) 335-4445

Hours: April–November, daily 6 AM–9 PM

Cost: Free

Website: www.co.washington.wi.us/departments.iml?Detail=417

Directions: Rte. 144 northeast four miles to County Rd. A, turn east and follow the signs.

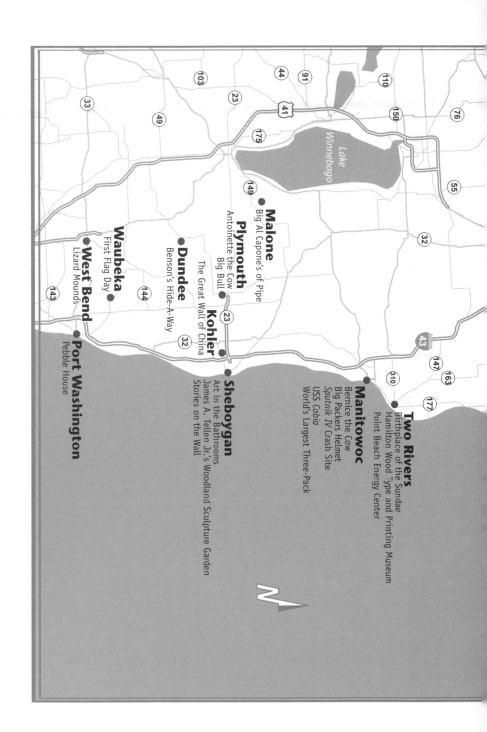

Malone
Big Al Capone's of Pipe

Plymouth
Antoinette the Cow
Big Bull

Kohler
The Great Wall of China

Dundee
Benson's Hide-A-Way

Waubeka
First Flag Day

West Bend
Lizard Mounds

Port Washington
Pebble House

Sheboygan
Art in the Bathrooms
James A. Tellen Jr.'s Woodland Sculpture Garden
Stories on the Wall

Manitowoc
Bernice the Cow
Big Packers Helmet
Sputnik IV Crash Site
USS *Cobia*
World's Largest Three-Pack

Two Rivers
Birthplace of the Sundae
Hamilton Wood Type and Printing Museum
Point Beach Energy Center

Lake
Winnebago

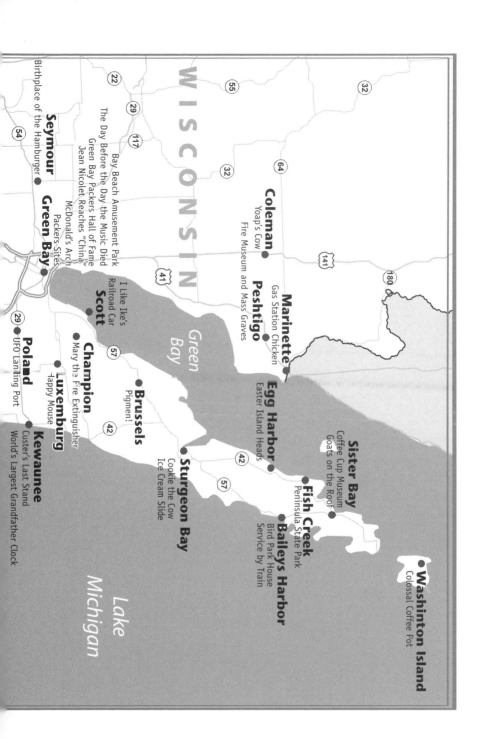

WISCONSIN

22
55
32
29
117
32
64

Seymour
Birthplace of the Hamburger

54

Green Bay

Bay Beach Amusement Park
The Day Before the Day the Music Died
Green Bay Packers Hall of Fame
Jean Nicolet Reaches "China"
McDonald's Arch
Packers Sites

29

Coleman
Yoap's Cow

Peshtigo
Fire Museum and Mass Graves

Marinette
Gas Station Chicken

141

180

I Like Ike's
Railroad Car

Scott

41

Green Bay

57

Champion
Mary the Fire Extinguisher

Poland
UFO Landing Port

29

Luxemburg
Happy Mouse

Brussels
Pigmen!

42

Egg Harbor
Easter Island Heads

42

Sister Bay
Coffee Cup Museum
Goats on the Roof

Fish Creek
Peninsula State Park

57

Baileys Harbor
Bird Park House
Service by Train

Kewaunee
Custer's Last Stand
World's Largest Grandfather Clock

Sturgeon Bay
Cookie the Cow
Ice Cream Slide

Lake Michigan

● **Washinton Island**
Colossal Coffee Pot

Milwaukee

Milwaukee is a fun town, and it's much more international than its beer-and-brat reputation would suggest. It has been home to such widely divergent personalities as Golda Meir and Liberace, is the birthplace of the typewriter and the Harley-Davidson motorcycle, and has public monuments to duck squatters and Joan of Arc. Milwaukee has played a role in two failed assassination attempts on presidential candidates, is the hometown of Laverne and Shirley, and has plenty of downtown parking. What more could citizens want?

Though Milwaukee is the most cosmopolitan city in Wisconsin, there's still a bit of the small-town sucker in its blood. Take, for example, a panic which swept the city in 1862. Somehow a rumor got started that Confederate troops were advancing on the city from the north. Geography-challenged "refugees" streamed in from nearby Waukesha and the Milwaukee Chamber of Commerce urged citizens to save themselves by fleeing in boats across Lake Michigan. Luckily, before the flotilla was launched, somebody consulted a map and questioned the reports from the war front.

Couldn't happen today? What about the strange case of Gary Medrow? This Milwaukee resident was arrested for calling local women at random and asking them to pick up family members and carry them around the house. Before he was apprehended he had convinced dozens of women to submit to his unique request.

Maybe beer is a factor in all this strange behavior. Milwaukee isn't called Brew Town for nothing. Still, there is plenty of weirdness in Milwaukee that can't be traced back to alcohol. This chapter offers many examples for your amusement.

Milwaukee
Cass Park

The Cheshire cat–like archway at the entrance to Milwaukee's Cass Park is the first of many psychedelic sculptures found around this playground. Kids can climb on the back of a floppy-eared sea serpent or stand on the feet of an Izy Bird. What's an Izy Bird? "Whether you are 2 or 102, short or tall, big or small, black, yellow, white, red, or brown, the Izy Bird reminds us we are all special." Kind of like Mister Rogers, but with feathers instead of sneakers and a cardigan.

Where's Alice?

The whole park has an *Alice in Wonderland* feel to it. Even the lamp posts have been transformed into big-billed birds. No doubt this will be a gathering place for boomers and their young grandchildren, where the kids will have to convince their grandparents they are not experiencing some sort of acid flashback.

Cass Park, Pleasant and Cass Sts., Milwaukee, WI 53202
No phone
Hours: Daily 8 AM–10 PM
Cost: Free
Directions: North from downtown on Cass St. to Pleasant St., one block east of Van Buren St.

Coffee Cup Pizza

You've heard of flying saucers. Here's your chance to see one . . . and a cup, too. The enormous cup and saucer wedged into the façade of this northwest-side pizzeria was originally installed to advertise the Milwaukee Coffee Company, but Starbucks did a number on them (and most coffee shops), and they eventually folded.

Today the place sells meatball and sausage sandwiches, lasagna, and some of the best thin-crust pizza around. Coffee? Not so much. But thankfully, Caradara's has left the cup and saucer in place, even if it confuses a few customers.

Caradara Club Pizza Restaurant, 5010 W. Vliet St., Milwaukee, WI 53208

Phone: (414) 476-7700

Hours: Always visible; restaurant, Tuesday–Thursday 4–10 PM, Friday–Saturday 4 PM–midnight, Sunday 4–9 PM

Cost: Free; pizza, $9–18

Website: http://caradaroclubpizza.com

Directions: Four blocks west of Rte. 41.

Fonzie's Statue and Arnold's Drive-In

When *Happy Days* premiered in 1974, the general plot was supposed to revolve around the Cunninghams, a 1950s Milwaukee family, and Richie Cunningham's friends, who hung out at Arnold's Drive-In. But then a minor character, Arthur Fonzarelli—the Fonz, or Fonzie—showed up and took the show in an entirely different direction. The lovable former hoodlum soon moved into the apartment over the Cunningham's garage and became entangled in increasingly preposterous scenarios, like jumping a shark on water skis and battling an alien named Mork with his thumbs.

There is no 565 North Clinton Drive—the Cunningham's address—in Milwaukee. The home seen in the opening credits is actually located in Los Angeles. There is a Clinton *Avenue* on the city's north side, but it's not a residential street—it runs through a business district. Arnold's Drive-In was based on the Milky Way Drive-In in suburban Glendale, which has since been torn down and replaced with a Kopp's Frozen Custard—a fairly close approximation to Arnold's, at least as far as its menu goes.

In 2008 a bronze statue of the Fonz was unveiled along the Riverwalk by Henry Winkler. The artwork was sponsored by TV Land and local *Happy Days* lovers. Penny Marshall and Cindy Williams attended the ceremony. Hopefully they'll get their own Milwaukee monument soon.

Fonzie Statue, Riverwalk, 117 E. Wells St., Milwaukee, WI 53202

No phone

Hours: Always visible

Cost: Free

Directions: South of Wells St. on the east side of the river.

Kopp's Frozen Custard, 5373 N. Port Washington Rd., Glendale, WI 53217

Phone: (414) 961-3288

Hours: Daily 10:30 AM–11 PM

Cost: Free; fountain, $2.25–7; meals, $4–7

Website: www.kopps.com

Directions: Two blocks south of Silver Spring Dr., one block east of I-43.

Sit on it!

Gertie the Duck Statue

How easily people get distracted! Though World War II was not yet over, a bird captured the nation's attention in the spring of 1945. Workers were rebuilding the Wisconsin Avenue Bridge downtown when they discovered a mother duck protecting a nest of eggs on one of the pilings. Rather than move the mallard, crews halted construction until the eggs hatched. City residents named her Gertie, and when her six ducklings burst forward they were christened Pee Wee, Dee Dee, Freddie, Mille, Rosie, and Black Bill.

By the time they were old enough to move on, these babies were paddling through a world free from Hitler. Their fresh beginning seemed to announce the nation's postwar determination. A statue of Gertie and her children was erected on the Wisconsin Avenue Bridge in 1997 by the architecture firm of Eppstein Uhen. The original statue had only Gertie and two of her offspring, but two more ducklings were added to the bridge in 1999.

Wisconsin Avenue Bridge, Wisconsin Ave. and Water St., Milwaukee, WI 53205

No phone

Hours: Always visible

Cost: Free

Directions: On the north side of the Wisconsin Ave. bridge, between Water St. and Plankinton Ave.

Golda Meir's Childhood Homes

Golda Meir's family, the Mabowehzes, fled pogroms in the village of Pinsk near Kiev in 1906 and ended up in Milwaukee. "Goldie" was just eight years old, but already showed personality traits that would lead her to be the Israel's first female prime minister. She was enrolled at the Fourth Street Elementary School (now Golda Meir Elementary School, 1555 N. Martin Luther King Dr., (414) 212-3200, www2.milwaukee.k12.wi.us/meir/) speaking almost no English, but graduated as valedictorian a few years later. And though her parents objected to her continued education, in 1912 she enrolled at North Division High School (1011 W. Center St., (414) 267-4900, www2.milwaukee.k12.wi.us/north/) without their blessing. It didn't last long.

When her mother arranged a marriage between Goldie (just 14 at the time) and the 30-something "Mr. Goodstein," Goldie hopped a train to Denver where her sister was living in a tuberculosis sanitarium. Two years later she returned with a husband of her own choosing. The Meirs lived in Milwaukee until 1921.

First Milwaukee home, 623 W. Walnut St., Milwaukee, WI 53212
No phone
Hours: Torn down
Cost: Free
Directions: Approximately where Walnut St. crosses I-43.

Second Milwaukee home, 750 N. Tenth St., Milwaukee, WI 53233
No phone
Hours: Torn down
Cost: Free
Directions: At Tenth St. and Juneau Ave.

Holler House

Most bowling alleys serve alcohol, but how many *bars* have their own lanes? Holler House is for the most part a tavern; the bowling alley seems like an afterthought. But it wasn't. On the contrary, it was a visionary idea, as these are the oldest bowling lanes in the United States!

Holler House only has two working lanes in the basement, and the pins are set by hand. The approach to the lanes isn't a direct shot, so you must line up crooked to the pins. If you've had a few brews, you'll probably be more crooked than you need to be. Despite this irregularity, Holler House has hosted its own competitive leagues.

Bowlers from around the country once came to Milwaukee to visit the Bowling Hall of Fame in suburban Greendale, but that museum has since moved to St. Louis. Second on the visitors' lists were always a couple of beers and games at Holler House. Both Traci Lords and Larry the Cable Guy have made the pilgrimage.

2242 Lincoln Ave., Milwaukee, WI 53215
Phone: (414) 647-9284
Hours: Tuesday–Sunday 4 PM–late; call ahead to see if lanes will be open, often closed in summer
Cost: $1.75 per line
Directions: At 21st St. and Lincoln Ave., on the north side of Forest Home Cemetery.

Koz's Mini Bowl

Though it has twice as many lanes as Holler House, the bowling at Koz's Mini Bowl is downsized in every respect. The lanes are 16 feet long, rather than the standard 60 feet, and the pins are 9 inches tall, not 15 inches. The balls, which have no holes, are about the size of grapefruit. It all makes for some high-scoring games, even with the beer.

Minibowl establishments used to be all over Milwaukee, but today this place, owned and maintained by Duwayne Kosakoski, is the only one that remains. You're welcome any night, but Thursday night is league play; you'll have to be content just watching.

2078 S. Seventh St., Milwaukee, WI 53204

Phone: (414) 383-0560

Hours: Daily 6 PM–2 AM

Cost: $3 per line plus $1 pinsetter tip

Website: www.kozsminibowl.com

Directions: Two blocks west of I-94, just north of Becher St.

Ladybug Club Ladybugs

Despite their cute appearance, ladybugs can be quite a nuisance—once they've invaded they make themselves at home. Example? One of Milwaukee's downtown buildings has been overrun, and they're still here. The six-story office tower east of the Riverwalk once housed a nightclub called the Ladybug Club. It was outfitted with three oversize insects on the front facade, and though the club is no longer in business, the beasties remain.

Still here.

Ladybug Building, 618 N. Water St.,
  Milwaukee, WI 53202

No phone

Hours: Always visible

Cost: Free

Directions: Between Michigan St. and Wisconsin Ave., east of the Riverwalk.

Laverne & Shirley

On TV, Laverne De Fazio and Shirley Feeney lived in a basement apartment on Knapp Avenue, and while there isn't a Knapp Avenue in Milwaukee, there is a Knapp *Street*. Close enough. Knapp Street runs through a gentrified neighborhood just north of downtown and these days would no doubt price out brewery workers and Lenny and Squiggy types. If living here was one of their dreams, they wouldn't have been able to make them all come true.

Filmed on a Hollywood backlot between 1976 and 1983, the closest Laverne or Shirley got to Brew Town was in the opening credits, in which there are quick shots of a few local landmarks such as Milwaukee City Hall and the Pabst Brewing Company. The latter stood in for Shotz Brewery as the pair's blue-collar employer; today it is being developed as a business and retail complex.

Basement Apartment, 730 Knapp St., Milwaukee, WI 53202

No phone

Hours: No basement apartment exists here

Cost: Free

Directions: Between Cass and Van Buren Sts., two block north of State St.

Milwaukee City Hall, 200 E. Wells St., Milwaukee, WI 53202

Phone: (414) 286-CITY

Hours: Always visible

Cost: Free

Website: http://city.milwaukee.gov

Directions: Two blocks east of the river, downtown, at Kilbourn Ave.

Pabst Brewing Company (today The Brewery), 915 W. Juneau Ave., Milwaukee, WI 53233

Phone: (414) 274-2880

Hours: Always visible

Cost: Free

Website: www.thebrewerymke.com

Directions: Just east of I-43, just south of Rte. 145.

Mitchell Gallery of Flight

Knowing that most airline passengers don't want to think about the *Hindenburg* before boarding, the Mitchell Gallery of Flight chose a different airship to put on display: the *Graf Zeppelin II*. Trouble is, the 22-foot replica hanging in the museum looks almost identical to the *Hindenburg*—the two were sister ships. Several artifacts from the doomed sibling displayed nearby don't help.

But the Mitchell Gallery isn't just about flaming gasbags. They've got tributes to Wisconsin aviators, including Richard Bong (page 42), Richard Lovell, and (of course) William "Billy" Mitchell. There are also dozens of propellers, aircraft models, airport models, and a tribute to the Space Shuttle *Columbia*. It's a great way to spend those two hours before departure.

General Mitchell International Airport, 5300 S. Howell Ave., Milwaukee, WI 53207

Phone: (414) 747-4503

Hours: Whenever the airport is open

Cost: Free

Website: www.mitchellgallery.org

Directions: In the airport's Concourse C.

WELCOME TO CLEVELAND

If you've ever flown into **General Mitchell International Airport,** be sure to scan the roofs of the neighborhood's houses. Back in 1978, local smartass Mark Gubbin painted "Welcome to Cleveland" on the flat-top roof of his building at 2893 South Delaware Avenue. Pilots and passengers coming in from the north have been confused ever since.

The Muskrat Group and the Typewriters

It is hard to imagine there ever was a time when museums didn't have dioramas. But today's standard practice is a relatively new innovation. In 1890, schoolteacher Peter Engelmann suggested placing stuffed animal specimens in a natural setting and talked to taxidermist Carl Akeley about it. The result was the world's first diorama, the Muskrat Group, still on display on the first floor of the Milwaukee Public Museum. Akeley went on to be known as the "Father of Modern Taxidermy" because he invented many of the processes and methods still in use today.

The Milwaukee Public Museum is a wonderfully weird institution, mixing art, culture, and natural history. Within a display you'll see stuffed creatures, human mannequins in ethnic garb, indigenous art, and excavated artifacts—something for everyone! It also has the world's largest dinosaur skull, a Costa Rican rainforest, and a full-size re-creation of the old streets of Milwaukee.

The museum is also home to the world's largest collection of typewriters, more than 700, though they're not all on display. The typewriter was invented in Milwaukee between 1867 and 1873 at 318 West State Street by Christopher Latham Sholes, aided by Carlos Glidden, Samuel Soulé, Henry Roby, and Mathias Schwalback. The first prototype was introduced in 1869 and established what is today known as the "universal keypad"—QWERTY. Sholes' efforts were funded by James Densmore, who eventually bought out Sholes's shares and made millions with the Remington & Sons Company. Despite his enormous contribution to society, Shoales died poor in 1890, and was buried in Milwaukee's Forest Home Cemetery (2405 W. Forest Home Ave., (414) 645-2632, www.foresthomecemetery.com).

Milwaukee Public Museum, 800 W. Wells St., Milwaukee, WI 53233

Phone: (888) 700-9069 or (414) 278-2702

Hours: Daily 9 AM–5 PM

Cost: Adults $14, seniors (60+) $11, teens (13–17) $11, kids (3–12) $10

Website: www.mpm.edu

Directions: One block north of Wisconsin Ave. on Eighth St.

The Safe House

The entrance to this establishment seems harmless enough: a sign on Front Street reads INTERNATIONAL EXPORTS, LTD. SINCE 1868. But these are no ordinary exporters, for they deal in human cargo, moving spies and secret agents through Brew Town.

"Do you know the password?" That's what they'll ask you when you enter a room with what looks like an old office switchboard. If you're not the clandestine type you can achieve entry by demonstrating covert behavior, just ask your operator what to do. If you pass the test, a secret passageway opens and you're allowed into the Safe House, Milwaukee's not-so-secret watering hole for top-secret agents.

The Safe House's specialty drink menu gets you started: the Incognito, the Silencer, the Goldeneye, the Under Cover Girl, and the Spy's Demise. After 6 PM you can order the Ultimate Martini which is shaken, not stirred, as it passes through the restaurant in a glowing pneumatic tube. The club is filled with clandestine devices like a CIA phone booth with 99 background sounds to disguise your true location, two Mata Hari outposts where female guests can spy on their dates, a chunk of the Berlin Wall, and a machine gun donated by John Wayne. When you're ready to leave, ask your server to point out the Secret Escape Route.

Not what it seems.

779 N. Front St., Milwaukee, WI 53202

Phone: (414) 271-2007

Hours: Bar, daily 11:30 AM–2 AM; dining, Sunday–Wednesday until 9 PM, Friday–Saturday until 10 PM

Cost: Meals, $9–30

Website: www.safe-house.com

Directions: One block north of Wisconsin Ave., on the east side of the river.

DON'T ATTRACT SUSPICION!

To be a truly successful double-naught spy, you have to avoid situations that might blow your cover. Getting arrested is a good way to be exposed, so if you're snooping in Wisconsin, here are a few laws to obey:

➡ Only one person may occupy a bathtub at a time.

➡ You cannot kiss on a train.

➡ It is illegal to sing in a bar.

- ➡ To walk on train tracks, you must either be a railroad worker or a reporter.

- ➡ You may not cut a woman's hair.

- ➡ It is illegal to marry your first cousin, unless the bride is older than 55.

- ➡ By law, every working lumberjack is entitled to a bathtub.

St. Joan of Arc Stone

Need a place to cool down on a warm day? Try touching the magic Joan of Arc stone in the Medieval Chapel at Marquette. According to legend, a statue of the Virgin Mary rested on this rock where Joan of Arc prayed just before being burned at the stake. As she rose from her meditation she kissed the rock. Ever since, this stone has been cooler than the stones around it. Don't believe it? Feel it for yourself!

The stone was not part of the original chapel, officially known as the Chapelle de St. Martin de Sayssuel. The chapel once stood 12 miles south of Lyons, France, in Chasse and was built in the 15th century. The French had abandoned it and Gertrude Gavin, daughter of a US railroad baron, bought and moved it to her family's Jericho estate on Long Island in 1927. The special stone was bricked into the wall to the left of the altar while the chapel was being rebuilt.

In 1965 the chapel was moved a second time when it was donated to Marquette University. Unless services are going on, doubting Thomases are welcome to test the stone, still cold after all these years. First, place your hand on the vertical (nonholy) stone; then touch the holy base.

Marquette University, 14th St. and Wisconsin Ave., Milwaukee, WI 53233

Phone: (414) 288-6873

Hours: Monday–Saturday 10 AM–4 PM, Sunday noon–4 PM; services at 10 AM and noon when school is in session

Cost: Free

Website: www.marquette.edu/chapel/index.shtml

Directions: Behind the Memorial Library on Wisconsin St.

A man's home is his not always his castle.

Ship Ahoy!

Edmund B. Gusdorf long dreamed of the seafaring life—cruising the high seas, sailing to exotic ports of call, swordfighting with pirates. But sadly, Gusdorf was a salesman, and his job left him little time for that type of foolishness. Instead, he engaged in a different type of foolishness: building a home that looked like a ship.

In 1926 Gusdorf constructed and christened the *Edmund B*, a 72-foot landlocked ship in a northside neighborhood. The one-bedroom home has an upper deck, a fireplace where the boiler room should be, and a 30-foot lighthouse to keep it from running into water, one assumes. The *Edmund B* is about 60 feet from the Milwaukee River, but it's a long 60 feet.

3138 N. Cambridge Ave., Milwaukee, WI 53211

Private phone

Hours: Always visible

Cost: Free

Directions: Three blocks north of Locust St., at E. Hampshire St.

Spencer Tracy's Boyhood Homes

As a star in Hollywood's studio system, Spencer Tracy's early history was given a healthy scrubbing by publicists. Born in Milwaukee on April 5, 1900, he was portrayed as a scrappy altar boy when in fact he was more of a thug-in-training. By the time he reached eighth grade he had attended between 15 and 18 elementary schools on the south side of the city, mostly because he had gotten in so many fights with his classmates. Following an argument with his father, he tried to burn down the family's Prospect Avenue home. It is no longer standing . . . but not because of anything Spencer did.

When the Tracy family fell on hard times in 1912, they moved to a home on St. Paul Avenue at 30th Street. It would be the first of many homes and apartments in which the family would live over the years. Only two of those homes remain and are listed below. In his teen years Spencer became friends with another teenager, Bill O'Brien, and the two joined the Marines together after the United States entered World War I.

On returning, O'Brien convinced Tracy to study acting with him at Marquette Academy. It was a good move for both of them. Tracy went on to be nominated for an Oscar nine times, winning twice, and O'Brien would change his first name to what people remember today: Pat O'Brien. He is best known for playing the Irish-Catholic priest in every movie ever made.

2970 S. Kinnickinnic Ave., Milwaukee, WI 53207

No phone

Hours: Private residence; view from street

Cost: Free

Directions: Just north of Rusk St.

2447 S. Graham St., Milwaukee, WI 53207

No phone

Hours: Private residence; view from street

Cost: Free

Directions: Between Wilson and Graham Sts.

OTHER MILWAUKEE BABIES

Heather Graham: January 29, 1970

Woody Herman: May 16, 1913

Al Jarreau: March 12, 1940

Jane Kaczmarek: December 21, 1955

Steve Miller: October 5, 1943

Pat O'Brien: November 11, 1899

Charlotte Rae: April 22, 1926

William Rehnquist: October 1, 1924

Tom Snyder: May 12, 1936

Bob Uecker: January 26, 1935

Gene Wilder (born Jerome Silberman): June 11, 1933

Teddy Roosevelt Near-Assassination Site

It was a good thing Teddy Roosevelt was both long-winded and near-sighted—it saved his life. On a campaign trip to Milwaukee as the Bull Moose candidate for president, Roosevelt was shot by a deranged bartender on October 14, 1912.

It happened outside the Hotel Gilpatrick (333 W. Kilbourn Ave.). Teddy had been stalked for 2,000 miles through eight states by New York tapster John Schrank (who had spent the previous night at the Argyle Lodging House on Third St.). It was here that the would-be assassin finally got within six feet of the Rough Rider. Schrank claimed William McKinley had come to him twice in dreams and implicated Roosevelt in his own assassination. "Let not a murderer take the presidential chair. Avenge my death!" McKinley commanded from beyond the grave. If that weren't reason enough, Schrank was a George Washington fanatic, and hated the idea that a lesser man dared run for a third presidential term, one term more than the Father of Our Country.

Though he aimed at Roosevelt's head, Schrank's arm was deflected by a bystander. Instead, the .38-caliber bullet hit Roosevelt in the chest where it was slowed down by a 50-page speech (folded twice) and eyeglass case in Teddy's breast pocket. The bullet lodged two inches into his chest, just touching his lung, but did not hit his heart. The crowd wanted to lynch Schrank, but Roosevelt calmed the mob by talking directly to his attacker. Roosevelt went on to make his 90-minute speech at the Milwaukee Auditorium (today the Milwaukee Theatre, 500 W. Kilborn Ave., (414) 908-6000, www.milwaukeetheatre.com) before going to Johnston Emergency Hospital, bragging, "You see, it takes more than one bullet to kill a Bull Moose!"

Roosevelt was later moved to Mercy Hospital in Chicago to recover. He died six years later with the bullet still lodged in his chest. Schrank was sent to the Northern Hospital for the Insane in Oshkosh (page 83) and then transferred to the Central State Hospital for the Criminally Insane in Waupun in 1914. He died there in 1943, angry that another Roosevelt, FDR, had been elected to a third term in 1940.

Hyatt Regency, 333 W. Kilbourn Ave., Milwaukee, WI 53203
Phone: (414) 276-1234
Hours: Torn down; Hyatt on the site today
Cost: Free
Website: http://milwaukee.hyatt.com
Directions: Between Third and Fourth Sts.

ANOTHER GUN-TOTING STALKER/VOTER

Milwaukee janitor Arthur Bremer shot George Wallace in Laurel, Maryland, on May 15, 1972. In the years leading up to his crime Bremer had attended classes at Milwaukee Area Technical College (700 W. State St., (414) 297-MATC, http://matc

.edu/) and worked locally as a busboy. He had been following various presidential candidates around the nation during the preceding 18 weeks, but Wallace was the first politician he could get close to.

As part of Richard Nixon's infamous "Dirty Tricks" campaign, special counsel Chuck Colson *on Nixon's orders* sent soon-to-be Watergate burglar E. Howard Hunt to Milwaukee to plant McGovern campaign material in Bremer's filthy apartment. Yet FBI agents had already entered Bremer's apartment looking for evidence, and they left it open and unguarded. Two reporters then ransacked the place. Realizing they had made an error, the FBI returned and sealed the crime scene, barring Hunt from entry.

Tripoli Shrine Temple

It looms over Wisconsin Avenue like a vision from *The Arabian Nights*. Two stone camels guard the entrance to a North African mosque topped by a 30-foot gold onion dome flanked by two smaller domes, with minarets on each of the building's four corners. No, you're not in Libya, but on the west side of Milwaukee at the state's largest temple for the Ancient Arabic Order of the Nobles of the Mystic Shrine, better known as the Shriners.

Tripoli Shine Temple was planned and constructed between 1925 and 1928. The

The best place to park your camel in Milwaukee.

interior of the building is as elaborate as the outside, every square inch covered in Islamic patterned tiles and furnished with matching chairs, tables, and cabinetry. The architectural details of the temple are described in a self-guided tour book available at the office.

The temple is the focal point of Milwaukee's most visible fraternal organizations, a division of the Masons. The Shriners' primary charitable purpose is to raise funds for children's hospitals specializing in orthopedic afflictions and burns. And if they have some free time to putter around parades in miniature VWs, what's the harm? The Tripoli Temple is also home to the world's longest bicycle, though it is not assembled for viewing. The 37-foot bike was built at Marquette in 1994 and can transport 36 fezzed Shriners at a time.

3000 W. Wisconsin Ave., Milwaukee, WI 53208
Phone: (414) 933-4700
Hours: Monday–Friday 9 AM–5 PM
Cost: Free
Website: http://tripolishrine.com
Directions: At the corner of 30th St. and Wisconsin Ave.

Wacky Shack

If Abraham Lincoln can be a vampire hunter, why can't Teddy Roosevelt battle dinosaurs? Turns out, he might have no choice. A statue of the Rough Rider sits on a bench in front of a weirdly decorated Milwaukee home, and just over his shoulder three velociraptors creep up from the backyard along a pathway marked with bowling ball flowers. Teddy does have some backup—a half-dozen cowboys and Indians surround the porch—but none of them are looking in the right direction. Then again, maybe the dinosaurs aren't even hungry; both the Hamburglar and Mayor McCheese, who stand behind the beasts, remain unmunched.

Cherry and N. 33rd Sts., Milwaukee, WI 53208
Private phone
Hours: Daylight hours
Cost: Free
Directions: One block north of Vliet St. on 33rd St.

World's Second-Largest Four-Faced Clock

After it was erected in 1962, the four-faced Allen-Bradley clock on Milwaukee's south side became widely known as the Polish Moon. This was not intended to imply that local residents felt their immigrant neighbors were punctual or time-conscious, just easily fooled.

Frankly, it's understandable somebody could mistake this clock's 40-foot-diameter faces for the Earth's satellite—this thing is BIG, and no matter where you stand you can always see one beaming face. For years the Allen-Bradley held the title of the world's largest four-faced clock, as well as the world's largest non-chiming clock. A clock erected in Mecca in 2010 now holds both titles.

1201 S. Second St., Milwaukee, WI 53204

No phone

Hours: Always visible

Cost: Free

Directions: Four blocks south of Rte. 59, one block west of Rte. 32.

Milwaukee, Menomonee Falls, Tomahawk
Hog Heavens

You don't have to see a Harley to know you're in its presence . . . just listen. That signature *blop blop blop* from the V-twin motorcycle's tailpipe sounds like a Mozart symphony to the ears of Hog lovers everywhere.

The Harley-Davidson Motor Company was founded in a Milwaukee garage in 1903. That year, William Harley and Arthur Davison built only three bikes. But two world wars made the company a force to be reckoned with, shipping 90,000 bikes to Allied troops in World War II alone. Nostalgic former GIs fueled commercial sales in the 1950s and '60s. Yet when more and more American manufacturers closed their doors or moved overseas, it looked like Harley-Davidson might get back to a three-bike-a-year operation. But, thanks to a hardworking labor force and a loyal customer base, Harley-Davidson survived the recessions of the 1970s and '80s and today is bigger than ever.

The company must be doing well, because in 2008 it opened a multizillion-dollar state-of-the-art museum in Milwaukee. Visitors can explore the history of the company, ride virtual Harleys, compare hundreds of engines and gas tanks from years gone by, view motorcycle-themed art, see 450 different restored models going back to Serial Number 1, and dine in the Motor Restaurant, black tie optional, but black clothes encouraged.

Harley-Davidson Museum, 400 W. Canal St., Milwaukee, WI 53201

Phone: (877) HD-MUSEUM

Hours: Friday–Wednesday 10 AM–6 PM, Thursday 10 AM–8 PM

Cost: Adults $16, seniors (65+) $12, kids (5–17) $10

Website: www.harley-davidson.com

Directions: East of Sixth St., just southeast of the I-43/I-794 interchange.

For those who would like to watch today's models being assembled, there's a power train factory in suburban Menomonee Falls, and it's open for tours. You have two options; you can either take the 30-minute Factory Tour on Monday or take a 90-minute Steel Toe Tour on Wednesday, Thursday, or Friday. The longer tours depart from the museum, and they provide the shuttle.

As the name states, this factory builds only engines and transmissions; then it ships them out for final assembly in either York, Pennsylvania, or Kansas City, Missouri—760 and 560 miles away, respectively. Road trip! Both of those facilities are open to the public as well.

W156 N9000 Pilgrim Rd., Menomonee Falls, WI 53051

Phone: (877) 883-1450

Hours: Factory Tour, Monday 9 AM–2 PM; Steel Toe Tour (leaves from museum), Wednesday–
    Friday 9 AM and 12:15 PM

Cost: Factory Tour, free; Steel Toe Tour, adults only (12 and up) $38 (includes museum admission)

Website: www.harley-davidson.com/en_US/Content/Pages/Factory_Tours/pilgrim.html

Directions: Exit Rte. 41 northbound on Pilgrim Rd. (County Rd. YY).

If you travel upstate, there's also a Harley-Davidson factory you can tour in Tomahawk. It specializes in fiberlass and plastic components—saddlebags, windshields, that sort of thing. The tours last about one hour.

Tomahawk Operations, 611 S. Kaphaem Rd., Tomahawk, WI 54487

Phone: (877) 883-1450

Hours: Friday 10 AM–2 PM

Cost: Free

Website: www.harley-davidson.com/en_US/Content/Pages/Factory_Tours/tomahawk.html

Directions: Exit Rte. 51 westbound on Somo Ave. (County Rd. D/Rte. 86).

SUBURBS

Colgate
Paul Bobrowitz, Artist

It sometimes seems that anyone with a chainsaw or a welding torch can make it as an artist in Wisconsin—there's an insatiable demand for totem pole bears and yard birds made out of shovels and rakes. But there are a few exceptions, and Paul Bobrowitz is one of them.

You'll find him in as close to the middle of nowhere as you can be, yet still near Milwaukee. His home and studio are off a cul-de-sac north of Merton. When you pull into his driveway you know you're somewhere unique. Robotic figures made of propane tanks line the lane, ending at a studio barn covered in metallic suns, moons, and everything else in the universe.

Bobrowitz's yard is filled with more than 300 sculptures, many of them kinetic and best appreciated on a windy day. Most of the pieces are for sale, so if you don't see a price tag, ask, or make Bobrowitz an offer.

N93-W29174 Woodchuck Way, Colgate, WI 53056

Phone: (262) 538-1495

Hours: Call ahead

Cost: Free

Website: www.bobrowitzsculpture.com

Directions: Turn right (south) on Dieball from County Line Rd. (County Rd. Q), then turn right (west) on Woodchuck Way.

Cudahy and Milwaukee
Sinking Caddies

A pink flamingo lawn ornament is hard to ignore. A full-size pink Cadillac, broken in half and jammed in the ground, is impossible. That's what Rick Serocki had in mind when he designed his front garden with a 1955 Fleetwood as its centerpiece. And Serocki didn't stop there. Over the years he has added whatever oversize ornaments he could find. Fire hydrants, bronzed toy soldiers, a minigolf skull, a Hamburglar, pink pigs made from propane tanks, a Big Boy statue, a purple snowmobile (with rider), and a great white shark on his garage. Far from a junkpile, they complement the well-manicured lawn, flower beds, and shrubs. The neighbors probably love it!

A unique sense of style.

4531 S. Lake St., Cudahy, WI 53110
Private phone
Hours: Always visible
Cost: Free
Directions: On Rte. 32 (Lake St.), just north of Layton Ave.

Oddly enough, this isn't the only broken Cadillac lawn decoration in the area. A second Fleetwood, this one a powder blue 1959 model, can be found in the front yard of Tony Balistrieri and David Jones of north Milwaukee. Its front end and tail are not aligned, making it look as if there are really two cars planted in the ground. To add a touch of realism, they wired up the headlights and fed the exhaust from their clothes dryer out through the tailpipe. Unfortunately, the too-long pipe overheated and burned up the appliance; the tailpipe is no longer operational.

But that setback didn't slow them down. They later installed half of a red 1969 Volkswagen Beetle bursting through the front fence. Their dogs can enter the car from the backyard and sit in the driver's seat and confuse passersby. They also have a burned-up Model A emerging from a large fitzer.

2959 N. Humboldt Ave., Milwaukee, WI 53212
Private phone
Hours: Always visible
Cost: Free
Directions: Two blocks south of Locust St., just west of the Milwaukee River.

Fox Point
Fox Point Art Yard

Mary Nohl was a shining example of human independence in the face of adversity. While her family had owned this beachfront property since 1924 and built a home here in 1943, it wasn't until she began creating yard art in 1968 that a few local boneheads began taking notice. Nohl's organic art had a primitive, Easter Island–like feel to it, made of concrete, driftwood, and items she'd discovered on the shore. Rumors circulated that Mary was a witch and that the statues she created were somehow involved. The pieces suffered constant vandalism until Nohl was forced to surround her property with a high chain-link fence topped with razor wire.

The only thing witchy about the soft-spoken woman was the word "BOO" embedded in her front steps, put there to ward off intruders. Though sometimes lumped with naive environmental artists, she was definitely not untrained; Nohl was a 1938 graduate of the Art Institute of Chicago and taught junior high for some time. Her work was extremely personal, and she never sold a piece. She lived frugally, and much of her inherited wealth was donated to several art programs in southeast Wisconsin.

Nohl died on December 22, 2001. Her home was willed to the Kohler Foundation, which has prevented it from further vandalism, as well as locals who want to see the place bulldozed. Recently listed on the National Register of Historic Places, it is not yet open to the public . . . but you can see over the fence.

7328 N. Beach Dr., Fox Point, WI 53217
No phone
Hours: Private residence; view from street, daylight only
Cost: Free
Directions: Beach Dr. east from Lake Dr. (Rte. 32), take a right at the fork, follow along the shore until it takes a right turn and heads back inland.

Germantown

Bast Bell Museum

Sila Lydia Bast wasn't just a bit of a ding-dong, she was a *big* ding-dong. During her 92 years on the planet, this Germantown native collected more than 5,000 bells of all shapes and sizes from around the world. Today they're all on display in and atop glass cases, hanging from the rafters, and swinging from a silo converted to a bell tower outside. A map covered in pins shows all the countries that have bells in the collection.

The Bast Bell Museum is part of the Dheinsville Historic Park, nine acres filled with relics of a bygone era. It is home to the Germanton Historical Society's genealogy archives, the Christ Church Museum, and the old Fire Hall. Every June they host a Rendezvous with ax-throwing voyageurs, and every September they host Germantown Hunsrucker Oktoberfest with beer-swigging locals and a Dachshund Dash wiener dog race.

N128 W18780 Holly Hill Rd., PO Box 31, Germantown, WI 53022
Phone: (262) 628-3170
Hours: May–October, Wednesday–Sunday 1–4 PM
Cost: Adults $6, seniors $5, kids (5–12) $2
Website: www.bastbellmuseum.com
Directions: Just east of Maple Rd. on Holy Hill Rd.

Greenfield

Organ Piper Pizza

You don't find many Wurlitzer organs these days except for in ballparks, hockey rinks, and old movie theaters. But in Greenfield you can chow down on thin-crust pizza while enjoying a concert from a live organist.

The organ itself is not entirely a Wurlitzer, but has been cobbled together using parts from around the country, including many pieces from old Kimballs. As explained in detail on its website, "Three smaller Wurlitzer organs were incorporated into this chestwork—a 2-manual (or "keyboard") 6-rank organ (or "sets of pipes"), a 3-manual 9-rank organ, and a 3-manual 12-rank organ. This completes 27 ranks on 5 chests plus an independent 3-rank Mixture as found in church organs totaling the entire organ at 30 ranks." Make sense? They've also incorporated dozens of "toys"—a telephone bell, horse hooves, a tom-tom drum, a slide whistle, castanets, sleigh bells, an ooh-gah horn, a Chinese gong, a mallard duck chorus, and (of course) a cowbell. It all makes for a loud and entertaining evening.

4353 S. 108 St., Greenfield, WI 53228

Phone: (414) 529-1177

Hours: Tuesday–Thursday 5–9 PM, Friday 4–9:45 PM, Saturday noon–9:45 PM, Sunday noon–8:45 PM

Cost: Pizzas, $10–20

Website: www.organpiperpizza.com

Directions: Three blocks north of I-43 and Layton Ave., west of I-894.

New Berlin
Easter Island Head

A local mystery.

Quite a bit of mystery still surrounds the enormous heads (called *moai*) found on Easter Island in the South Pacific, including how these heavy artworks, some weighing more than 80 tons, were moved from the quarry where they were carved to their final destinations.

Less mysterious is the head found on the front lawn of this suburban Milwaukee home—it was made on site out of concrete. It stands about 10 feet tall and is shielded by an even taller tree. And though it was clearly erected to draw attention, the current owners aren't too keen on tiki-loving hipsters stopping by for mai tais. Gawk from the road.

15400 W. Cleveland Ave., New Berlin, WI 53151

Private phone

Hours: Always visible

Cost: Free

Directions: Just east of Moorland Rd. on the north side of the street.

St. Francis

Dobberstein's Lourdes Grotto

Before he went off to Iowa to become Mr. Bigshot Grotto Maker, Paul Dobberstein was a student at St. Francis de Sales Seminary in Milwaukee. While training here in 1897 he contracted double pneumonia. He promised the Virgin Mary to build a grotto in her honor if she helped him recover. She did, and Paul kept his word.

Dobberstein's first grotto was a simple stone-and-concrete cave near his seminary's cemetery. The grotto is 10 feet tall, has no special features, and over the years fell into disrepair. But it has since been rehabilitated as the Lourdes Grotto. Isn't it amazing what a statue and a few candles can do?

Dobberstein used the skills he developed here to build the massive Grotto of the Redemption in West Bend, Iowa, which in turn inspired Father Mathias Wernerus to build the Dickeyville Grotto in Wisconsin, which in turn spawned the Paul and Mathilda Wegner Grotto, the Rudolph Grotto and Wonder Cave, and so on, and so on . . . Dobberstein was a true Johnny Grotto-seed, and this was his first.

St. Francis de Sales Seminary, 3257 S. Lake Dr., St. Francis, WI 52325

Phone: (414) 747-6400

Hours: Call for permission

Cost: Free

Website: www.sfs.edu

Directions: Just south of Oklahoma Ave.; from the entrance, follow the road to the left of the gymnasium, walk down the cinder road to the cemetery.

West Allis
Liberace's Birthplace

One of the world's greatest showmen, Waldziu Valentino Liberace, was born in humble West Allis on May 16, 1919. He was the only surviving child of a pair of twins, weighing in at a whopping 13-plus pounds. His father was a french horn player with the International Harvester Band at the Schlitz Palm Garden. His mother knew she had given birth to a genius . . . and she was right. At the age of 14 "Lee" got his first gig at Milwaukee's Little Nick's (Muskego and Mitchell Sts.) using the stage name Walter Busterkeys, and he went on to win music competitions across the state.

Liberace was very popular at West Milwaukee High School (51st St. and Greenfield Ave., since closed). The school held an annual "Character Day" where students were required to come as a famous or historic person. Liberace won three years running, first as Haile Selassie, then as Yankee Doodle, and finally as Greta Garbo. He graduated in 1937 and before long was touring the country. To look around West Allis today, you'd think Liberace took every last rhinestone when he left.

1649 60th St. (formerly 635 51st St.), West Allis, WI 53214
Private phone
Hours: Private residence; view from street
Cost: Free
Website: www.liberace.org
Directions: At 60th and Mitchell Sts., three blocks south of National Ave.

West Allis and Cedarburg
Pagoda Gas Stations

It looks like a Chinese take-out restaurant, a small pagoda with a bright red roof at a busy intersection, but it is actually a former gas station. Wadham's Oil & Grease Company built the structure in 1927, back when automobile touring was all the rage. The goal was to attract customers who were looking for adventure, or at least something different, when they filled their tanks. The company built more than 100 stations with a similar look.

At the time it closed its doors it was known as the Frank Seneca Service Station. Unlike what happens with so many abandoned roadside wonders, the pagoda was later restored. Today you can peer through the windows

With unleaded you get eggrolls.

to see what an old station once looked like. It is guarded by a department-store dummy in a grease-monkey uniform.

Frank Seneca Service Station, 1647 S. 76th St., West Allis, WI 53214

No phone

Hours: Always visible

Cost: Free

Directions: At the corner of 76th St. and National Ave.

Another Waldham's pagoda station can also be found in the Milwaukee suburbs, and this one is being used. The structure was built a year earlier than the West Allis station, and it is currently owned by a jewelry company.

Pagoda Fine Jewelry, N58 W6189 Columbia Rd., Cedarburg, WI 53012

Phone: (262) 376-8730

Hours: Always visible

Cost: Free

Directions: At County Rd. T.

SHERMAN PERK

Speaking of old gas stations converted for other purposes, here's another classic fill-'er-up that'll fill you up with java these days: **Sherman Perk** in Milwaukee (4924 W. Roosevelt Dr., (414) 875-PERK, http://shermanperkcoffeeshop.com). Housed in the former Copeland Service Station, this coffee shop has much cleaner bathrooms than the original.

MONSTER TOUR

W isconsin has long been the stomping grounds for many classic monsters. Ignore the obvious frauds, like the stuffed merman once on display in a Milwaukee museum. Think instead about genuine ghouls: vampires, werewolves, sea serpents, pig men, and Bigfeet, as well as a critter found only in Wisconsin, the Hodag. And don't forget that human monster, Ed Gein, who still inspires horror movies and nightmares more than 50 years after he first dug up bodies in Plainfield.

Monster reports vary greatly, depending on the source. Who saw what, when, and where is less important than the fact that somebody saw *something*, and they saw it in Wisconsin. You might, too, on this Monster Tour. Just be sure to lock your car doors.

Various Towns

Bigfoot!

Native Americans call it Windego. Others prefer Sasquatch. To most, it's just Bigfoot.

The first documented case of a modern Wisconsin Bigfoot was in 1910 at **Mirror Lake**. A hairy humanoid followed a 10-year-old-girl through the woods, though it never harmed her. In 1936, another was seen digging into an Indian burial mound along Route 18 near **Jefferson**.

In the 1960s and '70s there was a rash of sightings. Farmers were amazed to see a Sasquatch vault a barbed-wire fence near **Fremont** in June 1964. The creature repeated the jumping trick at the intersection of Routes 89 and 14 west of **Delavan** in July 1964. Bigfoot was seen twice more in **Fremont**, first on October 19, 1968, and then on November 30 in Deltox Marsh when several hunters were almost knocked off their feet as the monster ran past them. Apparently none of these gun-toting men thought to bag what would have been one heck of a trophy.

Bigfoot was reported to be in **Benton** in August 1970, **Fort Atkinson** in 1972, **Frederic** in December 1974, **Cashton** in September 1976 (sometimes called the Cashton Creature), and **St. Croix Falls** a month later. Children staying in a cabin near **Plainfield** were terrorized by a hairy creature in August 1981. Another Sasquatch was seen squatting over roadkill on Route 106 in **Jefferson County** in the summer of 1992 and then attacking a passing car. A Bigfoot harassed a **Frankfort** family in 1991 and 1992 by eating their chickens and peeping in their windows.

Today, Bigfoot is often sighted near **Rice Lake**. On November 3, 1997, it left 17-inch footprints near the Christy Mountain Ski Area, and in 1999 was seen hiking up a hill north of town, off Route 53. Another sighting took place at a cabin off County Road F near **Lugerville** on November 29, 1997. A newspaper deliveryman spotted Bigfoot carrying a goat on County Road H, $^7/_{10}$ of a mile west of County Road K north of **Granton** on March 28, 2000. It was also spotted twice near Lima Marsh east of **Milton** in 2005.

But by far the best report of a Wisconsin Bigfoot is described in a book entitled *Story in the Snow* by Lunetta Woods (Galde Press, 1997). The book is written from the perspective of Yesoda, a female Sasquatch, who visits a woman and her family in an undisclosed rural location in 1994. Yesoda reveals that she, her lifelong companion, Kunta, and others like her are "shape-shifters," taking on the form of any creature in nature. They disguise their tracks as those of rabbits, deer, and various reptiles. Yesoda and Kunta warn the woman's children through dreams that a gargoyle lives in their grain silo. She also reveals that Bigfeet protect the rest of us by moving rocks to align with the "electrical grid pattern surrounding Mother Earth."

They sure do keep busy.

Bigfoot Files: www.bfro.net/GDB/state_listing.asp?state=wi

Directions: Follow the directions listed above, and keep your nose peeled for the smell of a skunk.

BIGFOOT?

The mascot for Lake Geneva's **Big Foot Archers** is, not surprisingly, Bigfoot. Though the organization was named after Potawatomi Chief Big Foot, it wouldn't have been appropriate for members to be firing their arrows at a human target, dead or alive, so they built a nine-foot-tall furry Sasquatch instead. Visit them at N960 Hillside Road, (262) 275-3889, www.bigfootarchers.com. If you're visiting the Wisconsin Dells, there's another fake Bigfoot sticking out of the roof of the ticket shack for **Bigfoot Zipline Tours** (1550 Wisconsin Dells Pkwy., (608) BIG-FOOT, www.bigfootzip.com).

Elkhorn
Werewolf!

Werewolf? Here wolf! This lupine monster has been spotted so often along the same country road in southern Wisconsin that it has been dubbed the Bray Road Beast.

It was first sighted in 1936, digging in an old Native American burial mound. But not until a report in 1991 of frightened drivers near the intersection of Bray and Hospital Roads northeast of Elkhorn did the monster get any attention. The report coaxed many locals into admitting they'd been seeing the creature for years. The beast sometimes walked on its hind legs, but other times galloped on all four of its humanlike appendages. The same year, citizens discovered a sacrificial altar and the mangled remains of several local pets. Were the events connected? Had somebody summoned up the sinister forces of Hell?

It appeared so, and the beast became more aggressive. On Halloween night in 1991, the Bray Road Beast jumped onto the trunk of a teenager's car after she thought she'd run over an animal. It held on for some distance before tumbling off the swerving vehicle, scratching the trunk.

The Bray Road Beast was soon traveling to other locales. In August 1992 a driver on Route 106 northbound, just past County Road D near Hebron, saw the monster jogging through a cornfield looking for prey. Hebron is 20 miles north of Elkhorn, so the Bray Road Beast was apparently on the loose.

Then, in February 1993, the Bray Road Beast endorsed State Representative Chuck Coleman for the First Congressional District. It even appeared in a campaign photo shaking Coleman's hand. No joke. Voters weren't amused, impressed, or frightened; Coleman lost the Republican primary.

Where wolf?

Bray Rd., Elkhorn, WI 53121
No phone
Hours: After dark
Cost: Free
Directions: Two miles northeast of the Rte. 43 intersection with Rte. 12, on Bray Rd. at the intersection with Hospital Rd.

Hubertus

Bearwolf!

Back in 2006, Steve Krueger had the unenviable job of picking up roadkill in Washington County. On November 9 of that year, he pulled over at 1:30 AM to collect a dead deer on Highway 167 just outside the entrance to the Holy Hill shrine near Hubertus. Krueger had just lifted an 80-pound carcass into his pickup bed and had gone to the cab to retrieve a tag and fill out some paperwork when he felt the vehicle shake. Looking in his rearview mirror, he saw a large bearlike creature with a canine head—a bearwolf!—helping itself to the freshly killed meal.

Krueger didn't waste a second before throwing the car into drive and hightailing it out of there. The deer was lost, as was an ATV ramp that fell off the tailgate. When he returned later that morning, both the deer and the ramp were nowhere to be found.

So stop on by, late at night. Maybe you'll find them.

Holy Hill and Carmel Rds., Hubertus, WI 53033
No phone
Hours: Always visible
Cost: Free
Directions: On Rte. 167 (Holy Hill Rd.) on the north side of the Holy Hill shrine.

Madison
The Mendota Monster!

Loch Ness's Nessie might be better known, but this Wisconsin underwater monster get points for toughing out the frigid northern winters. Reports of a 20-foot creature in Lake Mendota have been circulating since the 1860s, having been first spotted near Governor's Island (on the northern shore) by a husband and wife, the Parks. Twenty-odd years later, in 1889, a fisherman near Picnic Point (at the northern tip of University Bay) caught a glimpse of it. Then, in July 1892, it attacked a rowboat carrying mailman Billy Dunn and his wife near Livesey's Bluff, leaving fang marks on a paddle Dunn used to defend himself. Clearly this was not a shy, harmless sea serpent! In 1897 it was blamed for eating a dog that was swimming in the lake, and was fired upon twice by salesman Eugene Heath near the eastern shore. Heath said the creature came after him and that the bullets he shot bounced off its scales.

Despite this aggressive behavior, the Mendota Monster might just be lonely and looking for companionship. In 1917 a University of Wisconsin student was sunning herself on a dock off Picnic Point when she felt something tickling her toes. At first she thought it was her randy boyfriend, but it turned out to be the snake-like tongue of the Mendota Monster! The woman screamed and the creature retreated. Monster sightings continued into the 1920s, and locals gave it the nickname Bozho, short for Winnebozho.

Lake Mendota, Madison, WI 53706
No phone
Hours: Summertime is best
Cost: Free
Directions: Just north of the UW campus.

Mineral Point
Password? Vampire!

Allen Ludden, future *Password* host and husband to Betty White, was born in Mineral Point on October 5, 1918. When he died in 1981, his body was returned here to spend eternity . . . with a vampire!

The Mineral Point Vampire was spotted only once, on March 30, 1981, by policeman Jon Pepper in Graceland Cemetery. This bloodsucker was less Anne Rice and more Bela Lugosi. He donned a black cape, had a pale, white face, and was extremely tall. Could it have been Ludden, back from the grave? Not likely. Ludden was a short man.

Graceland Cemetery, W. Fair St., Mineral Point, WI 53565
No phone
Hours: Daily 9 AM–5 PM
Cost: Free
Directions: East of Ridge St., two blocks south of Fountain St.

Brussels or Duvall
Pigmen!

Be careful what you wish for—it could backfire! According to local legend, some time in the late 1800s, a Belgian farmer near Brussels cursed a local pastor when his rich uncle left him nothing in his will. (Why he cursed the *pastor* is unclear.) Much to his surprise, the curser became the cursee. The farmer's furniture would rearrange on its own, sometimes accompanied by faraway music. Worse yet, he kept running into pigs with men's faces. He was so rattled that he went to the pastor and asked how he could get it to stop. Build a roadside shrine, the holy man said. The farmer did, and the curse lifted.

For years the small chapel stood along Route 57, but when the highway was widened it was moved to a local cemetery. Trouble is, nobody seems to agree which cemetery chapel it is today, the Chapel of St. Ghislane in Brussels or the Chapel of St. Hubert in Duvall. They're both a little spooky.

Chapel of St. Ghislane, St. Michael's Cemetery, Misere Rd. and County Rd. J, Brussels, WI 54204
No phone
Hours: Daylight
Cost: Free
Directions: North of County Rd. J on Misere Rd., southeast of town.

Chapel of St. Hubert, St. Francis de Paul Cemetery, Duvall Rd. and County Rd. Y, Duvall, WI 54217

No phone

Hours: Daylight

Cost: Free

Directions: South of County Rd. Y on Duvall Rd.

Plainfield
Psycho!

When it comes to psychos, Ed Gein was a groundbreaker. The product of an overbearing mother, a cruel father, and an abundance of time to himself, Ed Gein was, to put it mildly, odd. His mother did her best to keep Ed away from women for Biblical reasons and in doing so warped her son's psyche. Ed was left to form images of the outside world from dime paperbacks and mom's fire-and-brimstone advice. This was not a good strategy.

When his mother died in December 1945, Ed snapped. In 1947 he began robbing women's graves in the Plainfield Cemetery. He dug up Mrs. Sherman, Mrs. Everson, Mrs. Eleanor Adams (whose grave, just in front of Augusta's, was later reopened to confirm Ed's story), Mrs. Bergstrom, Mrs. Evans, and Mrs. Sparks, and he removed body parts as souvenirs. He also violated the nearby Hancock and Spiritland cemeteries. Ed then began tailoring a human bodysuit for himself, with the ultimate goal of becoming a woman. At night he would put on his macabre outfit and dance around in the moonlight.

When there weren't enough fresh bodies in the local graveyards, Ed resorted to murder. He is known to have killed two women, but there were perhaps more. The first victim was Mary Hogan, owner of Hogan's Tavern in nearby Pine Grove, just north of Plainfield in Portage County. He murdered her after closing time on December 9, 1954, and brought her home in his truck. But it was for a second murder, Bernice Worden, that Gein was eventually apprehended. He shot Worden in her Plainfield hardware store on the opening day of deer season. It was November 16, 1957, and most of the town's men were off hunting. So was Ed. Police traced a store receipt for antifreeze back to Gein at his grisly farmhouse.

Cops discovered Worden hanging from her heels, headless and dressed out like a deer, in Ed's barn. Inside his house were soup bowls made from skulls, chairs and lamps upholstered with skin, a box of salted noses, nine masks made from women's faces and adorned with lipstick, a pair of lips hanging from a window shade, a drum made with a coffee can with two skin heads, and a bed adorned with bones and skulls on the four bedposts. Mrs. Worden's heart was sitting in a pot on the stove. Her head was in a bag with nails driven into its ears; Ed planned to hang it with twine on a wall. In all, police believed there were the remains of 15 women in the house.

Then there was Ed's mother's room. It had been sealed at her death and wasn't reopened until the police got out the crowbar. Everything was exactly how she left it, but with a thick layer of dust. Ed hadn't touched a thing. Starting to sound familiar?

Ed's Former Land, Aniwa Ln., Plainfield, WI 54966

No phone

Hours: Always visible; view from road

Cost: Free

Directions: West on Rte. 73, left on County Rd. KK, right on Aniwa Ln., between Third Ave. (County Rd. KK) and First Ave. (the county line).

Gein was sent to the Central State Hospital, an insane asylum in Waupun (now named the Dodgeville Correctional Institute, 1 W. Lincoln St.). An angry local mob torched Gein's home on March 20, 1958, after rumors circulated that it would be purchased at auction and reopened as a house of horrors. Only Gein's 1949 Ford sedan survived. It toured in a Midwest sideshow throughout the 1960s, billed as the "Ed Gein Ghoul Car: The Car That Hauled the Dead from Their Graves." Human evidence collected from the home was buried in 1962 in an unmarked grave at the Plainfield Cemetery.

At a 1968 trial, Gein was found guilty of murdering Bernice Worden but was declared insane in the sentencing phase. He spent his remaining years in the loony bin, transferring from Central State to the Mendota Mental Health Institute in Madison in 1974. He died of respiratory failure on July 26, 1984, and was buried back in Plainfield where it all began . . . next to his dear old mother. His chipped and defaced tombstone was stolen in June 2000 and later turned up in Seattle. It is currently in the possession of the Waushara County Historical Society.

Even if you've never heard of Gein before, you'll recognize him as the inspiration for *Psycho*, *The Texas Chainsaw Massacre*, *Deranged*, and *Silence*

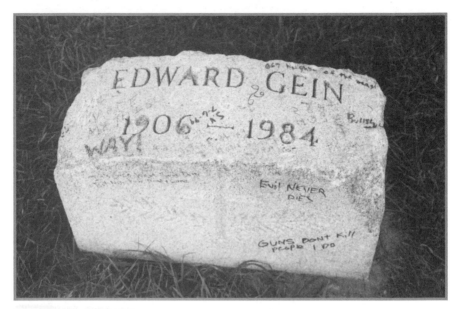

Ed was a groundbreaker.

of the Lambs, among others. Ed has been transformed into the modern American monster.

Plainfield Cemetery, Fifth Ave., Plainfield, WI 54966

No phone

Hours: Daily 9 AM–5 PM

Cost: Free

Directions: Follow frontage road (Fifth Ave.) north along Rte. 51; Ed's plot and his mother's are to the right of the central car path, near the back.

Rhinelander
Hodag!

The Hodag (*Bovine spirituallis*) is a rare and elusive beast found only in the swamps of northern Wisconsin. It received its name because it looks like a cross between a horse and a dog. The Hodag has a spiny, horned backbone, a serpent's tail, and legs without knee joints. Because of this, it cannot lie down, so it must sleep leaning against a tree. To capture a Hodag, just chop down the tree. Hodags eat only white bulldogs, and only on Sunday.

Hodag or Hoax-dag?

The first reported sighting of a Hodag came from German immigrants led by Gene Shepard near the headwaters of Rice Creek in 1896. Shepard cornered it in a cave and chloroformed it with a rag on a bamboo pole. He then put it on dimly lit display. Shepard's Hodag was seven feet long and three feet tall, and was later discovered to be a cheap hoax: a horse-hide stretched over a wooden body with bull horns glued to its back. Its movements were controlled with hidden wires pulled by Shepard or his kids. The Hodag was later destroyed when Shepard's resort on Ballard Lake caught fire.

But that wasn't the end of the Hodag. Shortly after the blaze, another one was spotted on the property of George DeBoyle near Lake Creek, on August 5, 1952. Before being captured, it ripped the shirt off DeBoyle and knocked out little Donny Decor, a fearless lad. The Hodag was placed in an open-bed cart and brought to town, and today you can see it at the Rhinelander Logging Museum. On close inspection it appears rather . . . wooden.

Enthusiasm for this town's unique critter has not subsided. Maybe Shephard's was a Hoax-dag, but there has to be another one out there somewhere. Today, Rhinelander calls itself the "Home of the Hodag" and has made the monster the high school's mascot. Businesses in town include the Hodag Bar, Hodag Sewing Center, Hodag Express Lube, Hodag Towing, Hodag Auto Sales, Hodag Learning Center, Hodag Lanes, Hodag Pump & Pantry, Hodag Bait & Tackle, Hodag Landscaping, Hodag Music, and, just in case, Hodag Gun & Loan. An enormous fiberglass Hodag has been erected near the Chamber of Commerce building along the river (with smaller Hodag statues scattered around town), and every year the town throws a Hodag Festival.

Hodag Statue, Rhinelander Chamber of Commerce, 540 W. Kemp St., Rhinelander, WI 54501

Phone: (800) 236-4FUN or (715) 365-7464

Hours: Always visible

Cost: Free

Website: www.explorerhinelander.com

Directions: On Rte. 8 (Kemp St.) just west of the river.

Rhinelander Logging Museum, Pioneer Park, Rte. 8, Rhinelander, WI 54501

Phone: (715) 369-5004

Hours: June–August, daily 10 AM–5 PM

Cost: Free; donations accepted

Website: www.rhinelander-resorts.com/loggingmus/logging.htm

Directions: At the intersection of Kemp St. and Oneida Ave.

Monico

Rhinelapus, the Green Monster!

The trouble with so many Wisconsin monsters is that they're elusive, showing themselves mainly to lonely nighttime drivers, drunken teens, and trailer park folk. But not the Rhinelapus, Monico's Green Monster—it's right in the middle of town!

Guy Dailey found the creature in the 1940s along Monico Creek. Some say it is a twisted root mass from a long-dead tree, but Dailey believed it was a petrified Rhinelapus—a freaky hybrid of a rhinoceros, an elephant, and an octopus. The three-legged ogre was moved to town and placed under a protective canopy next to Dailey's Lake Venus Tavern. For years it served as a jungle gym for kids whose parents were inside drinking.

After cryptozoologists (or somebody) linked it to the nearby Hodag, the Rhinelapus was painted green. And after the Venus Lake Tavern closed its doors, the monster was donated to the town for its "care and feeding." Sadly, the folks of Monico have penned it up behind a tall chain link fence, making climbing and photographing it next to impossible.

Monico Community Park, 1668 Rte. 8, Monico, WI 54501

No phone

Hours: Always visible

Cost: Free

Directions: On the north side of Rte. 8, opposite County Rd. V.

Will that fence really hold it?

EPiLOGUE

*N*ow for the bad news on Wisconsin's weird roadside attractions: they're short-lived. Mother Nature takes its toll on the sites, and old age does the same to the proprietors. Property values, "good taste," and cranky neighbors all work against those who look at the world a little differently and want to share it with the rest of us.

Sometimes attractions are put to sleep or abandoned by their creators. A satanic art environment called Devil Dance near Pittsville was left to decay, and nothing remains. Only two green men from Dave Siedler's Alien Presence near Tomahawk survive, standing under the eaves of a shed, not much of a presence at all. Ask about the Miniature Village built in Black Earth by Gilman Mikelson and the response is usually, "Here? In Black Earth?" Yet the Lilliputian town does exist, overgrown with weeds, off a county road west of town.

Basic economic laws of supply and demand have killed a few Wisconsin museums and sites. Biblical Gardens couldn't compete with the water parks in the Dells, and fiberglass Jesus statues ended up on the auction block. Spring's Green's American Calliope Center tooted its last note, sold off its instruments, and turned the building over to a storefront ministry. The Park Lane Railroad Museum in Dellwood ran off the rails and will not likely reopen. And the Wisconsin Folk Art Museum did its best to attract city slickers with fur-bearing trout, but they couldn't find as many suckers as they used to. It has since closed its doors.

Several of the attractions found in the first edition of this book—Storybook Gardens, Carl's Wood Art Museum, Wax World of the Stars, the Pyramid Supper Club, the World of Miniature Buildings, Serpent Safari, the *Midwest Hiawatha*, and the Wonder Spot—are now gone. Kaput, finis, sayonara. You had your chance.

The Kohler Foundation has funded and coordinated impressive restorations of some of the Wisconsin sites listed in this book, but with limited resources, has had to focus on locations of artistic or historic merit. That's admirable and appreciated, but who's out there saving the fiberglass cows, the stuffed albino muskrats, and the cheesemobiles? Nobody, that's who. If you don't get in the car and see them now, *today*, you may never be able to tell your grandchildren you ever saw the World's Largest Penny.

ACKNOWLEDGMENTS

The first road trip I ever took was to Wisconsin, just a short trip up through Kenosha and Racine to get away from Chicago for an afternoon. Wisconsin is a beautiful state, and though I am obligated as an Illinois resident to rib its inhabitants, it is hard to escape the fact it produces some of the nicest people in the Midwest. While researching the first edition of this book, I ran out of gas west of Madison, and before I could lock my doors and hike off to a station, a guy named Terry pulled over, drove me to a pump, and brought me back to my car. For all Chicago has to offer, they don't have roadside assistance for spaced-out drivers, and for that reason alone, I love Wisconsin.

This book would not have been possible without the assistance, patience, and good humor of many individuals. My thanks go out to the following people for allowing me to interview them about their roadside attractions: Mike Bjorn (Mike Bjorn's Fine Clothing and Museum), James Franklin Brunette (J. F. B. Art and Math Museum), Byron Buckeridge (Concretion Museum), Fran Burt (Rock in the House), Joan Cook (Wegner Grotto), John Cronce (Jockey International), Lloyd and Leonore Dickmann (Happy Tales Books), Tom Diehl (Tommy Bartlett's Robot World), Elmer Duellman (Elmer's Auto and Toy Museum), Ted Dzialo (National Freshwater Fishing Hall of Fame), Curt Evans (Chevy on a Silo), Tom "Dr. Evermor" Every (the *Forevertron*), Catherine Goetz (Hamburger Hall of Fame), Buck Guthrie (Toy Train Barn), Kenneth Haeuser (Prairie Moon Museum), Richard Hanson (Warner Brothers in Cement), Helmi Strahl Harrington (A World of Accordions Museum), Gordon Johnson (the Painted Forest), Tara and Scott Joles (Dells Bells Wedding Chapel), James Frank Kotera (Big Ball of Twine), Frank Kovac (Kovac Planetarium), Duwayne Kosakoski (Koz's Mini Bowl), Tom Kupsh (House on the Rock), Gail "Princess of Power" Lamberty (the Evermor Foundation), Barry and

Patti Levenson (Mustard Museum), Mark "Mad Man" Madson (Truck in a Tree), Don McClellan (Rocks for Fun Café), Maria McKay (Museum of Woodcarving), Dave Pflieger (World's Largest Grandfather Clock), Craig Powell (Hamilton Wood Type and Printing Museum), Rick Rolfsmeyer (Grandview), Jim Schauf (F.A.S.T. Corporation), Judith Schulz (Spinning Top Exploratory Museum), Lisa Stone (Friends of Fred Smith), Fred Theisen (Little Bohemia), Marge Timmerman (Dickeyville Grotto), Bob Tohak (UFO Landing Pad), Peggy Van Gilder (Moccasin Bar), Jim Van Lanen (Hamilton Wood Type and Printing Museum), Bill Vienneaux (the Sawdust Factory), Doug Watson (Watson's Wild West Museum), Laura Weingandt (End of the Line), and Clyde Wynia (Jurustic Park).

Additional thanks go to Nancy Moulton of the Kohler Foundation. Without her fact-checking and editorial advice on the environmental art sites restored by the Kohler Foundation, I might not have given these remarkable works or their creators their proper due. I have also had the pleasure of working with Jim Draeger of the Wisconsin Historical Society, who pointed me in the direction of a few places I'd never heard of.

For research assistance, I am indebted to the librarians in the Wisconsin communities of Amery, Appleton, Eagle River, Fish Creek, Genoa City, Kenosha, Lake Geneva, Lodi, Medford, Mineral Point, Montello, Sparta, and Sun Prairie. Thanks also to the chambers of commerce in Bloomer, Burlington, Cumberland, Eagle River, Elmwood, Green Bay, La Crosse, Lake Geneva, Mercer, Mineral Point, Onalaska, Port Washington, St. Germain, Sauk City, Sun Prairie, Waupun, Winneconne, and the Wisconsin Dells.

An extra special thanks goes out to Travis Strasburg, owner of North Country Taxidermy, who allowed me to use the photo of the deer hunter on the cover of this book.

Friends, family members, and complete strangers willingly volunteered to act as models for the photographs in this book: Jim Frost, Patrick Hughes, Eugene Marceron, Clyde Wynia, James Frank Kotera, and Don McClellan. Thank you, all.

To my Cheesehead friends, Gianofer Fields, Julie Froman, Tim Murphy, and Ellen Ryan, I hope I did your home state justice. And to Jim Frost, thanks as always for your support, encouragement, and hours behind the wheel.

ReCOMMeNDeD sources

*I*f you'd like to learn more about the places and individuals in this book, the following are excellent sources.

Introduction

General Wisconsin Guides: *History Just Ahead* by Sarah McBride, ed. (Wisconsin State Historical Society Press, 1999); *Forgotten Tales of Wisconsin* by Martin Hintz (History Press, 2010); *Odd Wisconsin* by Erika Janik (Wisconsin Historical Society Press, 2007); *It Happened in Wisconsin* by Michael Bie (TwoDot, 2007); *Weird Wisconsin* by Linda S. Godfrey and Richard D. Hendricks (Barnes & Noble, 2005); *Awesome Almanac—Wisconsin* by Jean Blashfield (B&B Publishing, 1993); *Strange Wisconsin* by Linda S. Godfrey (Trails Books, 2007); *Famous Wisconsin Authors* by James P. Roberts (Badger Books, 2002); *The WPA Guide to Wisconsin* by the Federal Writers' Project (Minnesota Historical Society Press, 1941); *The Wisconsin Almanac* by Jerry Minnich, ed. (Prairie Oak Press, 1999); *52 Wisconsin Weekends* by Bob Puhala (Country Road Press, 1997); *Wisconsin: The Story of the Badger State* by Norman K. Risjord (Trails Books, 1995); *Wisconsin Literary Travel Guide* by the Wisconsin Library Association (Wisconsin Library Association, 1989); *Wisconsin Lore and Legends* by Lou Russell and John Russell (Oak Point Press, 1982); *Wisconsin Lore and Legends* Volume II by Lou Russell and John Russell (Oak Point Press, 1982)

Wisconsin Ghosts: *The Wisconsin Guide to Haunted Locations* by Chad Lewis and Terry Fisk (Research Publishing Company, 2004); *Wisconsin Ghosts* by Beth Scott and Michael Norman (Heartland Press, 1980)

Wisconsin Shrines and Grottoes: *Sacred Spaces and Other Places* by Lisa Stone and Jim Zanzi (School of the Art Institute of Chicago Press, 1993)

Strange Events and Phenomena: *The W-Files* by Jay Rath (Wisconsin Trails, 1997)

Chapter 1

Paul Bunyan: *Paul Bunyan* by Esther Shephard (Sandpiper, 2006)

Old Abe: *Old Abe, Eagle Hero* by Patrick Young (Kane/Miller, 2010)

John Dillinger: *John Dillinger* by Dary Matera (Da Capo, 2005); *Dillinger's Wild Ride* by Elliott J. Gorn (Oxford, 2009); *Dillinger* by G. Russell Girardin (Indiana University Press, 1994)

Smokey Bear: *Smokey Bear 20252* by William Clifford Lawter Jr. (Lindsay Smith, 1994)

Fred Smith's Concrete Park: *The Art of Fred Smith* by Lisa Stone and Jim Zanzi (Price County Forestry Department, 1991)

John Heisman: *Heisman* by John Heisman and Mark Schlabach (Howard Books, 2012)

Museum of Woodcarving: *My Brother Joe the Woodcarver* by Lucy Barta McKay (Museum of Woodcarving, 1976)

Richard Bong: *Aces High* by Bill Yenne (Berkley Trade, 2010)

Dr. Kate and the Million Penny Parade: *Dr. Kate* by Rebecca Wojahn (Wisconsin Historical Society Press, 2009)

Chapter 2

Harry Houdini: *The Secret Life of Harry Houdini* by William Kalush and Larry Sloman (Atria, 2007); *The Life and Many Deaths of Harry Houdini* by Ruth Brandon (Random House, 1993)

Joseph McCarthy: *A Conspiracy So Immense* by David Oshinsky (Oxford 2005); *Joseph McCarthy* by Arthur Herman (Free Press, 2000)

Wisconsin Death Trip: *Wisconsin Death Trip* by Michael Lesy (University of New Mexico Press, 2000)

Garden of Eden: *Found at Last* by Reverend David O. Van Slyke (Garden of Eden Preservation Society, reprint from 1886)

Necedah Apparitions: *Revelations and Messages* by Mary Ann Van Hoof (For My God and My Country, 1966)

Apostle Clock: *The Apostles Clock Video* by the Oshkosh Public Museum (Oshkosh, 1998)

Birthplace of the Republican Party: *Grand Old Party* by Lewis Gould (Random House, 2003)

Gasoline Alley: *Sundays with Walt and Skeezix* by Frank King (Sunday Press, 2007)

Sculptureville: *Public Sculpture in Wisconsin* by Anton Rajer and Christine Style (SOS! Wisconsin, 1999)

Chapter 3

General Dells Guide: *Hidden History of the Wisconsin Dells Area* by Ross M. Curry (History Press, 2010); *The Wisconsin Dells* by James Laabs (Prairie Oaks Press, 1999)

Circus World: *Badger State Showmen* by Fred Dahlinger and Stuart Thayer (Circus World, 1998)

International Crane Foundation: *Cranes* by Janice M. Hughes (Firefly Books, 2008); *Crane Music* by Paul Johnsgard (University of Nebraska Press, 1998)

Belle Boyd: *Belle Boyd in Camp and Prison* by Belle Boyd (LSU Press, 1998)

H. H. Bennett: *H. H. Bennett, Photographer* by Sara Rath (University of Wisconsin Press, 2010)

Chapter 4

Honey Bees: *The Beekeeper's Bible* by Richard A. Jones and Sharon Sweeney-Lynch (Stewart, Tabori & Chang, 2011)

Passenger Pigeons: *The Silent Sky* by Allan W. Eckert (iUniverse, 2000); *Passenger Pigeons* by the State Historical Society of Wisconsin (State Historical Society of Wisconsin, 1976)

King James (Strang): *"God Has Made Us a Kingdom"* by Vickie Cleverley Speek (Signature Books, 2006); *Assassination of a Michigan King* by Roger Van Noord (University of Michigan Press, 1997)

Dickeyville Grotto: *Dickeyville Grotto* by Susan A. Niles (University Press of Mississippi, 1997)

Wisconsin Dairyland: *Cheese* by Jerry Apps (University of Wisconsin Press, 2004); *The Master Cheesemakers of Wisconsin* by James Norton and Becca Dilley (University of Wisconsin Press, 2009)

Orson Welles: *Orson Welles: The Road to Xanadu* by Simon Callow (Viking, 1995)

Andy Gump: *Andy Gump* by Sidney Smith (Reilley & Lee, 1924)

Aztalan: *Aztalan* by Robert Birmingham and Lynne Goldstein (Wisconsin Historical Society Press, 2005); *The Lost Pyramids of Rock Lake* by Frank Joseph (Galde Press, 1992); *Atlantis in Wisconsin* by Frank Joseph (Galde Press, 1995)

The *Forevertron*: *A Mythic Obsession* by Tom Kupsh (Chicago Review Press, 2008)

Frank Lloyd Wright: *Frank Lloyd Wright* by Meryle Secrest (Alfred A. Knopf, 1992)

House on the Rock: *House of Alex* by Marv Balousek (Waubesa Press, 1990)

Chapter 5

Bombing at Sterling Hall: *Wisconsin Crimes of the Century* by Marv Balousek (William C. Robbins, 1989)

Thornton Wilder: *Thornton Wilder, An Intimate Portrait* by Richard Goldstone (Saturday Review Press, 1975)

Otis Redding: *Otis!* by Scott Freeman (St. Martin's Griffin, 2002)

State Capitol Building: *Wisconsin Capitol Fascinating Facts* by Diana Cook (Prairie Oak Press, 1991)

Bob La Follette: *Fighting Bob La Follette* by Nancy C. Unger (University of North Carolina Press, 2000)

Mustard Museum: *The Wurst of the Proper Mustard* by Barry Levenson, ed. (The Mustard Museum, 1993)

Georgia O'Keeffe: *O'Keeffe* by Jeffrey Hogrefe (Bantam Books, 1992)

Chapter 6

Green Bay Packers: *When Pride Still Mattered* by David Maraniss (Simon and Schuster, 1999)

Eisenhower's Train: *The Eisenhower Collection of the National Railroad Museum* by P. H. Dudley, et al. (National Railroad Museum, 1990)

Sputnik: *Sputnik* by Paul Dickson (Walker & Company, 2011)

USS *Cobia*: *Final Patrol* by Don Keith (NAL Trade, 2006)

Peshtigo Fire: *Firestorm at Peshtigo* by Denise Gess and William Lutz (Holt Paperbacks, 2003); *The Great Peshtigo Fire*, Second Edition by Rev. Peter Pernin (State Historical Society of Wisconsin, 2000)

Jean Nicolet: *The Nicolet Corrigenda* by Nancy O. Lurie and Patrick J. Jung (Waveland Press, 2009)

Birthplace of the Hamburger: *Home of the Hamburger Celebration* by the Hamburger Hall of Fame (Self-published, 1989)

Chapter 7

Gertie the Duck: *The Story of "Gertie"* by Harris Nowell (Journal Company, 1945)

Golda Meir: *Golda* by Ralph G. Martin (Charles Scribner's Sons, 1988)

Spencer Tracy: *Spencer Tracy, Tragic Idol* by Bill Davidson (E. P. Dutton, 1987)

Teddy Roosevelt: *The Attempted Assassination of Teddy Roosevelt* by Stan Gores (State Historical Society of Wisconsin, 1980)

Harley-Davidson: *The Encyclopedia of the Harley-Davidson* by Peter Henshaw and Ian Kerr (Chartwell Books, 2010); *Harley-Davidson Century* by Darwin Holmstrom (Motorbooks, 2004)

Wisconsin Filling Stations: *Fill 'er Up* by Jim Draeger and Mark Speltz (Wisconsin Historical Society Press, 2008)

Les Paul and the Electric Guitar: *The Early Years of the Les Paul Legacy, 1915–1963* by Robb Lawrence (Hal Leonard, 2008)

Liberace: *Liberace* by Bob Thomas (St. Martin's Press, 1987); *Liberace, An Autobiography* by Liberace (G. P. Putnam's Sons, 1973)

Chapter 8

General Weirdness: *The Wisconsin Road Guide to Mysterious Creatures* by Chad Lewis (On the Road Publications, 2011); *Monsters of Wisconsin* by Linda S. Godfrey (Stackpole, 2011); *The W-Files* by Jay Rath (Wisconsin Trails, 1997)

Bigfoot: *Story in the Snow* by Lunetta Woods (Galde Press, 1997)

Bray Road Beast: *The Beast of Bray Road* by Linda S. Godfrey (Prairie Oak Press, 2003)

Ed Gein: *Deviant* by Harold Schechter (Pocket Books, 1989); *Edward Gein* by Judge Robert H. Gollmar (Pinnacle Books, 1981); *Ed Gein, Psycho* by Paul Anthony Woods (St. Martin's Press, 1995); *Psycho* by Robert Bloch (Tom Doherty Associates, 1959)

Hodag: *Long Live the Hodag* by Kurt Kortenhof (Hodag Press, 2006)

CiTY iNDeX

Site Index